PROBLEMS

In

REMEDIES

Damages — Equity — Restitution

By

Dan B. Dobbs
Professor of Law, University of Arizona

&

Kathleen Kavanagh
Associate Dean, University of Arizona College of Law

SECOND EDITION

TEXT IS PRINTED ON 10% POST
CONSUMER RECYCLED PAPER

5th Reprint — 2004

To Loretta and Colby

Preface

This edition adds more than 60 new problems for teaching remedies by the problem method. We have retained the core problems from the first edition, usually with changes in detail. We have added problems to create new issues. We have also added new settings and modernized some of the old ones. We think that teachers will find more variety and more choices among this array of problems. The book is still intended for teaching a basic remedies course by the problem method, but overall it probably offers more possibility for depth of analysis.

In the pure problem method, students begin with a problem and then turn to outside sources for help in resolving it. The outside source for which these problems are designed is the one-volume edition of DAN DOBBS, THE LAW OF REMEDIES (2d ed. 1993). However, these problems may be used profitably as a supplement to casebook or other more common methods of law school teaching or in Continuing Legal Education seminars, with or without the treatise.

We have striven to keep this book compact and to retain its character as a tool for pure problem method teaching. We have, however, added four cases that we believe will provide a useful foil for considering both problems and the cited textual sections.

The problems embodied in this book differ from the usual academic presentation in several ways. First, students are not initially confronted with an authoritative statement of "law," but with facts and human problems. Second, except in the four introductory chapters, the problems are not organized to present an orderly sequence of remedies rules. Instead, they are organized around diverse factual settings, so that the issues come to the student just as they come to lawyers in practice — helter-skelter. Although there is more organization than meets the incurious eye, the problems require students to work analytically, not on an organization dictated by the inexorable logic of a casebook.

relentless - constant

By looking at problems in their factual setting — as problems of personal injury or contract or economic loss — we hope to help make students remedy-conscious and also to draw on their best skills. We hope to connect the human side of law to the legal rules by starting with the human side. At the same time, we hope to present a complete picture of the main remedies and their workings.

We wanted the total package of problems to reflect a little bit of the amazing diversity of cases, clients and situations that face lawyers. Some of the people in our problems are behaving in traditional ways. Husbands and wives can be found vacationing or buying land together in our problems. Some other people seem more contemporary in their careers and living. We have enjoyed including all kinds of people. As in the first edition, their names reflect their family origins from around the world. Whatever their names, their characters, activities, and legal problems identify them as modern Americans and human beings for whom students can imaginatively provide some legal assistance.

For their help in research on these problems and in laborious efforts in proofing, we thank Paula Nailon and Julia Corty, each of the University of Arizona Law College Class of 1994. If any errors remain after their indefatigable efforts, they are due to a malevolent computer or to our own performance as the sole typists of the manuscript.

Dan Dobbs
Kathleen Kavanagh
Tucson, Arizona
April, 1993

Summary of Contents

TABLE OF CONTENTS

Subpart B. Remedies in Particular Settings

(A) Land (Mostly)

(1) Physical Integrity of the Land and Structures

(2) Possession, Use and Enjoyment

(B) Chattels (Mostly)

PART II

SUPPLEMENTARY PROBLEMS

TABLE OF CONTENTS

Clients and partners bring problems. Lawyers resolve these problems mainly by using skills of analysis, research, argumentation, and negotiation. Students working through a remedies course by attempting to resolve problems can gain a considerable legal experience by practicing these professional skills. Not many problems in litigation have answers until the courts finally resolve the case. Not all of the problems in this book have answers, either. However, by using analysis and argumentation, along with a modest bit of "research" in the remedies treatise, students should be in about the same position as the practicing lawyer who deals with a comparable problem.

The problem approach emulates, in a modest and gentle way, the chaos of practice. In the case law approach, the judge defines the problem and has already sifted the facts. In the ordinary practice of law, your client may not give you all the relevant facts; still less will your client correctly identify the legal issues. Lawyers in practice cannot be effective if they are passive. They must take initiative to find the right legal rules as well as the important facts.

In using the problems in this book, you can see that those in Part I furnish you references. These readings should help you begin analyzing the problem. But a warning: they are to some extent cumulative. Once you've read materials on, say, equitable discretion, you need to remember something about them so you will recognize a "discretion" issue when it arises again. In Part II you'll find the problems are even closer to real life: they give you no references at all. For those, you'll have to begin as lawyers begin, armed with analysis, a good book, and an index.

We hope you enjoy working at these problems. Many good lawyers have said that the problems they had in remedies were valuable, not only for working on skills of research, analysis, synthesis, and argumentation, but also for learning the "rules." We hope they will be valuable for you as well.

This book of problems is made to be used with the treatise, DAN DOBBS, THE LAW OF REMEDIES (2d ed. 1993) (3 vols.) or DAN DOBBS, THE LAW OF REMEDIES (2d ed. 1993) (one-vol. abridgement). Suggested readings will refer to the one-volume abridgement if it contains the relevant material. For convenience, citations to the one-volume edition will be given as DOBBS, TEXT § x.x (x). Occasionally the three-volume un-

1

abridged edition will be cited. In that case the citation form will be DAN
DOBBS, THE LAW OF REMEDIES § x.x (2d ed. 1993).

PART I

A SURVEY OF REMEDIES

Subpart A

The Principal Remedies and Remedial Rules

In this subpart we survey each of the main remedies by examining problems that concentrate on each remedy in turn, often in diverse factual settings.

CHAPTER 1

THE NATURE OF REMEDIAL QUESTIONS AND A SURVEY OF BASIC REMEDIES

A NOTE ON REMEDIES SUBJECT MATTER

The general questions of remedies law. The big remedies questions are: (1) What remedies are potentially available? What remedy should the plaintiff choose to pursue? and (2) What is the scope or measure of the remedies that might be awarded? What procedural or tactical incidents accompany the chosen remedy? If this is abstract, consider:

Four types of remedies. Remedies can be classified in many ways, but one useful classification says that there are four basic kinds of remedy: (1) *Damages*. The damages remedy is an award of money given as compensation for the plaintiff's loss, or, less often, to punish the defendant. (2) *Restitution*. A restitutionary remedy is an award of money, things or status given to prevent unjust enrichment of the defendant, but not necessarily equal to the plaintiff's losses. (3) *Coercive remedies*. Coercive remedies force the defendant to do something or to cease some activity. Coercive remedies are usually some form of injunction. They include specific performance of contracts. (4) *Declaratory remedies*. Declaratory judgments provide an official and authoritative determination of some disputed question.

Restitution = Property and contracts

3

Choosing a remedy and determining its scope. In any given case, the plaintiff might identify several possible remedies. She might be permitted to have *either* damages *or* specific performance but not both in the particular case. Part of her choice will depend upon the measure of damages or the scope of the specific performance decree. Some measures of damages might yield such a high recovery that the damages remedy would be preferable to the specific performance remedy. In other cases, the specific performance claim might put the defendant at such a disadvantage that the plaintiff would immediately achieve a superior tactical position in the litigation. This would be the case if specific performance would be more costly to the defendant than a damages award, for example.

This is the stuff of remedies. Remedy choice and remedy measurement are central not only to getting the best recovery but also to the tactics of litigation. Remedies is very much a litigation-oriented course. Remedies is also relevant to lawyer-planners, for example, to lawyers who draft contracts and who must forecast or contract about possible remedies.

Substance vs. remedy. Remedies law differs in focus from substantive law about rights and defenses. Remedies questions arise only when the lawyer can assume that rights will be established. So most problems in this book and in the field of remedies are decidedly NOT about whether the plaintiff has a right. They assume that the plaintiff has a right and go straight to the questions about the relief to be granted.

A remedial goal: vindicate the substantive right. At the same time, a very general goal of remedies is to vindicate the plaintiff's right. For this reason, the remedy should match the right and should be congruent with the right. If the plaintiff has a right to purchase 100 shares of AT&T stock from the defendant, that right is not vindicated by allowing the plaintiff to purchase 200 shares of AT&T stock or 100 shares of some other company. This point seems elementary but it can easily be overlooked. It has an important meaning. Remedies questions come into being after the substantive right has been established, but the appropriate remedy must reflect the size or scope of that substantive right. Sometimes the real remedies argument is one about the scope or nature of the plaintiff's right or entitlement. Once you know that the plaintiff's right was to purchase 100 shares of AT&T stock, you know a great deal about the remedy.

Practical constraints and conventional remedies. Remedies is a practical field. The ideal is to provide a remedy that vindicates, reflects, or matches the plaintiff's right, but the ideal may be costly or impossible to achieve. Sometimes the most important remedies rule is a practical compromise with the ideal or a convention that makes the ideal workable. Running through remedies questions are efforts to understand the proper scope of the plaintiff's right, to shape a remedy that matches the right, and then to decide what practical compromises are acceptable.

The example of the trespasser's vacation. Imagine, for example, that you own a cabin at the lake, a place to get away from time to time. Suppose that the defendant moves into it one weekend, knowing you won't be there. He happily occupies it for a little vacation of his own, but scrupulously leaves it clean. Your cabin is no worse for the wear. You undoubtedly have a right to exclusive possession of the cabin. You have lost something of that right even though you yourself did not want to use the cabin at the same time. Fixing a remedy for such a case may require us to recognize the ideal right to exclusive possession, but it may also require us to adopt some convention about measuring damages, since you did not actually lose any money or have to repair any harm. Identify the right, then find a remedy to match it if you can. Recognize acceptable remedial conventions or compromises when you cannot.

Public interests and remedial goals. Although remedies is presented here through problems grounded in the adversary system, lawyers ignore public interest at their peril. Realistic assessment of the judge's reaction to your arguments for a remedy or for a given scope to that remedy must include some awareness of public interests. Few judges would say, "The public be damned." Public policy will often oppose a remedy that provides more than full compensation, for example, or one that entails needless economic waste.

<u>*Three broad principles of remedial law*</u>. A number of problems recur frequently in remedies law. This paragraph identifies three of those problems by stating three very broad principles. *First*, **it is desirable to compensate for rights but to avoid either over- or under-compensation**. Easier said than done, as it turns out. *Second*, **it is desirable to avoid economic waste**. For example, we don't usually like remedies that require destruction of valuable goods. *Third*, **it is desirable to maintain a degree of efficiency in administering remedies**. We don't like to give a remedy that costs the defendant $100 but only benefits the plaintiff by $1, provided

we can find a better solution. You can consider these principles or attitudes as you go through these materials.

The problems in this book give you a chance to develop skill in recognizing remedial possibilities as an advocate, or occasionally as a planner-contract drafter and in working out the arguments, technical and otherwise, that you could present to a judge or to a negotiator for your adversary.

The problems in Chapter 1 are simpler than most. In most of them, you won't be required to choose among several remedies. Instead, you will get a chance to see some characteristics of the three most important remedies — damages, restitution and coercive remedies.

Problem 1-1

Perales v. Fenton

Fenton negligently ran a stop sign. As a result, his car collided with a car owned and operated by J. M. Perales, damaging the fender and door and also doing some frame damage. Perales' car was worth about $5,000 before the damage. She had three estimates made by reliable garages for the repair of her car. These ran from a low of about $6,000 to a high of about $7,000. You represent Perales. Fenton's adjuster has offered you $5,000 for the car damages. Should you accept?

Note

Damages awards usually aim at compensation. Can you determine what could count as "compensation" in this case?

Problem 1-2

Benton v. Henderson

Henderson stole Benton's 1929 antique auto. Benton spent $5,000 in tracking down Henderson and recovering the car. The car, though valuable, was worth less than $5,000 — probably about $4,000.

Reasonable

Benton tells you he spent so much money because after he had spent $1,000 locating Henderson, he thought he had him, but Henderson then moved on. Each time Benton would find the elusive Henderson, Henderson would escape his grasp. Each time Benton believed that he could get the car by spending only a few more dollars. Benton also tells you that he "loved that car," and would have spent even more if he had needed to. He is much relieved to have retrieved the car no worse for the wear.

look at elements of claim

Henderson has won some money and Benton wants to get some kind of attachment before suit because he fears Henderson will either spend it all or take off for parts unknown. You think you have grounds for attaching some part of Henderson's bank account but you don't want to overstate your claim because if you do, both you and Benton might be liable for a wrongful attachment. Should you seek try to attach assets valued at $4,000 or $5,000 or some other sum?

$5000 could be special claims

Note

take punitive into account

Notice that Benton spent more than the car was worth in tracking it down. Does that matter?

Problem 1-3

Zamora v. Damson

Damson stole an oil painting from Zamora. The painting was worth about $5,000. Damson sold the painting for $10,000 to a gullible client, though he managed to do so without actual fraud. What may Zamora recover from Damson?

Note

Are the legal goals here the same as those commonly encountered in other problems in this chapter? Can anything be said here for allowing Zamora to recover $10,000 instead of $5,000? Read the description of the four basic kinds of remedies above.

Problem 1-4

Green v. Dalstrom

Green deeded his farm to Dalstrom. Green did so because Dalstrom falsely represented to Green that if Green did not transfer the farm, the creditors of Green's son would be able to get it. Dalstrom told Green that the deed was legally only a mortgage for $10,000 and that this would keep the son's creditors from attaching the land. To show his good faith, Dalstrom actually gave $10,000 to Green, the amount of the supposed mortgage. In fact the paper signed by Green was an absolute deed. The land was worth at least $100,000. Dalstrom has recorded the deed. What exact remedy, or form of remedy, do you seek on Green's behalf?

Note

Consider all the alternative remedies, or forms of remedy, you think might be available. Once you have decided on the remedy you think you'd like most to get, try your hand at classifying it. Is it damages? Restitution? A coercive remedy?

Problem 1-5

Leary v. Langtree

Langtree, a contractor doing work on a nearby road, began removing gravel from land owned by Leary. Leary told him to get off his land, but Langtree refused to do so and kept taking gravel.

Langtree had no other feasible source. If Langtree is forced to haul gravel from alternative sources, it will cost him so much that he will not be able to complete the highway without losing enormous sums of money. Quite possibly he will not be able to complete it at all. The highway is important to the state and if Langtree suffers bankruptcy, the highway's completion will probably be substantially delayed. Construction work has disrupted business along the highway and has also cut down traffic and trade between cities connected by the highway.

Leary brought a suit in the Superior Court of Brandis County, a court having equity powers, and sought an injunction against further removal of the gravel, plus damages for gravel already removed. The gravel itself, however, is not worth much and Leary probably can recover very little by way of compensatory damages. The real issue is the injunction.

Note

1. The injunction sought in *Leary v. Langtree* is a *preventive* injunction, that is, one that would prevent harm in the future. Such an injunction is issued only if the defendant, by word or conduct, demonstrates that future harm is a real threat. If Leary had sought the injunction before Langtree had taken gravel or threatened to do so, it would have been denied. A *reparative* injunction would order the defendant to repair the harm already done, for example, to restore the gravel already taken. This is also a *mandatory* injunction, one that mandates an affirmative act as contrasted with a *prohibitory* injunction that mere prohibits conduct.

Key point

2. Why does Leary want this injunction? What will happen if it is issued? Think about real people.

3. A form of injunctive order not involved in *Leary v. Langtree* is the specific performance order. A specific performance decree orders the defendant to perform a contractual obligation. Contract obligations usually entail some affirmative action, so a specific performance decree is often analogous to, or a form of, a mandatory or reparative injunction.

Note: Some Other Basic Points

1. *Enforcement of remedies*. Notice that injunctive remedies (including specific performance) attempt to give the plaintiff the very thing to which he is entitled, not a money substitute. Injunctive remedies also differ from money remedies in the way they are enforced. Money remedies like the damages award are usually enforced by the sheriff or marshall who seizes the defendant's property under a writ, then, after appropriate notices, sells it. The resulting fund is used to pay the money damages award. Injunctive remedies, in contrast, are often enforced by contempt sanctions. In some instances, the defendant who disobeys an injunction may be jailed until he complies with its terms.

2. *Combining remedies*. Sometimes you can combine remedies, so don't think that you must select one and one only in all cases. For in-

stance, you might obtain specific performance of a contract if the defendant refuses to perform when performance is due. This will give you the performance to which you are entitled, but you might still have losses due to the delay. In that case, you might get *both* specific performance *and* damages.

3. *Secondary or helping remedies.* In some cases, secondary or helping remedies may be more important than the primary remedies identified here. For example, if you are entitled to damages or restitution as your primary remedy, a lien, attachment or *lis pendens* on the defendant's property may be the best way to solve many particular problems, as well as to prevent others.

4. *Remedies with particular names.* Several important remedies are not always easy to identify with one of the four categories listed above, because they are given names of their own. Ejectment and replevin, used to get possession of real and personal property, are technically neither damages nor injunctions. They are restitutionary actions of a sort, but hardly anyone will ever identify them in that way. Many remedies, like ejectment and replevin, are given unique names. Another example is "reinstatement"; this is a remedy for a person wrongfully discharged from a job in violation of Title VII. But reinstatement is merely a specific form of injunction. When you hear specific remedy names like that, try to see not only the specific relief given but also how it fits in the larger picture.

CHAPTER 2

THE COERCIVE REMEDIES: "EQUITY"

"Law and equity." At one time in England, two court systems operated side by side. One system was the common law, administered in such courts as the King's (or Queen's) Bench or the Common Pleas. The other was a system of "equity," administered in the Court of Chancery. The Chancery Court had a distinctive history, procedure, and style of thought.[1] Its remedies were strikingly different. Instead of rendering money judgments enforceable by the sheriff's seizure of assets, the Chancellor usually issued coercive orders such as injunctions. These might be enforced by the contempt power if necessary.

Jury trial. The most striking difference about an "equity" case today is that no jury trial right attaches to a purely equitable suit. In modern practice, "law and equity" have merged. American courts today usually exercise both the powers of the common law courts and the powers of the equity courts. Nevertheless, if the case is considered to be an equitable case, the parties have no right to a jury trial.

What cases are "equitable"? What is an equitable case, then? The terms equity and equitable are used in different ways at different times, so the answer is complicated. State courts might answer it somewhat differently from federal courts. However, you might begin with this rule of thumb: a case is equitable when the only *remedy* sought is equitable. That includes at least all cases in which the plaintiff seeks only an injunction.

Adequacy of legal remedy. The fact that the plaintiff asks for an equitable remedy does not mean that she will get it. Equity courts historically claimed the power to deny equitable relief as a matter of discretion. In addition, equity courts traditionally said that, with certain exceptions, they would not take a case at all if the legal remedy was adequate. Another formulation of this rule is that equity would not act unless necessary to prevent irreparable harm. This rule helped to minimize competition between the two court systems. One major argument today is whether that

---

[1] See 1 DAN DOBBS, THE LAW OF REMEDIES § 2.2 (2d ed. 1993).

rule is still needed after the two systems have merged, or whether, in fact, courts still actually apply the rule.

Policy and practicality. Sometimes courts say they are refusing to give an equitable remedy because the legal remedy is adequate. But in some such cases, you might think their reasons are different and that they might be acting on some perception of policy or practicality instead. For example, a court might refuse to issue an injunction against a lawsuit in another court. Interfering with other courts is serious business and likely to cause other problems. So there are good reasons of policy and practicality to refuse such an injunction. Those reasons don't seem to have much to do with the adequacy rule.

————

This chapter introduces the basic characteristics of "equity" cases. Remember as you work through the readings and problems that in most instances today you will go to the same courtroom and the same judge, regardless whether your claim is "at law" or "in equity."

You can find a brief overview discussing equity, equitable remedies, the different meanings of the term "equitable," and other basics in 1 DAN DOBBS, THE LAW OF REMEDIES § 2.1 pp. 55-66 (2d ed. 1993).

—————————

Problem 2-1

Hallows v. National Bank of Arifornia

1. Hallows and four other partners in the law firm of Riggs & Esteban decided to form their own firm. The Bank agreed in writing to provide certain loans to the firm-to-be, guaranteed by the individuals forming the firm. The money was necessary for initial capital outlays for equipment, rent, renovations and law books, and to stand in reserve to pay salaries until regular income could be assured.

2. Some of the loans would be made almost immediately (for initial capital); others would be available as needed for payment of current expenses until the income flow developed. In the latter category, even more money would be available from the bank if, but only if, the Hallows firm could demonstrate a certain level of billing hours. As to this level of

loans, the bank would have certain rights to inspect the firm's books and to demand changes in certain firm practices and procedures.

3. Hallows and her partners-to-be announced their departure from the Riggs & Esteban firm and made arrangements to sever all ties by April 15. Members of the Riggs firm were unhappy with the Hallows group, but the group had done nothing unethical in preparing to sever its ties. After these arrangements were made with the old firm, but while the Hallows group was still working there, the bank told Hallows that it would not make the loan after all. Negotiation was futile.

4. The Hallows group is now in limbo, unable to stay on with the Riggs firm but deprived of the capital it needed to open its own offices. Other banks in the city have refused to make any similar loan, although Hallows has not yet approached banks in other cities. Hallows feels an immediate loan is necessary. Some clients are likely to follow Hallows into the new firm if the firm opens immediately because that would mean those clients would have continuous service from lawyers who have generally handled their work. However, if the firm's opening is postponed, clients whose work has been done in the past by members of the Hallows group will not be able to turn to Hallows immediately and will become accustomed to new attorneys at Riggs (or in some other firm). In that case, such clients would probably not take their work to Hallows later and the new firm would probably be foredoomed to failure.

5. Hallows asks you to represent her and her group in a specific performance suit against the bank. What issues and arguments do you foresee and what is your estimate of the probable outcome? Please see DOBBS, TEXT § 2.5.

legal REMEDY IS IN ADEQUATE, would SUFFER SPECIFIC performance CAUSES IN a contractual SETTING! IRREPARABLE Harm DAMAGES wd under compensate, a contract is a promise (moral theory)

Problem 2-2

Burton v. Winter et al.

Fifteen years ago, Burton sold a large tract of 600 acres to Winter Developers. Burton reserved for herself and her heirs, the right to use certain described portions of the tract along the river. The types of uses were not specified. The provision was a valid part of the deed and binds Winter and all subsequent purchasers.

For a long time, Burton used the lands along the river mainly for social purposes: picnics and group outings. Winter developed the land as homesites, calling the area Wintergreen. Over the years, all of the hundreds of lots were sold and homes built on them. The river lands were conveyed to the Wintergreen Neighborhood Association as common lands for use of all lot owners, subject to Burton's reserved rights to use the lands for herself and her heirs.

Two years ago, the county completed a large park along the river running up to the boundary of the 600-acre tract. The park has become extremely popular. From the park's boundary line, Burton constructed a path along the river in her reserved use area. Along the path Burton set up several small businesses, including a cafe and a boat and bike rental.

Residents of the area have come to think of the lands as entirely theirs. They understand Burton's rights to use the lands, but had never considered commercial development possible. The deed's reservation does not explicitly limit the kinds of uses available to Burton.

Winter (the original grantee), the Wintergreen Neighborhood Association, and a group of the homeowners advised Burton that they would not permit entrants on the land from the park. Since park users were the only ones who would enter the reserved river lands and make use of Burton's commercial facilities there, this move would destroy Burton's businesses if it succeeded. Winter and the other defendants placed barriers at the park land boundary. Income naturally came to a halt and Burton closed the businesses, but did not remove the small buildings.

Two years later, after the park had been further improved and was even more heavily used, Burton brought a suit to force Winter, the Neighborhood Association, and the neighbors to remove the barriers and to permit unimpeded access.

A series of motions led the trial judge, Judge Green, to determine that (1) the reservation was valid and enforceable, so that Burton had a right to use the described lands along the river, and (2) Burton's right to use the land was not restricted as to purpose, so that commercial uses were reserved as well as purely personal ones. Judge Green then said, "I have some reservations of my own about this reservation." After the lawyers offered a little polite laughter, he went on to say that he would like to consider the possibility of limiting relief or even denying equitable relief altogether. On this point he asked attorneys on both sides for a memo.

Represent either Burton or the Wintergreen defendants, according to your preference or the class assignment. Consult generally DOBBS, TEXT §§ 2.4 (1), 2.4 (5). You may wish to scan § 2.3 (5) on estoppel and laches as well.

Thinking ahead: Suppose Judge Green considers all the memos and announces: "I'm going to refuse all injunctive relief as a matter of equitable discretion." If you are representing Burton, what steps will you consider? If you are representing Wintergreen, what is your response to those steps? For Burton's lawyers: now that you have reflected on potential next steps, do you make any immediate changes in your strategy right now?

[handwritten margin notes: "Equitable Estoppel"; "laches is a Defense for Wintergreen"; "Burton can RELY the legal REMEDY - enforcement of contract"; "Balance of Equities public park & commercial use"]

Problem 2-3

Estep v. McCauley

We represent Mr L. C. Estep. He owns his own home at 403 Oak Place. The house and lot are valued at approximately $300,000. There are a number of trees on the lot, including several large oaks probably 50 to 70 years old. These and other trees lie along the back of the lot abutting land owned by Mr. James McCauley. Mr. McCauley is about to cut the trees in question in the belief that he owns the land. In other words, we have a boundary dispute. McCauley has told his chain saw crew to cut in the morning. Estep feels it is very important to him to stop this. Please get it taken care of this afternoon. Please read DOBBS, TEXT §§ 2.11 (1) & 2.11 (2) & 2.11 (3).

Problem 2-4

Aarons v. Ballman Industries, Inc.

[handwritten margin note: "Dairy Queen doctrine"]

Ballman Industries operates a factory in Charlestown, Aresona. The factory is economically important to the town of Charlestown, where it is located, but it does emit smoke and particles. Some residents claim the smoke and/or particles are dangerous to health and it is true that the incidence of congenital anomalies with newborns is much higher in Charlestown than elsewhere in the state. Other residents of the town take the view

15

that the factory is as safe as it can be and that attacks on the factory threaten the economic well-being of the community. The community is in fact polarized on this issue.

The objecting faction has filed a suit in federal court, asserting claims both under certain federal statutes and under state nuisance law. Under state nuisance law, they claimed public nuisance with private damage and also private nuisances with damage. They sought (1) injunction against all operations of the factory, or in the alternative, an injunction effectively preventing discharge of any pollutants whatever; and (2) damages for past harms. The suit demanded a jury trial. Subject to further research, it appears that there is federal jurisdiction under the federal statutes and because of some diversity, and that there is "supplemental jurisdiction" over the state-law nuisance claims.

Ballman has expected this suit for some time. It does emit pollutants, but it tells its attorneys it has done everything possible to control them short of stopping production. It believes it is in compliance with federal law, but Ballman's attorneys believe there may nonetheless be a state-law nuisance. They also think damages are small. What they fear most is an injunction.

The Ballman attorneys are most concerned about the possibility that a federal jury would be unsympathetic to the defense. They feel a state-court jury in Charlestown would lean in favor of the defense, or that they would be divided because of their reluctance to damage an important industry that employs many local workers. But they think a federal jury, drawn from a large area with no real connection to Ballman, might be ready to "hang us at dawn," especially if the plaintiffs are able to get in evidence about the higher percentage of congenital abnormalities in the Charlestown area.

Represent either Aarons' group or Ballman. Analyze the narrow issue of jury trial. On the injunction aspects of the case, can the defense avoid a jury trial or not? Please scan DOBBS, TEXT § 2.6 (2), then read §§ 2.6 (3) & 2.6 (4).

Notes

1. *Merger*. The problems in *Aarons* arise from the fact that the old separate courts of law and equity have been "merged" almost everywhere. Merger raises questions about what kind of procedures, remedies, and analysis should be followed. For a general background or summary of merger, see DOBBS, TEXT § 2.6 (1).

2. *Equity jury trial and the Dairy Queen rule.* Although jury trial was not traditionally required or even permitted in equity courts, *Dairy Queen, Inc. v. Wood*, 369 U.S. 469, 82 S.Ct. 894, 8 L.Ed.2d 44 (1962), discussed in the readings, requires a jury trial in federal courts whenever a common law remedy is sought along with an equitable remedy and when the two remedies turn on common facts. What would be the common facts in this case on the damages and the injunction claim?

3. *Res judicata.* In general, in a completely merged system of law and equity, res judicata doctrines apply. Notice how res judicata and jury trial issues interact under *Dairy Queen*. Especially note *Parklane Hosiery Co. v. Shore*, 439 U.S. 322, 99 S.Ct. 645, 56 L.Ed.2d 552 (1979) and *Lytle v. Household Mfg. Co.*, 494 U.S. 545, 110 S.Ct. 1331, 108 L.Ed.2d 504 (1990), summarized and discussed in DOBBS, TEXT § 2.6 (4).

4. *Modification of equitable decrees.* The court's power to modify the injunction later on is related to its discretion to deny or shape the injunction in the first place. Under the federal standard, an injunction favoring the plaintiff may be modified to further the original purpose of the decree if "time and experience" show that will be necessary or desirable. A modification favoring the defendant may be justified if a significant change in factual or legal circumstances makes it inequitable to give the original decree prospective application. Should the modification be made by a judge sitting without a jury if both legal and "equitable" issues are involved?

5. *What is equitable?* The terms equity and equitable carry many meanings. Probably the most common idea is that a case or an issue is "equitable" when it is associated with equitable remedies, most of which are injunctions or variations on injunctions. Sometimes, however, courts and lawyers consider a case to be equitable when equitable discretion or ideas of justice are invoked as a substantive matter. For more on what is equitable for jury trial purposes, see DOBBS, TEXT § 2.6 (3).

Problem 2-5

Esquivel v. Simpson

Esquivel sued Simpson for specific performance of a valid contract under which Simpson was to convey Blackacre to Esquivel. The court ordered specific performance, but Simpson has refused to convey. Esquivel is afraid that Simpson will convey to someone else. You represent Esquivel. How should you proceed?

17

Problem 2-6

State Department of Civil Rights v. City of Truman

The City of Truman, Kansouri awards most of its major construction and repair contracts among four large construction firms, who are usually the only ones who bid on the jobs. Statutes require bidding and regulate the award. Three of the contractors directly or indirectly discriminate in hiring. Some of the discrimination is against women; some against minorities. All three of the contractors, including Dupres Brothers, Inc., are in violation of state and probably federal law. Various enforcement devices have been invoked to force them to hire more minorities and women. As a part of the effort to force these large firms to comply with the law, the Kansouri Department of Civil Rights has brought an action against them to impose certain hiring quotas. It has joined the City of Truman as a defendant. The only relief sought against the city is that it be enjoined from accepting any bids from any of the named contractor-defendants until they are shown to be in compliance with the state's anti-discrimination law. The city is in no way itself violating the law by accepting bids from these contractors.

You are an attorney for the city and have been asked to attend a conference with the city manager, the city council's committee on public works, and the head of the public works department. Be prepared to discuss whether the city should resist the injunction, to ask any necessary questions of fact, to outline the important considerations involved, and to take a position on the probable legal rights and legal outcome if the city does resist.

Read DOBBS, TEXT §§ 1.7, 1.8; § 2.8 (5); see also § 2.4 (7), sub. *Discretion and the Rightful Position: Discretion Limiting Rights* & sub. *Discretion to Expand Rights?*

———

CHAPTER THREE

BASIC PROBLEMS OF THE DAMAGES REMEDY

Problem 3-1

Story v. Grayson

Ricci & Alyen
Attorneys at Law

[File notes by Ernest Ricci]

Story owned a valuable llama used for breeding, known as Bambee. Bambee was one of the new-found Erasmus Llamas which had especially desirable qualities. One desirable quality was their disinclination to spit.

Bambee was put to stud at very good fees. Story paid $90,000 for Bambee a year ago. Bambee's market value now is between $110,000 and $130,000. Grayson stole Bambee at a llama show. Story, who knew that Bambee was gone but not that Grayson had him, expended $3,000 in trying to find Bambee. After several weeks, he gave up the intensive search and began searching for a replacement.

Story was unable to find llamas of the same breed in Bambee's price range. Story inspected a number of llamas of the somewhat comparable breed known as Machu Llamas. Prices among the Machu tended to run somewhat higher for animals that were otherwise comparable and Story ended up buying a Machu (not an Erasmus) Llama named Llamaha for $150,000.

Breeding farms that used Bambee and now use or consider using Llamaha will testify if needed that Llamaha is indeed comparable to Bambee. Story has discovered that Grayson was the thief who stole Bambee. Grayson is a llama breeder who has considerable assets. Ironically, however, Bambee is not among them; Bambee died a few weeks after Grayson stole him.

19

Story wants to sue Grayson. Grayson claims he took Bambee on loan and by agreement, but Story assures me that this is not true and that such a loan would be contrary to custom of the llama breeding and showing communities around the country. My notes of the interview with Story indicate that he lost some customers, maybe permanently, as a result of losing Bambee. He certainly lost some fees during the time it took to get Llamaha as a replacement. He will get the exact information for us, but he thinks the lost fees came to at least $10,000, possibly more.

Although I have not yet drafted a complaint, Marybeth Englard, representing Grayson, has talked to me about the case. She thinks that while Grayson won't admit the theft, he will settle for a reasonable sum. That caught me off guard, because we haven't worked up a memo or any detailed figures. We need to work up a memo on the measures and elements of damages.

Mr. Ricci asks you to work up the memo. Start by looking at DOBBS, TEXT §§ 3.2 & 3.3 (1)—3.3 (5). If you have time, you may find § 3.1 furnishes helpful background information and definitions. Likewise § 3.3 (6) may prove useful if you have time to read it.

Problem 3-2

Re Washington

Bedford, a building contractor, agreed by valid contract to build a house for Washington on Washington's land. The house was to be built according to plans and specifications furnished, and the total price was $200,000. Bedford performed his contract in all respects, except that, contrary to the express insistence of Washington and to the specifications and plans, he installed red ceramic tile in one of the bathrooms instead of the blue tile called for. The quality and make of the tile is the same as that called for in the specifications.

The value of the completed house standing on the lot is $260,000. The value of the house with blue rather than red tile would probably be virtually the same. It will cost $6,000 to rip out the red tile and install blue tile. Washington and his lender paid Bedford in installments as work was completed and withheld a total of $7,000 until the job was completed. Washington has now had an estimate for repair of the bathroom for $6,000 and has authorized payment of the withheld funds except for the $6,000 that would be needed to rip out the red tile and install blue. Bedford has now been paid $194,000 on the contract price. He has claimed the remaining $6,000. Washington has said he has a right to keep it as <u>damages</u>. After some dispute, Washington called us and said he'd follow our advice. Please call him back and tell him whether he owes the $6,000 or any part of it and bill him for your time.

Please read DOBBS, TEXT §§ 3.3 (6) & 12.19 (1).

Problem 3-3

Berwyn's Dress Shop v. Allyn-Thomas Leasing Corporation

Allyn-Thomas Leasing planned and built a shopping center, the Lakeside Mall. Long in advance of completion, Allyn-Thomas made leases with various business operations. It leased a certain space to Berwyn's Dress Shop for a base rental of $5,000 per month plus a percentage of the gross sales. The lease contained other normal provisions for shopping center leases. The leased space was to become available on September 1 of last year.

At the time the lease was signed, Berwyn's was an existing business with a location in the downtown area. However, the Lakeside Mall and two other nearby shopping centers were drawing most prime retail locations from the downtown area to the richer suburbs. Berwyn's main competitor, Dominick's, was moving to a shopping center, Northside Center, near the Mall. For this reason, Berwyn's felt it was important to move and to get established in the area ahead of Dominick's. Dominick's lease arrangements had it that Dominick's would open in the Northside Center on October 1 of last year. Berwyn's arrangement was therefore satisfactory to Berwyn, since it would put Berwyn's into the area well ahead of Dominick's.

Allyn-Thomas' contractor fell behind his schedule, though it was obliged to pay a rather stiff <u>liquidated damages</u> for delay. Berwyn's space was not available until January 1 of this year, well after Dominick's had opened in Northside nearby. In the meantime, Berwyn's lease downtown had run out and Berwyn's had no location available at all for about two

21

weeks. Goods were stored in a warehouse. Some of the goods were not suited to the only warehouse available and were stored at "owner's risk." Some of these were in fact damaged in the warehouse.

We represent Berwyn's. They tell us that they have lost customers and sales during the period without a retail outlet. They lost the advantage they sought to have with the Lakeside Mall lease, because they failed to gain competitive advantage over Dominick's. In fact, as a result of the delay, have actually *lost* competitive ground. Berwyn's accountants believe they can make reliable estimates as to these losses. The goods damaged in the warehouse cost another $1,500. Berwyn's is very angry because it could have had comparable space at Northside Center for about $4,000 per month and the same percentage of gross sales.

What damages can we recover for Berwyn's from Allyn-Thomas for its admitted breach of the lease?

Please read DOBBS, TEXT § 3.4.

Problem 3-4

Esterhazy v. Heyman

Heyman contracted with Esterhazy to provide Esterhazy a pasture of certain acreage and quality for pasturing Esterhazy's sheep. Heyman accepted the sheep at his pastures, knowing that the quality of alfalfa and other grasses was insufficient. This insufficiency was a breach of either an express or an implied term in the contract.

Shortly after acceptance of the sheep, Heyman informed Esterhazy of the insufficiency, which arose because of irrigation problems. Esterhazy replied, "Well, that's your problem; you got to pasture them right, or get grain elsewhere; we got a contract."

As a result of poor pasture, a number of sheep died, either of starvation or of disease brought on by low resistance due to underfeeding. Your client, Esterhazy, tells you, in addition to these facts, that he was short of funds at the time all this happened, and that Heyman had been the only person willing to pasture or feed on partial credit. When Heyman's pasturage proved insufficient, Esterhazy felt there was little he could do except to stand on the contract.

Esterhazy's sheep losses amounted to $15,000, all occurring after he knew of the insufficient pasturage. He says he could have bought enough feed for the sheep for $3,000, but that he simply did not have the money and could not borrow it. Heyman has offered $3,000 in settlement of all claims. Should Esterhazy accept this sum?

Please read DOBBS, TEXT § 3.9.

Problem 3-5

Mariakakis v. Bastian

Bastian discussed leasing a house from Mariakakis. Mariakakis agreed to accept $1,850 per month plus the cost of fire insurance, $600 annually. The parties prepared a lease. It provided that Mariakakis would maintain fire insurance on the premises. It specified various options about how the lease would be treated in the event of a fire. If premises could be reasonably repaired within the term of the lease, the lease would not terminate but Bastian would pay no rent during any period in which occupancy was not reasonably possible. If the premises could not reasonably be repaired and made habitable during the term, then the lease was terminated and obligations on both sides were discharged. The tenant's obligations were to pay rent ($1,900 per month), to exercise reasonable care toward the premises, and to return the premises in as good a condition as that in which they were found, ordinary wear and tear excepted. The lease contained other commonly used clauses.

Bastian paid the deposit and the first month's rent and moved in. During the second week, Bastian accidently set fire to the house while smoking in bed. He escaped unharmed, but the house burned down. Mariakakis had purchased insurance with the East Virginia Fire Insurance Company, payable to Mariakakis. The EVF paid the entire face amount of the policy which was in fact the actual value of the house. EVF, acting under a subrogation clause in its policy, then brought suit against Bastian claiming that he negligently destroyed Mariakakis' house and that EVF was

23

subrogated to Mariakakis' rights. The complaint demanded recovery for all sums expended by EVF in payment for the house.

You represent Bastian, the defendant. Please read DOBBS, TEXT §§ 3.8 (1) & 3.8 (2).

Problem 3-6

Le v. Bonnet

We represent Le. Bonnet is a medical doctor. Le was her patient. Bonnet negligently completed surgery and closed the incision in Le's abdomen without removing some "sponges" and a pair of scissors. It soon became apparent to Le that something was wrong. She consulted a second doctor, Dr. Goodwin. Goodwin performed a second operation to remove the equipment Bonnet had left in. Infection required several aditional days in the hospital. Le suffered pain, lost wages, and further medical bills as a result of this second operation. Her own medical insurance paid all but $1,000 of her $10,000 medical bills.

Bonnet's liability insurer has agreed to pay $1,000 on the medical bills and to make a satisfactory payment for pain and suffering and lost wages. This will pay all Le's out-of-pocket even after our fee is deducted. Should we press for the $9,000 or is that to be excluded because Le's insurer has paid for that portion?

Please read DOBBS, TEXT § 3.8 (1).

Problem 3-7

Mendel v. Murphy

Seven years ago, Jon Murphy was attempting to buy shares in a closely held corporation engaged in the manufacture of prescription drugs. This was the Pure Food and Drug Co., whose stock occasionally was sold over the counter. The last shares sold over the counter as of that time were shares sold a year earlier for $1,000 each. This was a lot of ten shares. At that time, the book value of the shares was approximately $950.

Murphy located one Ben Mendel, an 80-year-old man, who owned ten shares. In February he expressed an interest in buying the shares. Mendel said he was willing, but that he wasn't sure what the market price was these days. He said he had paid about $900 a share two or three years earlier. As later shown in Mendel's deposition, Murphy said something like, "Well, we're in the ball park anyway, we can get the exact value down later and I'll give you my IOU and you can go on and sign over the shares to me now." Mendel agreed to do this on the strength of Murphy's well-known standing in the area as a businessman.

The IOU was as follows: "I promise to pay today's market value for ten shares of Pure Food and Drug stock, purchased this date. Jon Murphy." The note was dated February 15, seven years ago. Mendel duly assigned the shares and made appropriate arrangements with the transfer agent. On February 16, Murphy pledged the shares to the First Kent Bank & Trust Co. of Chapelapolis to secure a loan of $8,000.

The book value at that time was $1,100, but no market in the shares could be established until over a year later when 15 shares were sold over the counter for $1,300 per share. Mendel had been demanding payment for some time and Murphy had repeatedly said he was agreeable to a payment as soon as they could agree on the price but that, in the absence of a market, all he could see to pay would be the $900 figure mentioned. Four years ago, almost three years after the IOU was signed, Mendel, represented by the Kirk firm, brought suit against Murphy. Murphy took the same position he always did: he admitted owing $900 per share but disputed any greater obligation. He said he had been willing to pay $900, at least from the time it became apparent to him and to Mendel that no more accurate price could be fixed.

Mendel's complaint asserted in the alternative these claims: (1) there was no contract because the parties had failed to agree on an essential term, namely the price; the court should compel reconveyance of the shares to Mendel by imposing a constructive trust or otherwise; (2) the agreement to assign the shares was procured by fraud, duress or undue influence, and the court should compel a return of the shares to Mendel by imposing a constructive trust or otherwise; (3) if there was a contract, there was an implied term to pay reasonable value for the shares, which was no less than $1,300 per share; (4) Mendel was entitled to interest on the value of the shares from the date of the IOU if he was entitled to recover on any of the first three claims asserted.

25

Various preliminary depositions and motions occupied the parties and their attorneys intermittently until two years ago, at which time, on the basis of depositions and admissions, Murphy's firm moved for summary judgment on the first two claims. There was a hearing, and after the judge had taken the matter under advisement, he entered a summary judgment for the defendant on the first two claims, holding that, as a matter of law, neither fraud nor undue influence nor duress had been established, and further that the parties had indeed reached a contract with "reasonable value" as an implied term of the contract.

At that point, Mendel was completely disenchanted with the legal system in general and his attorney in particular. He discharged the attorney and retained us to try his claim. We got the judge to set the remainder of the case for trial in January last year to determine the reasonable value of the shares. As we see it, Murphy has been using every form of delay possible and Mendel's first attorney wasn't energetic enough to get this small matter tried and disposed of.

We completed trial in February last year. It was really a series of non-jury hearings in which a number of experts testified as to value of the shares on the purchase date and again we felt that the defendant was dragging the matter out unnecessarily. Judge Esquivel concluded that the reasonable value of the shares on February 15 should control the liability, and that such value was $1,175 per share; he entered judgment in favor of Mendel and against Murphy for $11,750 with interest at 6% from the date of judgment until paid.

Esquivel declined to enter judgment for interest as we requested. Mendel wants to appeal. He is riled at the legal system and everyone concerned. I don't blame him. He was hard up and in fact there was a little evidence at trial that he had to borrow $5,000 at 10% interest three years ago. In addition it gripes him that Murphy has received the dividends on the shares, which in the seven years since the IOU have come to over $7,000. However, I don't want to let him appeal unless we have a real shot at getting something more for him. Please research the possibility that we could get interest.

———————

Problem 3-8

Harry's, Inc. v. Miracle Strip
Merchants Ass'n et al

The City of Charlesville, after many years of struggle, passed a comprehensive zoning ordinance with aesthetic requirements. One of these restricted the size, location, and other characteristics of business signs. The Miracle Strip, a boulevard of five miles or more, is one area that contains numerous signs in connection with the uninterrupted strip of businesses. The signs are large and bright and (the city claimed) were distracting to drivers. To some people (but not all), these signs appeared as a "jungle" or a "neon junkyard." Testimony before the city council contained both harsher and more tolerant terms.

Harry's, Inc., is a business located on the strip. Jasmin Belmont, who was the owner of Harry's, called a meeting of strip merchants to discuss the situation. Belmont wanted to oppose the ordinance on the ground that it was unconstitutional as an infringement of free speech or a taking of property or both. After two long evenings of discussion, however, the other merchants decided against bringing suit at the moment.

Belmont estimated that her signs cost no less than $10,000 and that she had invested even more in their upkeep. According to her, the total value of all the signs along the strip was in the millions. Since the signs would have to be scrapped under the ordinance, she retained the Dangerfield firm to bring suit to enjoin enforcement of the ordinance on constitutional grounds.

The suit against the city was successful: Judge Arlen issued the injunction and time has elapsed for an appeal. The Dangerfield firm, joined by Belmont, moved the court for an award of attorney fees against the city. The motion was denied and time for appealing that has also elapsed.

Dangerfield has asked our firm to determine whether Belmont or Dangerfield has a reasonably good chance of collecting a share of the fees from the other merchants. If so, we are retained to pursue that claim. According to Belmont and Dangerfield, the other merchants still have their signs up and the Harry's, Inc. suit has determined issues so broadly that there is no danger of any ordinance forcing the signs down except by the exercise of eminent domain powers with full compensation.

Please begin by examining DOBBS, TEXT §§ 3.10 (1) & 3.10 (2).

Problem 3-9

Wallace v. City of Rich Springs

The City of Rich Springs has operated its own electrical company or "department" since 1918. Rich Springs is now a large city with a modern sophisticated power distribution system. Electricity sales to citizens and other persons served by the system account for many millions in monthly revenue to the Rich Springs Electrical Utility.

Three years ago, Keith McLaughlin, a city electric engineer working for the utility, became concerned that citizens living near high voltage lines and transformer stations were being exposed to harmful electromagnetic radiation. He had two reasons for this concern. First, he became acquainted with people living near transformer stations because his job took him to those stations periodically. He began to realize that some of them showed a number of unhealthy symptoms and a surprising number were diagnosed cancer patients. Second, he had read scientific literature, some of which indicated that people subjected to electromagnetic fields around high voltage lines or transformer stations were or might be prone to suffer various cancers and other health problems.

McLaughlin did what he called a "home made" study, inquiring among people around the transformer stations about their health. This study was not in any sense scientific, but it did show a lot of health problems consistent with the idea that those most exposed were suffering as a result. McLaughlin reported this "study" and some of the scientific literature to his superior, the director of the electrical utility. The director, Felicia Steele, told McLaughlin to forget it.

Two years ago, some citizens became convinced that the transformers and high voltage lines were causing health problems for those living near-by, mainly in the form of various kinds of cancer. They called on Steele and she told them that there was no health hazard and that in any event there was no cost-effective way of eliminating either the transformers or high voltage lines. At the time of the meeting, Steele in fact had in her possession a scientific study that purported to show very substantial health risks for cancers, especially in children. However, she also had in her possession studies that indicated no connection between electromagnetic fields (EMF) and health problems.

A number of complaints continued to come in. Then about a year ago, over a period of several weeks, several children were diagnosed as suffering from leukemia, a form of cancer associated with EMF in some of the literature. One of those children, Mary Ann Wallace, died from the disease. Her father, Gene Wallace, has retained our firm to bring a wrongful death suit against the City of Rich Springs. We filed a suit against the city under the wrongful death and the survival statute. (As you know, under our law, the city is liable in tort for damages negligently caused by operation of a city utility, including a city water or city electric company.)

At Wallace's insistence, but most reluctantly, we also asked for an injunction to compel the city to take action on this health risk. Our reluctance was justified. The Rich Springs Senior Association, Inc., a group devoted to the interests of older citizens, intervened to oppose the injunction because they feared the alternatives. They feared that the city would raise electrical rates, if it were required to undertake expensive shielding or other actions to minimize the EMF risk. This would be especially harmful to those on fixed incomes. They took the position that the risk was non-existent or minimal in any event. So the injunction part of our suit has added a lot of trouble for us. Judge Brown refused to issue a preliminary injunction. The permanent injunction issues will abide the trial of the wrongful death claim.

The immediate problem is this: can we recover punitive damages? Please give me your researched opinion. See DOBBS, TEXT § 3.11 (1)

CHAPTER 4

RESTITUTION

● Peggy intended to deliver her motorcycle to an agent for Bill's Motorcycle Repair. She mistakenly believed that Duffy was an agent for that establishment and delivered it to him. Duffy was not an agent for anyone and he refuses to return the motorcycle.

● Penn owns a farm he calls Paris. While Penn was vacationing in Canada, Guinn moved onto the farm and claimed it as her own. She refuses to leave.

● Percy mistakenly believed that he owed his landlord $500 as rent for his last month on the premises. Acting under this belief, he mailed a check to the landlord, Leake. Leake deposited the check. Now Percy has discovered that he had paid the last month's rent with his initial deposit and that he owed nothing.

Peggy is entitled to replevin, a common law action that will allow her to recover the motorcycle. Penn is entitled to ejectment, a common law action that will put him in possession of Paris. Percy is entitled to recover the money in an action analogous to the common law action of *assumpsit* for money had and received.

All three claims can be viewed as claims for restitution. A judgment for the plaintiff would *restore* something to the plaintiff that belongs to the plaintiff in some important sense. Unless the defendant is obliged to make restoration (restitution) he will be unjustly enriched.

All of the claims are common law claims. They arose historically in law courts, not equity courts. The first two gave the plaintiff property, but not by injunction. Instead, they would give the plaintiff the motorcycle by having the sheriff seize it; or would give the plaintiff Paris by having the sheriff physically oust Guinn and put Penn in possession.

The first two claims are special in another way. They are grounded in the plaintiff's property interest. Peggy owned the motorcycle, Penn owned Paris. We know that Duffy and Guinn must give up the property even if they are innocent because we know that Peggy and Penn are the property owners. The third case is different. If Percy pays money to someone, it is not correct to say that the money is his property. In this case we must say that Percy can recover, not because he has legal title to the money and not because Leake is a wrongdoer, but because Leake has received a benefit that in good conscience belongs to Percy and that Leake will be unjustly enriched unless Percy is allowed to recover.

This last kind of unjust enrichment theory, not based on property ownership, was originally explained on the ground that the defendant had impliedly *contracted* to pay or repay the money. The implied-in-law contract was also called quasi-contract. Although you could have a genuine implied-in-fact contract, this one was wholly fictional, a way of saying that courts would impose a rule of law to prevent unjust enrichment. Because of the fiction, however, the claim was originally associated with the common law writ of assumpsit, by which contract claims were enforced. Its various forms are still often referred to as quasi-contract claims.

This kind of assumpsit or quasi-contract claim was adapted to a world in which increasing amounts of wealth were NOT in the form of tangible property. Replevin was used to recapture tangible chattels; ejectment to recapture real property. Wealth in the form of intangible property, money, and services did not fall within the scope of those actions. Quasi-contract or unjust enrichment claims appeared to fill the gap just when commercial life made intangibles the main form of wealth.

Before going on, take notice that restitution may involve actual contracts and it may involve wrongdoing by the defendant, but that neither contract nor wrongdoing is necessary to establish a restitutionary claim. In Percy's case, for example, the claim is based on the fact that Leake has money to which Leake is not entitled; he is unjustly enriched. You should also take notice that restitution does not necessarily entail "rescission" or avoidance of a contract. Percy's claim is again an example.

Restitution takes many forms. The restitution claims summarized above are all typical "law" claims, but some restitution can take place in an equitable format. One brief example: Suppose that by mistake you convey Blackacre to Dallem. Perhaps you had meant to convey Whiteacre but described the wrong property; or perhaps you had meant to convey to another person. Either way, however, Dallem got legal title and she re-

31

corded the deed. You are not the legal owner and not entitled to immediate possession, so ejectment won't work.

This looks more like Percy's situation, except that instead of giving money you gave land title. In Percy's case you could sue for money in an ordinary "law" claim. But how can you sue to get title back in your name? The answer is that you must ask the court to use the powers that were historically equitable in nature. You might think of asking the judge for an injunction requiring Dallem to reconvey the property, for instance. Your grounds would be the same as in Percy's case: if Dallem keeps the property, she will be unjustly enriched. In fact, lawyers will say you are seeking a "constructive trust," but the effect is the same. The judge will say that Dallem is a constructive trustee and therefore obliged to convey the property back to you and the judge will issue an order so requiring if necessary. You can see the equitable characteristics in the coercive order for reconveyance.

Problem 4-1

Hirsch v. Dawson

Dawson's land, although located in an arid western state, had always produced plenty of water from its wells. As a result, Dawson was able to raise cattle and grow crops with relative ease. Last year Hirsch, who lived in the east, inspected the land and discussed its purchase. He examined well records and the produce. After he went back home, Hirsch wrote Dawson several letters asking questions on particular subjects. Finally, six weeks ago, right after the earthquake, Hirsch called Dawson and they orally agreed to the purchase by Hirsch for $650,000. A week later Hirsch flew in and the deal was closed. Hirsch paid $650,000 and Dawson gave him a deed.

Water gradually dried up, however, and in a matter of a few weeks, the wells were all dry. Hydrologists concluded that the earthquake had shifted rock formations so that water had drained from what was formerly the aquifer from which the Dawson-Hirsch land drew its water.

We represent Hirsch, who wants to undo the deal. Hirsch believes that Dawson honestly did not know of the earthquake's effect. Dawson says he was not aware of any diminution in the water supply, as he had harvested his crops and sold off his cattle and was using little or no water at the time of closing. Use your general legal knowledge. On that basis, what is your opinion: (1) Has Hirsch any claim at all? On what basis? (2) What is his remedy if he has one?

Problem 4-2

Best Ins. Co. v. Roth et al.

Hans Roth owned a home. Best Insurance Co. carried fire insurance in the sum of $200,000. For reasons not particularly pertinent here, Roth was also insured against fire in the same amount by Pure Ins. Co. Both policies had an "other insurance clause," providing: ·

> The insurer shall not be liable for a greater proportion of any loss than the amount hereby insured shall bear to the whole insurance covering the property against the peril involved, whether collectible or not.

The Roth home suffered severe fire damages on the night of January 12, last year, while Roth and his family were in Florida on vacation. The Best Insurance Co., unaware of Pure's coverage, adjusted the loss and paid a total of $80,000 to Roth in full settlement. Roth seems to have been unaware of the Pure coverage; in any event he made no claim on it.

Shortly after the loss was paid by Best, Best discovered Pure's coverage. This was a few days before the expiration of the period in which Roth was permitted to make claim under the Pure policy. Best notified Pure that it had paid Pure's share of liability, sent Pure copies of all investigation, reports, proofs of loss, and requested that Pure pay its share over to Best. Pure made a noncommittal answer by telephone, at which time Best requested Roth to file proof of loss with Pure. Roth refused, saying he had not even realized he had two coverages and certainly did not intend to claim twice. Best was unable to explain adequately to Roth and the time for filing proof of loss expired without his having made any claim against Pure. Shortly thereafter, Pure formally notified Best that it would not honor Best's claim, in spite of the pro rata clauses in both policies.

Thereupon, Best brought an action naming both Pure and Roth as defendants, praying $40,000 from Roth, or in the alternative, $40,000 from

33

Pure. Its premise was that Roth was never entitled to more than $40,000 from Best. Each defendant answered denying liability generally.

Roth, in addition, specifically pleaded that, of the insurance funds received, he had used $30,000 in repairing the damages done to the house, and had left some portions unrepaired in order to pay for emergency medical care for his wife, Laura, who had suddenly been stricken with a serious disease requiring medical resources far beyond the family income. Roth specifically pleaded that he had no financial resources available, and that all funds paid by Best to him had been spent as described. He prayed dismissal of Best's claim. In a separate paragraph, he sought to plead, demanding payment under the Pure policy in the event Best's claim against Pure was denied, and acknowledging that if he recovered under this cross-claim Best would be subrogated to the recovery. Pure answered this cross-claim denying liability on the ground that proof of loss had not been filed by Roth within the time specified by the policy as a condition precedent to liability.

Your firm represents Best. Can you construct a good case for Best against (a) Roth and (b) Pure? Should we support Roth's claim against Pure? Read the survey of restitution ideas in DOBBS, TEXT § 4.1 (1) – 4.1 (4).

Notes

1. Is Best's claim here different in any essential particular from Percy's claim against Leake in the example above?

2. Ask yourself whether Roth committed any wrong or violated any contract. If not, is he nevertheless unjustly enriched? Work out the pros and cons of your answer.

3. If Roth is, prima facie, unjustly enriched, are there any considerations that might counsel a judge against imposing liability?

———————

Problem 4-3

Kaufmann v. Bacall

Kaufmann is a housepainter. Work has been slow, although he is an excellent painter. Last April 17 he decided to paint a house he found at 5641 Via Condesa. It needed paint. He repainted it in its original color and did an excellent job. When the owner, Bacall, returned home he found a house that looked much better and was worth at least $1,000 more than it had been in the morning. Kaufmann asked for payment. Bacall at first refused, then called our firm. Does he owe this? He'll pay it if you say so.

Problem 4-4

Amstell v. Waddell

Waddell orally agreed to sell his farm to Amstell for $600,000. They were to see a lawyer together and arrange the exact terms. Waddell agreed that, as it was planting season, Amstell could begin any planting he wanted to immediately. Amstell entered the farm and spent $2,000 in planting grape vines.

Waddell came out to the slopes one day and told Amstell that the deal was off. The two had never seen the lawyer and there was no writing. Waddell apologized, but said he could not bring himself to leave the farm after all.

Amstell purchased another farm nearby, this time with full documents. He has moved into possession of that farm and is happy enough with it. However, he wants to be paid for improvements he made on Waddell's farm. What additional information do you need to determine the appropriate amount of restitution?

35

Problem 4-5

Polnitz v. Polnitz

Anna Mae Polnitz was the sole fee owner of a 200-acre farm. She died leaving the farm to her husband, Abraham and her three children. The children were grown and lived in their own homes. Abraham continued to live on the farm as he had done before. When he was 75, Abraham moved in with his daughter Amy and sold the farm. He received $200,000 in cash, but he did not reveal the price to his children and none of them asked either about the price or their share. Abraham invested the entire $200,000 in stock of the Prague Glass Company. Last year he died and the stock was discovered. He had placed it in his name and Amy's with right of survivorship. As the survivor, Amy is now the sole legal owner of the stock. Its market value is $300,000.

We represent Amy's two brothers, James and John. They are not sure, but they feel that somehow they should have received something from Abraham. Amy has admitted to them that Abraham made cash contributions to her household while he was living there.

See DOBBS, TEXT § 4.3 (2).

Remedies in Particular Settings

With this subpart, we begin to look at problems in a different way. Instead of concentrating on restitution, damages, or injunctive relief, these problems concentrate on fact-situations. Lawyers confronting fact-situations brought to them by clients must consider all remedial possibilities. So some of the problems in this part may involve more than one remedial possibility.

CHAPTER 5

REMEDIES FOR THE PROTECTION OF

INTERESTS IN TANGIBLE PROPERTY

A. Land (Mostly)

(1) Physical Integrity of the Land and Structures

Problem 5-1

Truitt v. Mallard

Mallard owned a large tract of good timber land, and he cut it extensively. Last year he entered upon Truitt's land, which adjoined Mallard's, and prepared to do further cutting. Truitt warned Mallard that he was trespassing. Mallard denied he was trespassing and claimed he was on his own land. He now states that he honestly believed this to be true at all times. Truitt pointed out the boundary some distance away, but Mallard denied the location of the boundary and stated his belief that the boundary was considerably farther away and that he was on his own land.

After Truitt warned Mallard, Mallard got his deed out and an old map and later paced off the markings before cutting timber. He erroneously located the boundary by this process, and, as a result he cut timber that was in fact on Truitt's land. At two different stages, he cut and hauled a large quantity.

The first cut was hauled in Mallard's trucks to a mill owned by Jeffreys and sold at the mill site to the Ft. Smith Paper Company for the sum of $23,000. The second cut was hauled to the Jeffreys Mill and rough milled at a cost of $10,000. Mallard then sold the rough milled lumber for $50,000 to two lumber dealers in the area.

Truitt has now discovered the timber cutting and wants to collect damages. The state has a timber trespass statute, imposing double damages for any timber trespass. Your first client interview with Truitt reveals that the market value of timber rights on the land cut over was probably in the neighborhood of $25,000.00. Such timber rights, had they been sold, would have given the buyer the right to cut for a five-year period. What damages should you, as Truitt's attorney, demand from Mallard? What would you accept in settlement?

Please see DOBBS, TEXT §§ 5.1, 5.3 (1) – 5.3 (3).

Note

1. *Case comparison.* In *Dethloff v. Zeigler Coal Co.*, 82 Ill.2d 393, 412 N.E.2d 526 (1980), cert. denied, 451 U.S. 910, 101 S.Ct. 1980, 68 L.Ed.2d 229 (1981), discussed in DOBBS, TEXT § 5.3 (3), a trespasser removed coal from a mine. He was held liable for the entire sale price he received, less a credit for some of the costs he incurred in removing the coal. But he was not credited with the full costs he incurred. Is there a punitive element in the recovery so calculated? If so, is the punitive element proportioned to the wrongdoing or bad faith?

2. *Multiple damages.* Many statutes mandate or permit multiplied damages for particular kinds of cases. Multiple damages statutes are discussed in 1 DAN DOBBS, THE LAW OF REMEDIES § 3.12 (2d ed. 1993). Are these useful or desirable? From the facts of *Mallard v. Truitt*, what problems can you see in construing such statutes?

3. *Surrogate or standardized damages.* Multiplied damages represent one form of positive-law, standardized, or surrogate damages. A standardized damages award is not measured by the actual losses of the plaintiff but is fixed in advance by statute. Sometimes the award is not fixed in advance but its *range* is fixed. The copyright statute, for example, authorizes statutory damages with a minimum of $500 and a maximum of $20,000.[2] Some statutes authorize recovery of stated amounts for each violation. Is there a place for standardized damages? If so, is it limited to statutory provisions or could courts themselves make a rule permitting standardized awards as one option?

---

[2] 17 U.S.C.A. § 504 (c) (1).

4. *Conventional damages measures.* Sometimes we believe we are measuring damages accurately when we are really applying well-accepted accounting or legal conventions about measurements. The most obvious cases of conventional measurements closely resemble standardized awards except that the conventional measurement uses a formula instead of a fixed amount. Some kinds of workers' compensation awards are like this. The formula might be something like this: "80% of the workers' average weekly wage."

Other conventions are much less obvious. Measuring market value of the plaintiff's llama in *Story v. Grayson* (Problem 3-1) for example, is not "wrong," but it reflects a conventional adoption of the market value test rather than a precise measure of the plaintiff's losses. If you do not believe that the market value test is conventional, consider whether it would represent any *actual* loss if the plaintiff had decided to leave the country and give the llama to the first stranger who comes by or to trade it for a handful of beans. As a practical matter, we need many conventions or positive rules in measuring damages. Can we with equal justice use standardized measures?

Problem 5-2

Levmore v. Learner

Levmore owned a farm. Some large old trees were on her property near the boundary line. A logger named Learner, who never surveyed but merely estimated the territory where he had logging rights, accidentally cut some of Levmore's trees, including one spectacular ancient oak.

When Levmore discovered that the tree had been cut, she immediately arranged to replace it with the largest oak she could arrange to plant. This was a very expensive replacement. It cost her $5,000, but she thought it worth the cost, even though the loss of the original oak only diminished the value of her property by $500 and its replacement would not raise the value of her property by any more than $500.

When she discovered that Learner had cut the tree, she wanted to sue. You represent her. Can you get the replacement cost for her? See DOBBS, TEXT §§ 1.9 and 5.2 (1).

Problem 5-3

Wang v. Dameron

Wang owns a large tract of wooded, hillside land. A spring high on the land is the source of Davis Creek, which in turn flows into the Gonalquin River. The spring, creek and river became polluted. Reconstructing, we now think this is what happened.

Dameron, using a back hill road, dumped a number of barrels and drums of toxic materials in the woods. These materials seeped through the ground and contaminated the spring. Although all remaining barrels and drums have been removed, it will cost a small fortune to clean the land so as to prevent further contamination. Estimated costs are not less than $1 million.

Wang has brought suit against Dameron for the cost of cleaning the land, demanding $1 million in compensatory damages plus $10 million in punitive damages. Wang has sued under a state tort law theory of trespass. No statute prevents or inhibits such a suit.

Both the Wright firm and the Rosenstiel firm have made you offers of employment. Without revealing any confidential information, Wright has told you it represents Wang and would like you to sit in on conferences because of your excellent recent remedies course. Rosenstiel has told you about the same except that it represents Dameron. Choose a firm. Comment on any remedies issues you see in the facts. Begin research by consulting DOBBS, TEXT § 5.2 (5) and any related material you might wish.

Problem 5-4

Segal Foundry v. The Fraser Corporation

Our client is The Fraser Corporation. The Fraser Corporation is a manufacturer of overhead cranes of the kind used in factories. Fraser contracted to deliver and install a certain crane in the Segal Foundry. Fraser installed the rails and supports on which the crane was to run, but workers on the site failed to fully rivet the supports. When Fraser was testing the crane, the whole structure collapsed; the crane, rails and supports, which run into considerable tonnage, crashed into a furnace or kiln. The furnace was substantially demolished.

It appears that Fraser, who is a self-insurer for this liability, was almost certainly negligent. We have gathered the following information about the damages issue:

1. The furnace was one built by Segal itself, designed for the particular factory. It is not an item purchasable on the market, and Segal has now rebuilt the furnace with its own labor. The direct labor costs came to $30,000. Materials costs came to $10,000. Segal accountants have also submitted papers indicating that, according to their figures, fixed overhead attributable to the cost of replacement is an additional sum of $ 4,500.

2. The plant income was reduced during the replacement period of the furnace. Gross income reduction was $6,000. However, two men were laid off during the replacement period and the plant saved their normal wages in the sum of $2,000

3. There was a small fire that burned out an office in the foundry. This seems to have resulted from the furnace's destruction. Segal had the office repainted at an expense of $400. It bought replacement desks and file cabinets at an additional cost of $1000.

Please prepare a memorandum on the damages issue. Keep in mind that we need this memorandum for negotiation. Consult DOBBS, TEXT § § 5.14 (2) & 5.14 (3).

Note

Clients do not always come with all the right information. Neither do senior partners asking for memoranda. Sometimes we omit relevant facts from these problems, just as clients sometimes omit them in their statements to their lawyers. This omission permits a wider scope for discussion, since you may have to make alternative assumptions to resolve a problem. It also puts you in a frequent role of the lawyer as the questioner who must first identify the information gaps before reaching a legal judgment or planning a strategy. Is there information of a more or less factual nature (as distinct from information about accounting practices) that you'd want to resolve this Problem? Can you formulate a precise question?

Problem 5-5

Seidel v. Brown

Seidel owns a tract of 300 acres, which he farmed for many years until he retired. He continues to live on the land, which has a small trout stream and two bass ponds. Up until recently, this has been quiet and fairly remote, but over the years the town of Chapelapolis has gradually grown in the direction of the Seidel tract. Seidel leases a portion of his farm to neighboring farmers when they have some special need for it, and he raises a small garden. Otherwise, the land is his "retirement home", and his main activities are gardening, fishing, and some raising of domestic animals.

Two years ago, Richard Brown, a large-scale housing developer, purchased a tract of 100 acres lying between the city limits of Chapelapolis and the Seidel tract. His workers began to clear and level this land for the purpose of laying out streets and homesites and building three- and four--bedroom houses.

In the course of clearing scrub and brush off the land, Brown's workers encountered mud and some low spots. The mud was impeding work significantly, and a foreman told the men to take some of the machinery onto adjoining unimproved land owned by Seidel, and to level some of the humps or high spots on the land and to bring the dirt over onto Brown's land and fill the low spots. The men did this, destroying some of the scrub timber on Seidel's land in the process, and using the dirt. A portion of the foreman's deposition taken after suit was filed and explaining why he did this is attached.

The machinery operators in general did a good job, and Seidel's land has increased in value by at least $50,000 as a result of the development on Brown's land, since Seidel's land has now become quite valuable for homesites. The destruction of scrub on Seidel's land did not cause any significant damage, and may have improved its value slightly for homesite purposes. The leveling improved the value of the land by at least $2,000 for its purpose as homesite property. However, Mr. Seidel objects for reasons of his own, which are indicated in more detail in his deposition, taken by Brown after suit was filed and attached hereto.

One of the machine operators lost control of one of the large grading machines, which ran into Seidel's barn, doing some fairly extensive damage. Seidel at this point discovered the presence of the men and angrily ran them off his land. The barn's siding was torn considerably, and a portion of the roof had to be replaced. The total repair cost of the barn was $3,000. Seidel immediately consulted our firm about bringing suit against Brown. After two consultations, we filed suit against Brown and, due to the hard line Brown took and his refusal to let us speak to his men, we decided to take depositions. A portion of the deposition of the foreman, Jim Cates, is attached. Brown responded by taking Seidel's deposition, and a portion of that, along with Brown's answer in pertinent part, is attached. Please let me have a memo as to damages or other remedies so I can start some settlement talk.

DEPOSITION OF JIM CATES

[From pages 6-7 of the Deposition]

Questions by Jones Davis, for the plaintiff.

Q. Now, Mr. Cates, just why was it you decided to enter on Mr. Seidel's land?

A. Well, we had this machinery and men rented, and we had to keep it going or just stand to lose what it costs us if you have it sitting around doing nothing.

Q. You mean you had to have fill dirt, and there wasn't anything for the machinery to do until you had it?

A. Yes, sir, that's right, that's just what I do mean; $500 a day worth of machinery and men sitting around is what I'm paid not to get.

Q. All right, Mr. Cates, why didn't you just get fill dirt somewhere else?

A. Well, for one thing, Mr. Brown, he was out of town, and he has the money for things like that, or I guess he does. Anyway, I don't. I can't just go hire Mr. Brown some new expenses without his okay. I did that once, and let me tell you, I'm not about to do that again.

Q. Was there any other reason?

A. What do you mean?

Q. You said, "For one thing." Was there any other reason why you couldn't get fill somewhere else?

A. I reckon so. I don't know if you know the problem around this area, but it's mostly flat and low, and there's a lot of drainage problems, and everybody needs fill around here and nobody has it to sell. So you have to have it hauled from up around the Elbow Lake area, and you have to go up and wait until the old boy up there has a truck available, he's running four trucks now all day long, but that's not enough, so you have to wait until you can find a truck or use one of his, and then you have the haulage cost, I've got to use one of my men and that costs something, or I've got to pay haulage. Well, the dirt and haulage would have run me about, oh, I'd say around $150 altogether at least.

Q. So you figured it wasn't so unreasonable to go over and borrow a little from Seidel, and I guess you probably had in mind how much you'd save on the machinery, keeping it working instead of idle.

A. Yes, sir.

Q. How much was that?

A. Well, I'd figure a day's time at least, that's $500 right there. If you can't find a truck, or you have to wait much up there at Elbow Lake, you've got two days time before you know it.

Q. So altogether, you figured $500 for one day's time, and at least $150 for the haulage costs?

A. Yes, sir.

Q. And maybe another $500 and more haulage costs?

A. Yes, sir.

Q. Altogether I figure that runs at least $650, and maybe more like $1,200?

A. Yes, sir, at least something like that.

. . . . .

[Portions of the deposition relating to Cates' authority as an employee and the negligence of the grader driver in damaging the barn and other issues are omitted as not relevant to this memo.]

FROM THE DEPOSITION OF WILLIAM SEIDEL

[From pages 3-4 of the Deposition]

Questions by Oliver Khazan, attorney for the defendant Brown.

Property Interests

Q. Mr. Seidel, at the request of Mr. Brown and myself, you permitted an appraiser to look over your land, and he told you that your land, as it stood before Brown's development, was worth about $150,000. Is that right?

A. Yes.

Q. And he also told you that, as a result of Brown's development on the adjoining land that your property would be worth at least $200,000 for homesites now?

A. Yes.

Q. And he was right, wasn't he, you don't deny that, do you?

A. No, I don't deny it, but I don't want to sell the property. I want to live on it and fish on it and as far as I am concerned, Mr. Brown and his cheap houses can go to hell.

Q. Mr. Seidel, did the appraiser -- that was Mr. Hermann, wasn't it?

A. Yes.

Q. Did Mr. Hermann tell you that the removal of dirt on your land also improved its value as homesites?

A. Yes, he did. He said, "Mr. Seidel, your land has been improved by $2,000 by that simple grading, because that's good drained land now and just right for homes," and I said, "Mr. Hermann, that may be so, but I don't want no homesites, and I know for a fact it will cost me at least $500 to put that land back the way it was, you know, to build it up again and put the scrub back and so on." So how do you figure it's worth more if I ain't going to put houses up there? How do you figure it's worth more if I'm going to spend money and break my back putting dirt back the way it was?

Q. How old are you, Mr. Seidel?

A. I'm 71 years old as of last month, January 3.

Q. Is anyone living with you?

A. No, my daughters are both married and moved away.

Q. Are you well?

A. I've got a little arthritis and a few old man's problems, but I'm alive.

Q. Ever been in the hospital?

45

A. Had a heart attack last year and spent a little time there.

Q. And nobody's living with you?

A. No.

Q. When you get sick, what do you do for help?

A. One of my daughters comes to stay a while.

Q. Where does she come from?

A. Orlando.

Q. That's about 1000 miles?

A. Probably.

Q. How long can she stay? Does she have children?

A. Well, maybe two weeks. She has to take care of her children.

Q. So if you get sick longer than that, what will you do?

A. Well, maybe move into a rest home or a hospital, depending.

Q. Or move in with your daughter in Orlando?

A. Or the one in Arkansas.

Q. So you might be selling that land of yours someday.

A. Someday I've got to die. But that's someday.

Q. That's all, Mr. Seidel.

EXCERPTS FROM THE ANSWER OF RICHARD BROWN

[Formal portions and portions not relevant to this memo are omitted here.]

VII.

The entire tract owned by the plaintiff, William Seidel, has been improved in value by the sum of at least $50,000, by virtue of the defendant's development of adjoining lands, and by reason of this increase in value, the defendant is not liable in any sum whatever to the plaintiff. If the defendant is liable in any sum, he is entitled to set off this increase in value of the plaintiff's land.

VIII.

The tract of land owned by the plaintiff, William Seidel, has been improved in value by reason of the grading and leveling done by the defendant's servants, by the sum of at least $2,000. By reason of this increase in value the plaintiff is not entitled to recover any sum from the defendant. If the plaintiff is entitled to any sum from the defendant, then the defendant is entitled to set off this increase in the value of the plaintiff's land.

IX.

The defendant admits that machinery operated by Bill Goode did in fact strike the plaintiff's barn and admits that the cost of replacing and repairing the barn was $3,-000, as alleged in the complaint. The defendant continues to deny that Bill Goode was his employee or that Goode was operating within the scope of his employment, but says that in any event, the value of the barn immediately before the impact was $8,000, and its value immediately after the impact was $7,000, and that the defendant is not liable, if at all, in any sum more than the difference between its value immediately after and its value immediately before.

X.

The defendant further says, while continuing to deny that Bill Goode was his employee or operating within the scope of his employment, that after repair, the barn appreciated in value and was worth $11,000, by reason of the fact that the roofing and timbers damaged were old and depreciated and the roofing was old and depreciated, and by reason of the further fact that these items were replaced and repaired with new materials that will last longer. By reason of these improvements in value, the plaintiff has no loss resulting from the impact of the grading machinery and the defendant is not liable for any sum due to this impact.

XI.

The plaintiff failed to minimize his damages resulting from the leveling and grading of his land and from the impact on his barn in that he could remove the remainder of the barn for very little cost with a resulting improvement in his land for homesite purposes, and in that he could sell his land in its leveled state for homesite purposes at an increase in value.

The highest and best use of the land is for such purposes, and the plaintiff is under a duty to use his land for the highest and best purposes or to claim damages only on the basis of such purposes.

Readings already completed will be relevant but you may also wish to scan for other relevant materials.

Notes

1. *Comparison case 1: "L" Investments, Ltd. v. Lynch*, 212 Neb. 319, 322 N.W.2d 651 (1982). Defendant's vehicle struck plaintiff's building and damaged a wall and some windows. Repair costs were $2,640, but there was no evidence as to the diminished value. The trial court dismissed the claim because plaintiff had not proved that cost of repair was less than the diminished market value. *Held*, reversed. With certain qualifications, "the measure of damages for its negligent damage is the reasonable cost of repairing or restoring the property in like kind and quality. . . . . . While certain of the writers, including Dobbs, and perhaps some courts, argue that right of recovery should be without limitation [ ], we believe the award for such damage should not exceed the market value of the property immediately preceding the damage to the property. It seems that one ought not to be able to recover a greater amount for partial destruction than one could recover for total destruction."

2. *Comparison case 2: Weld County Bd. of County Com'rs v. Slovek*, 723 P.2d 1309 (Colo. 1986). The defendant was responsible for flooding the plaintiff's land. *Held,* reduced market value of land after flooding by defendant was not necessarily the only measure of damages; the plaintiff can recover cost of restoration in an appropriate case. Although economically wasteful remedial expenditures must be avoided, the diminution in market value is not necessarily a ceiling on repair cost recovery. Nor is the pre-tort value of the property. The cases for allowing repair costs in excess of diminished value cannot be reduced to a set list.

3. Notice the difference between (1) the pre-tort value of the property and (2) the diminished value of the property as a ceiling. Do you think that the Nebraska Court in *"L" Investments* meant that the pre-tort value was the *only* ceiling?

4. *Valuing land.* How can you put a "market value" on land, or say that it was diminished or increased in value? There would be a market in land if many parcels were identical and people regularly bought and sold some of them, or if you auctioned the particular plot to a substantial group of bidders. But land does not sell frequently and sale of one parcel does not necessarily say much about the value of a parcel next to it. Land is necessarily valued less by actual markets than by a construct in which courts accept opinion testimony of owners and experts, or data such as evidence of comparable sales. Sometimes, too, they attempt to estimate "market" value by figuring the income that the land could bring. These ideas are discussed in a section

called "Constructing Market Value: Definitions and Evidence," in 1 DAN DOBBS, THE LAW OF REMEDIES § 3.5 (2d ed. 1993).

(2) Possession, Use and Enjoyment

Possession of land facilitates many other things. Sometimes you might want to protect your possession of land for more or less symbolic reasons. At other times, however, possession of land is chiefly significant for economic reasons, as where land is used in the production of income.

On other occasions, possession of land is a means of effectuating personal fulfillment or privacy or some social or political goal. So sometimes interference is less a direct matter of trespass or even nuisance than it is a matter of interference with contract, an invasion of privacy, or an attack on one's civil rights. Some cases like this may be found in Chapters 6 & 7 below, although they resemble or may actually involve some kinds of trespass.

Problem 5-6

Morlacci v. Weber

We represent Martin Morlacci. Georgia Weber and Martin Morlacci are citizens and residents of this state, though they were not close neighbors and did not know each other.

Morlacci had long ago acquired a deed to 200 acres of land in the State of Montorado, adjoining this state to the west. Weber also has a deed that appeared to convey to her some of the same lands in Montorado.

Weber was originally unaware of Morlacci's claim. Three years ago, Weber, believing herself to be on her own land, set up a farmer's market stall every Sunday on the Montorado land, selling produce to travelers. She gradually expanded and now sells a wide variety of tourist materials, including films, T-shirts, CDs and other items. The stall proved immensely profitable, and in last year Weber built a small permanent building on the land near the road. Her gross income has steadily increased, even though she operates only on weekends.

Our position: Weber was in fact on land claimed by Morlacci. None of the land in the area was developed except for Weber's business. Morlacci recently discovered all this while driving in Montorado. He demanded that Weber get off his, Morlacci's land. Weber said it was her own land. Morlacci returned home and consulted us. Title records seem to bear out our contention that the land probably belongs to Morlacci under the law of Montorado, and we have so advised him.

Morlacci says he has never been able to do anything with the land. He has no prospects for leasing it or selling it. He suggests that maybe you could force Weber to buy it, since she has used it. Alternatively, he wants to get Weber off the land. He says he is short of cash, and if you can't get Weber to buy the land, he wants to get Weber off the land, collect as much damages as possible, and hopefully recover interest and enough to pay your fee. Morlacci is an old and valued client whom we represent mostly in connection with his business. Please plan an action on his behalf. Considering both tactics and remedial value, what remedy or remedies will you seek?

See DOBBS, TEXT §§ 5.10 (1), 5.10 (3) (ejectment and injunction); 5.8 (2), 5.8 (3) (damages) & 5.9 (restitution). "Jurisdiction" to affect foreign land titles is considered briefly in § 2.7. You may wish to consult parts of § 2.9 (4).

Note

Comparison case: The only entrance to a spectacular cave is on the defendant's property. Most of the cave occupies a position on property of the plaintiffs, whose property adjoins the defendant's. The defendant makes profits selling tickets to see the cave. The plaintiff has no access to the cave on his own property, and the defendant has nothing to interest customers if he confines them to the portion of the cave under his own property. On facts similar to these, a well-known case allowed the plaintiff to recover the defendant's profits. *Edwards v. Lee's Adm'r*, 265 Ky. 418, 96 S.W.2d 1028 (1936), discussed in DOBBS, TEXT § 5.9.

Problem 5-7

Mills Realty Corp. v. Ferber Industries, Inc.

Mills Realty Co. owns and operates a relatively new 16-story office building in the City of Ellensborough, a city of 500,000. Two sides of the building are composed chiefly of glass. This was designed with several purposes in mind. One was to admit substantial light so that the use of electricity during daylight hours could be minimized. Another was to improve morale of office workers.

The use of extensive glass areas created some special problems, however, as well as special advantages and savings. One problem was the problem of window cleaning. Mills planned for this in advance of the building's construction by contracting with Gramble Bros., an independent contractor, to clean windows periodically at a fixed rate. The contract also called for Gramble to do more frequent cleanings than those specified in the contract when Mills demanded it. For such additional work, Gramble would be paid an hourly rate, but, due to Mills' large contract, the hourly rate would be about 2/3 the hourly rate normally charged for window washing. Finally, the contract also called for window repair and replacement by Gramble on a regular basis. Here again, repair and replacement was to be furnished at about two-thirds of the normal price, due to Mills' large volume work.

Two years ago, Ferber Industries completed construction of a large factory in Ellensborough, about one-half mile from the Mills Building. Ferber employed about 1,500 workers in various capacities in the manufacture and distribution of rubberized silicone and aluminum fratchits. Even as the building was completed, there was talk of expansion. Ferber's payroll constituted a substantial boost to the local economy.

During the first year of Ferber's operation, it became apparent that, in spite of considerable efforts in smokestack design, the use of electronic and mechanical filters and other devices, the Ferber plant's operation would produce immense clouds of dark smoke containing many microscopic particles. The smoke, blown by prevailing winds, drifted directly to the Mills Building, where, for reasons explicable by engineers, it tended to circle the building, striking first one glass wall and then the other.

51

The physical presence of the smoke was quite a serious matter in itself. However, as days wore on it became clear that, even when the plant was not operating, the smoke had darkened the windows quite substantially. Later it was discovered that the smoke was depositing, not merely the normal grime capable of being washed off, but also particles which, due to chemical content, became more or less permanently embedded in or stuck to the glass. At any rate, normal window washing could not remove them.

As a result of the physical presence of the smoke itself and its deposits on the windows, visibility through the windows was substantially cut. This affected the morale of many office workers. In addition, the electrical supply, furnished by Mills to all tenants, was increased substantially to make up for the reduced daylight in the offices.

The physical presence of the smoke while it was actually drifting near the building caused two other problems. First, it clogged the heating and air conditioning units of the building, necessitating additional repairs. It also caused a substantially less efficient use of these systems, with a resulting increase in electrical costs for their operation. Again this was a cost borne by Mills under the terms of the lease. Second, the physical presence of the smoke itself caused a number of office workers to suffer extreme nausea and lost time from work. This also caused morale problems to tenants who employed them.

You represent Mills. You have concluded that in all probability Ferber's activities constitute a nuisance. Since you initiated discussion with Ferber, they have done additional work and now believe that in the very near future they will be able to make one improvement: they will be able to reduce the microscopic particles in the smoke substantially, so that permanent damage to the glass areas of the Mills Building can be halted. You have concluded that, though this is a gain, the remaining problems will still constitute a nuisance.

Accordingly, you are preparing to file suit against Ferber. It appears to you at this time that Mills will need to replace about 80% of all glass in the building because of damage done that cannot be corrected by mere window washing, and that windows will require washing about twice as often as before, even if Ferber is able to make the improvements mentioned above.

Consider to what relief you will be entitled. What relief will you ask for as a matter of tactics? What relief would you settle for? Move as quickly as you can on this one; the client's tenants are beginning to complain bitterly and to talk of constructive eviction. If rents are withheld by large numbers of tenants, the financing on the building could collapse.

Problem 5-8

Cronin v. Marquez

✓Cronin and Marquez were adjoining landowners in the City of Ellensborough. A city zoning ordinance designated the area as "residential family dwelling". Rules applied by the ordinance for such areas provided that no building should be located closer than 15 feet to the property line as to any portion of the building, and that no building should reach a height of more than 35 feet at any point.

Marquez owned a lot facing north, with sidelines running north and south. Cronin owned the lot immediately to the west of Marquez. This also faced north and had sidelines running north and south. Marquez built his house on his lot first. A few months thereafter, and before a paved road was installed in front of the lots, Cronin began building his house. Cronin had selected plans from a mail order company and had them worked on by a local architect for a flat fee. However, the architect was not employed to supervise construction and did not attempt to do so.

The plans called for a house of such a size that the architect gave directions to the contractor to construct its easternmost foundation on a line parallel to the lot's sideline and exactly 15 feet from the line. This would have met the requirements of the zoning ordinance. A survey was made and the lines laid out in accordance with this. However, the beginning point of the survey was run from an assumed boundary of the road in front of the lots. This was not paved, and though there were stakes marking the road, they were "guesswork stakes," set out by the developer to mark an approximate location for cutting a temporary road, not surveyor's stakes. When the Cronin lot was surveyed, however, the surveyor assumed that the road stakes marked the line of the road, and made his survey from there. This led to a miscalculation of the sideline by a substantial margin and the house foundation as a result was laid out, not parallel to the sidelines, but at an acute angle to them.

The southeast corner of the foundation, and all that rose above it, actually crossed four inches over onto the Marquez lot. While the work was in progress, the Cronins decided they liked the deck or balcony on the eastern side so much that they wanted to extend it. They were ignorant of the zoning ordinance requirements, and merely spoke to the contractor about extending the balcony. An agreement was reached that he would widen the balcony for a certain price and that he would also extend a cantilevered roof proportionately to cover a part of the extended balcony. These two things were done. None of the parties knew it, but the extended balcony on the east violated the sideline requirement, almost reaching the property edge on one end and transgressing the 15-foot rule for its entire length. The extended roof also caused a problem. The roof had been designed at an angle sloping to a point upward and outward over the deck. The contractor had simply extended it outward over the increased balcony width. This projected the roof into the sideline area and also projected it two feet over the 35-foot maximum height.

None of this was noticed when a certificate of occupancy was furnished by the City of Ellensborough and the Cronins moved in. Shortly after this, the Cronins and Marquezs began to have difficulties. The Marquezs accused the Cronin's teenage son of being a dope pusher and of attempting to seduce the Marquez's teenage daughter, represented by them to be a clean-living and virtuous young person. After this opening gun in the neighborhood warfare, things went downhill rapidly. Eventually the Marquezes had a survey made of the line between the two lots and discovered both the encroachment on their land and the zoning ordinance violation. They have filed a suit demanding a mandatory injunction to force Cronin to remove the encroachment and also to make the balcony and roof conform to the zoning ordinance. They are also demanding damages incurred by them as a result of the ordinance violations and the encroachment.

You have been retained to represent the Cronins. It would cost a substantial sum to remove the encroachment and much more to remove a portion of the house proper from the sideline area. After consulting with the building inspector at Town Hall, you discovered the Town occasionally misses these things and seldom does anything about them, but occasionally insists on enforcement of the ordinance even where the Town itself has issued a certificate of occupancy.

Your investigation also indicates that Marquez never objected while the building was going on, that his motive in objecting probably resulted from the neighborhood quarrel, and that Marquez himself probably built his own house into the reserved sideline area on his eastern boundary (not on Cronin's side). The architect consulted by Cronin tells you that he explained the sideline requirement to Cronin and also that he altered the original plans to keep the roof line within the requirement and explained that to Cronin, too. Cronin doesn't deny this; he merely says he doesn't understand such things. You aren't very sure that negligence can be proved against the surveyor, Richard Lineberger. But you wish to consider the possibility. Would he be responsible, if at all, for the damages? More immediately, what defenses can you assert against Marquez? What kind of settlement would you be prepared to accept, assuming the following figures represent the various economic interests involved:

(a) Removal of the encroachment alone, without complying with the sideline requirement, will cost about $5,000. This would reduce the value of the house and lot by about $4,000.

(b) Removal of the encroachment plus removal of all portions of the house (foundations, walls, balcony and roof) from the sideline area, plus repair and re-building as necessary, would cost about $12,000 and would reduce the value of the house and lot by about $12,000.

(c) Removal of the balcony from the sideline area would cost about $500 and would reduce the value of the house and lot by about $750. Re-building of the roof to conform to the height requirements would cost about $500 and would not substantially affect the value of the house.

(d) Both lots are expensive and desirable. The value of the Marquez lot is probably not substantially reduced by the Cronin's house location because Marquez's own house is on the far eastern side of his lot, away from Cronin's.

(e) Cronin's house could be made to conform with all rules if he could purchase a strip along the west side of Marquez's lot a width of 15 feet, 4 inches. Such a strip would be worth, on the market, about $7,000.

See DOBBS, TEXT § 5.10 (4).

Notes

1. Is the right of choice involved in this kind of case just as it is in the housepainter case?

55

2. *Comparison case*: *Leonard v. Stoebling*, 728 P.2d 1358 (Nev. 1986). The defendant extended his house in a way that blocked the view of the plaintiff in violation of a building restriction. Although the Architectural Control Committee gave its approval to the defendant's plans, the court ordered an injunction to compel restoration of the plaintiff's view. It said:

> A mandatory injunction is a stern remedy. It is therefore incumbent upon the trial court upon remand, to structure the injunction so as to accomplish the restoration of appellants' view with the least degree of detriment to respondent. However, if a modification of respondent's addition will not achieve the status quo, then the offending structure must be removed in its entirety.

The court may have believed that the defendant misled the Architectural Committee.

3. *Slocum v. Phillips Petroleum Co.*, 678 P.2d 716 (Okl. 1983). A pipeline was installed several feet over onto the owner's land. He recovered several thousand dollars in compensatory damages. The award of punitive damages was reversed because there was no bad faith or oppression, only negligence. The court upheld the trial court's denial of a mandatory injunction. This is most of the discussion: "Owner's use of his property has not been substantially affected and his damages are fairly compensable. The cost of removing the pipeline would be substantial and cause a hardship and it would be unconscionable to require Phillips to remove the pipeline."

(B) Chattels (Mostly)

Problem 5-9

O'Malley Mfg. Co. v. Handelsman et al.

O'Malley purchased a carload of fratchits from Ferris Fratchit Co. Fratchits, used in several kinds of manufacturing businesses, were temporarily in extremely short supply. O'Malley paid cash and prepaid all freight. Ferris Fratchit loaded the fratchits in a car supplied at Ferris' plant by the Carolina-Pacific Railroad. The car was then locked and carried over the Carolina-Pacific line along with various other cars.

A different car was carrying goods to Handelsman Co. Handelsman was in desperate need of fratchits. It could not manufacture its goods without them and it could not pay creditors without continuously manufacturing and selling goods. Handelsman was simply in no position to wait for supplies.

The car for Handelsman was carried to the tracks outside Handelsman's plant for unloading. The O'Malley car carrying the fratchits was on a siding nearby. Carolina-Pacific intended to carry both of those cars and others in the O'Malley direction so the O'Malley car and others were on a siding until Handelsman unloaded. Handelsman bribed an employee of Carolina-Pacific to unlock the doors to the O'Malley car and during the night Handelsman employees unloaded all the fratchits. The doors were closed and relocked.

The O'Malley car arrived at O'Malley's empty, as everyone discovered when the locked car was opened. Handelsman had done a good job of covering up and it took a month to get evidence about what happened. All the O'Malley fratchits had been used in manufacturing Handelsman's product, Zurikers. In fact, all the Zurikers made using the O'Malley fratchits were in the warehouse ready to ship as soon as Handelsman received the purchase price from buyers.

O'Malley paid $1 each for the fratchits. Because of the short supply, they increased steadily in market price. When Handelsman got the fratchits, fratchits were selling at $1.50 when they could be found at all. When O'Malley located the Zurickers, fratchits were selling at $2. O'Malley thinks the supply is stronger now and expects the price to drop below a dollar by June.

See DOBBS, TEXT §§ 5.13 (1) – 5.13 (3). You may be able to use rules or principles you have already mastered in some aspects of this problem.

Problem 5-10

Astley v. Wolodsko

A small vessel named *The Dauntless* was owned by the U. S. Government. It was a famous ship, having been involved in a historical naval exploit, but it was no longer valuable as a working part of the fleet. The government determined to sell it under sealed bids. It received a bid from Ms. Emily Astley for the sum of $100,000. This was the high bid. The scrap value of the ship was probably at least twice this sum, though this is debatable. There were few other bidders and all bid lower than Astley.

Astley had the ship towed to a berth in Wilmington, East Carolina where she put the ship on exhibit near the retired Battleship *East Carolina*. She offered a tour with various historical lectures, slides, etc. She charged $3.00 per customer. This went on for one week, during which time she took in, gross, about $900, and netted an operating profit of about $500, although some of her time was devoted to the operation. At the end of one week, due to the negligence of the Wolodsko Factory, which lay adjacent to the ship's berth, there was a tremendous explosion and the ship was blown to bits.

Astley knows of no one to whom she might have sold the vessel except for scrap. Had she continued to operate the ship as a floating museum a market might have been created, but at the time it was destroyed there was none.

Wolodsko concedes liability. For how much is it liable?

Consult DOBBS, TEXT §§ 5.16 (1) – 5.16 (3).

Note

1. If there is no actual market in property, could you construct an estimated price or value from elements that potential purchasers would consider in determining their offering price? For instance, if you know the income of property, can you somehow project the price people would be likely to pay to secure property producing such income?

2. If replacement or repair is possible but expensive should the plaintiff recover replacement costs when no market value is provable or when replacement or repair costs more than provable market value? In *O'Brien Bros., Inc. v. The Helen B. Moran*, 160 F.2d 502 (2d Cir. 1947), the United States was responsible for sinking the plaintiff's vessel. It was wartime, and no replacement was available. For this reason the plaintiff raised the vessel and repaired at great cost. Because no vessels were bought and sold there was no market, but figuring original costs of purchasing the vessel and depreciation, one might estimate a market value. The court insisted that the plaintiff's recovery be limited to the diminished market value. Why not allow recovery of reasonable replacement costs? Could you suggest a rule stating the conditions for recovery of replacement costs in cases like this one?

3. What if the property does not produce income or its potential income cannot be estimated? Suppose the property is your family photograph album or your great-grandmother's diary?

Problem 5-11

Gaard v. Stem

Gaard took his male cat, Tom, to the vet (Stem) and left the cat overnight. When he came for the cat the next day he found that Stem had castrated the animal. It is not clear at this point whether Stem misunderstood Gaard's requests, whether he mixed up Tom with some other cat, or whether he acted maliciously. Gaard is highly upset and wants to sue. He admits that he purchased Tom from the Humane Society for $10 and that no one would buy the cat. However, Gaard loved the animal. Stem's insurer says it would pay a small sum as a nuisance settlement, but even conceding liability it says we are not entitled to more than $10. Is this worth pursuing? See DOBBS, TEXT § 5.16 (3). You can also consult § 5.15 (3).

Problem 5-12

Stein v. Eastern Express

Our law firm represents Lewis Stein.

Lewis Stein is an American artist who regularly produces and sells paintings. He is well-recognized and very productive. He is represented by several established galleries in different cities, and several major museums own at least one of his paintings.

Although he has experimented with a variety of thematic material, with different kinds of paints, and quite a variety of subject matter, his paintings exhibit a style that usually marks them as "Steins" no matter what their content or theme.

In January, he consigned six paintings to the well-known Stellar Gallery in Philadelphia. He packed the paintings himself and shipped them via a private shipping company, Eastern Express. Eastern damaged all six paintings. The paintings were in an Eastern van, ready for transport, when an Eastern forklift driver and the van driver got into a heated argument over methods and timing of loading the van. The van driver turned away from the forklift driver, got in the driver's seat of the van, leaned out, and made a rude gesture. He attempted to drive away, but the enraged forklift driver rammed the van with the forks. The fork tore all six of Stein's paintings.

In recent years, Stein has been able regularly to sell all of his paintings at the prices demanded. By mutual agreement with the Stellar Gallery, the price on each of the six pictures was to be $75,000 each. The gallery would have retained 40% of the sale price and would have absorbed all expenses incident to sale and promotion, including the cost of flying Stein from his home in Hartford, Connecticut to Philadelphia for an Opening.

Stein has also sold pictures in galleries in Los Angeles, Houston, New York, Boston, Paris and Milan. Prices in some of these galleries tend to run as much as one-third higher, but fewer pictures are sold in some of those locations. Because Stein feels it important to cultivate a national audience, he places pictures in Philadelphia even though they do not usually bring as high a price as pictures sold in New York or Houston. Eastern Express admits liability. Their investigation and negotiations with Stein reveal the following additional facts.

First, Stein could repair the pierced paintings or have it done by a restorer. This would entail bringing the canvas back to a flat position by gluing a flat backing on the reverse side. Some degree of repainting of the canvas after "restoration" could be done by Stein or he could leave them in the "restored" condition without additional repainting. Either way, most of the value of the paintings would be retained. It is even possible that because of the damage, and because of Stein's growing reputation, some collectors might even buy the damaged-and-repaired paintings more readily or for a higher-than-normal price. Certainly the paintings would sell for no less than $50,000 in the Philadelphia market.

Second, it would be possible for Stein to scrap the paintings themselves and repaint the identical "subject matter" by copying them. This would be time-consuming, but this solution would produce the full value of the original paintings. In that case, the value of Stein's time would be lost. That value could be figured by taking his present annual income from paintings and dividing that by the number of hours he works. With the resulting dollars-per-hour earnings, it would be possible to estimate the cost of Stein's copying of the damaged paintings. His casual estimate was that it would cost him about $10,000 for each painting. He added, as the adjuster reported, "that $10,000 is the dollar cost; the psychic cost would be billions."

As the last statement indicates, Stein objects to repainting. He also objects to selling the damaged paintings. He insists that, artistically, they have been destroyed and that he must be permitted to supervise their complete shredding and be paid their full value. Eastern, on the other hand insists that it is liable only for the diminution in value of the paintings, that Stein must minimize damages by repair, or that, in the alternative, it will pay full value and take the pictures for resale in their present condition or in the condition to which Eastern may restore them.

Consult DOBBS, TEXT § 5.16 (4).

Problem 5-13

Valentine v. Fitzhugh

Harry Fitzhugh negligently drove his car into the rear end of John Valentine's car while both were exiting an Interstate highway. The Valentine car was badly damaged, though Valentine was not personally injured. The car was towed to the one service station in the nearby town. The proprietor, Meany, agreed to repair the car for a reasonable price. When asked for an estimate, he agreed to make one out and mail it to Valentine, who lived about 100 miles away. There were no other nearby repair shops. The car could have been towed about 50 miles to the town of Phillips, where several qualified repair shops existed. This would have been relatively expensive, but otherwise feasible.

After a week, Valentine, who had intended to use his car for selling vacuum cleaners door to door, called Meany. Meany said he had not had time to make an estimate, but would "guarantee" reasonable repair costs and could get the car repaired and driveable within another week. Valentine said he didn't think this would suit either his own collision insurance company or the liability insurer for Fitzhugh. However, he couldn't find either adjuster, and he called Meany back and authorized the repair at the guaranteed "reasonable" price.

At the end of the week, Meany had not completed repair. He said he had to order a part, which had not come. This sort of pattern persisted for a total of six weeks. Meany refused to let Valentine remove the car once he had begun repair (the first part of the second week) because he had a repairman's lien. At the end of the sixth week, Meany announced the car was ready and demanded payment for it in the sum of $600. Valentine found both his adjuster and Fitzhugh's, but both refused to pay on the ground that there had been no competitive estimate, and on the further ground that the car, even if reasonably repaired for $600, was not worth more than around $500 to begin with. In addition, Fitzhugh's adjuster refused to pay Valentine's demand for $100 a week rental on a substitute car.

Valentine actually rented a car at this price for four of the six weeks and tried to do without one for the remaining two. After this refusal, Valentine borrowed money from the bank and paid off Meany. This took a week, so he was without his car a total of seven weeks. He is paying 8% interest at the bank and does not expect to be able to pay off the loan for six months. The Meany repair was defective, and Valentine has spent another $50 having it adjusted at a local shop. You represent Valentine in his claim against Fitzhugh. Fitzhugh's adjuster will see you this afternoon. What, exactly, do you think you can claim and collect on?

See DOBBS, TEXT §§ 5.12 (1) – 5.12 (2).

Problem 5-14

Beltran v. Massengill's Body Works

Beltran bought a vintage, classic car, which he rebuilt and to which he added certain design elements of his own. When that was done, he painted the car's body with a unique design in many colors, which completely covered the body. The complex design included some stylized figures and faces but was mostly abstract. The result was stunning and beautiful. The car itself was a valuable classic car. As painted it would command an added price.

Beltran had purchased the special paints for this work on credit from Massengill's Body Works. He owed Massengill $350. Although he had promised to pay within 30 days, he had not done so and the debt was 60 days old. Massengill saw the car in Beltran's driveway. He entered the car, started it by means unknown, and took it to his shop, where he locked it away.

After he locked the car in a garage, Massengill found a wooden musical instrument from Peru in the back seat of the car. He also found a stencil that Beltran had used for painting some of the flowing lines on his car. Massengill took the stencil and tried it out, painting a car in his shop by using it. He liked the results and has continued to use it in his business, although he only paints a few stripes, not a complete design.

The flute was a different story. He took it home and showed it to his brother, Dale. Without Massengill's knowledge, Dale took the flute, which was worth $200. Dale, who was a fast talker, sold it to a tourist for $300. Dale bet the money on a horse which lost the race. The next day Massengill asked Dale about the flute and he admitted these facts.

Beltran was out of town at the time and was not immediately aware of the "repossession" (as Massengill called it). When he got home two days later he found a note from Massengill demanding immediate payment and threatening sale of the car. He called Massengill, who told him about Dale's theft of the flute and apologized, but insisted upon immediate payment. He said he would sell the car unless payment was forthcoming. Beltran pointed out that Massengill had no title, but Massengill said he would dismantle the car and sell it for parts if necessary.

Beltran does not have the money, although the car itself is valuable. He is upset and angry and threatening to take some friends to Massengill's to retrieve his car by force and to leave a little damage behind in revenge unless we can get the car back. We represented Beltran before on a minor criminal charge when he was 17. He's 23 now and has stayed out of trouble. His work on the car is creative and serious and shows an ability to stay with something productive. Although you can understand why he's angry, this progress could all go down the drain if he gets so angry that he breaks into Massengills. Can we get the car back right away? Remember that Beltran has no cash.

CHAPTER 6

INTERFERENCE WITH ECONOMIC RIGHTS

"Economic rights" and "economic interests" are terms of art here. You have economic interests in your property and even in your own good health. However, some economic interests stand apart from your physical well-being and from your tangible property. For instance, someone may use your picture in an advertisement. This does not infringe any tangible property you own nor does it hurt you in a physical way. If you have a right in such a case it is what we will call an "economic right."

Many important kinds of cases fall into the category of economic interests. Besides cases dealing directly with money and credits, economic rights are implicated in trademark, copyright, and patent cases; in interference with business and contract cases; in job rights cases; and in lawyer malpractice cases — to suggest a sample. In many other cases, economic rights are mixed with highly personal rights considered in the next chapter. For example, a libel may cause your client to lose a job, definitely an economic interest.

Economic rights can be infringed in many ways. Some ways economic rights are infringed are considered in separate chapters. The most notable of these include misrepresentation and breach of contract. Even if we put contract and fraud cases in separate chapters, we are left with too many kinds of economic rights to consider fully here, and some of them are rather specialized besides.

So we cover a few samples. Rights in money and credits are more like intangible economic rights than tangible property rights, so interests in money are included here. So are interests in business opportunities and contract rights with third persons.

Problem 6-1

Koch v. Jackson World Travel Agency

Koch decided to take a world cruise. In January she deposited $20,-000 with Jackson World Travel Agency toward the cost of the cruise tickets. Jackson deposited the check in its bank account with the Arifornia National Bank. Deposits of other would-be travelers were also placed in this account.

A week later, Koch discovered that Jackson was financially shaky and that it had not actually purchased the tickets or deposited any sum with the cruise line. Koch consulted a lawyer, Anna Montaño, who notified the bank that Koch claimed a trust or lien interest in the fund on deposit. At this point, no one claims that Jackson is guilty of any kind of actionable fraud. Although Jackson perhaps should have deposited funds like Koch's in a trust account rather than in the agency's own account, Jackson did not attempt to embezzle or spend the money for its own purposes.

We represent the bank. Bank officers have told us that the total fund is $50,000, but that Jackson has owed the bank $55,000 for over a year and that they are ready to transfer Jackson's entire balance in partial payment of Jackson's debt to the bank. The bank is entitled to do this under its customer and loan agreements with Jackson if the funds are in fact Jackson's. To the extent that Koch or others have an interest in the funds, legal or equitable, the bank of course has no rights in them.

The bank tells us that there was a balance of $30,000 in the account when a deposit of $20,000 was made in late January. Presumably that deposit represents the payment Koch made to Jackson. The Jackson agency actually closed up the day after the Koch deposit and no other transactions, in or out, have taken place.

Should the bank make the transfer of the Jackson account funds to itself in partial payment of Jackson's debt? Please read DOBBS, TEXT §§ 6.1 (1) — 6.1 (4).

Problem 6-2

Quinn v. Naron

Naron embezzled $10,000 from Quinn on a single occasion. He deposited the embezzled monies in his bank account on Thursday. His account contained a balance of $5,000 at that time. On Friday he withdrew $10,000 and bought 10,000 state lottery tickets. On Saturday night, one of the tickets was the sole winner in the lottery. It paid cash of $1 million. The state's check for that sum reached Naron the next Thursday and he deposited it the same day. The following day Quinn discovered the embezzlement.

You represent Quinn. What can you do for Quinn here?

Problem 6-3

Connecticut Indemnity v. Rapallo

Erdmann embezzled $100,000 from her employer, Rapallo. Connecticut Indemnity had issued a fidelity bond which in essence guaranteed the employer against loss by the unfaithful employee. Connecticut paid Rapallo $100,000 under the provisions of this bond. Rapallo discovered that of the $100,000, Erdmann had directly invested $50,000 in a parcel of land identified as Blackacre. Rapallo brought suit to impose a constructive trust on Blackacre and prevailed in this litigation. About the time the judgment was entered, oil was found in the same strata on nearby property. Rapallo has been offered $200,000 for the property. Connecticut has learned this and has demanded that Rapallo pay it the $200,000.

Represent either Rapallo or Connecticut. If your professor agrees, try this procedure. Make your basic analysis, with or without writing. Consult DOBBS, TEXT § 4.3 (4) in the process. When you've completed that, you should have a first estimate of your client's legal position. Now discuss settlement with one of the counsel for the opposing party.

Were your analyses close enough that you can probably reach a settlement? If not, try to determine why your analyses are far apart. Do you think either counsel could have made a biased assessment? If that happened, will it be beneficial to that counsel's client? If it was not bias of counsel, consider whether your settlement was difficult because counsel gave too much weight to uncertainties in the law. How should uncertainty be dealt with when you are estimating the settlement value of a case?

Problem 6-4

Paolo Ghiberti & Co., Inc. v. Speer

New York counsel for Paolo Ghiberti & Co., the stockbrokers, have asked us for an opinion as to Paolo Ghiberti's rights under our law.

1. Speer owned shares of stock in, and was manager of, Fiberco, a manufacturer and seller of fiberglass and fiberglass products, including boats, house siding, mobile homes, bathtubs, and the like. Speer began to play the stock market, using the brokerage firm of Paolo Ghiberti, members of the NYSE. He was not particularly successful, and in fact, regularly lost money on schemes to get in and out of the market quickly.

2. Apparently as a result of his losses, or perhaps because he liked to gamble, he began to intercept checks made out to Fiberco from buyers who were paying off accounts. Since he had authority to endorse and deposit the checks to the Fiberco account, he began to endorse these checks and receive cash or endorse them and deposit them to his personal account.

3. The bank, Charlesville National Bank, had never been authorized to permit deposits of Fiberco checks into any account but Fiberco's, and the bank, or an officer who acted on its behalf, was aware that Speer was depositing large sums to his own account in this fashion. Speer used his account to invest quite heavily in the stock market through Paolo Ghiberti.

4. The result of this was that Fiberco's books showed that its accounts receivable were unprecedentedly high. That is, its books showed that credit customers were not paying promptly and that collectively they owed large sums to Fiberco. Neither the treasurer, the chief accountant, nor any other company officials instituted any checks on this situation. Nor did they safeguard deposits in any way. However, the annual independent audit by a CPA, which would occur in May, would routinely seek to verify accounts receivable. That action by auditors would inevitably lead to the discovery that debtors had in fact paid for their orders and that

they did not owe what the books showed. From this, auditors would quickly discover the embezzlement by Speer.

5. To avoid this discovery, Speer wanted to get the money he had embezzled back into the Fiberco accounts and to credit customers who had paid. He wanted to do this before April 30, after which auditing would begin.

6. In early April, Speer ordered $2,600,000 in stocks through Paolo Ghiberti. He put up no money at all at the time the order was placed. The arrangement was that Speer would pay the balance in cash within five working days of the order. Five working days (one calendar week) later, Speer delivered his check on the Charlesville National Bank for the balance due in the sum of $2,600,000. This was accepted by Paolo Ghiberti and deposited in their bank account.

7. Later on the same day, Speer ordered a sale of "his" stock at prevailing prices. In fact, prices were down and the stock sold for only $2,000,000. Paolo Ghiberti delivered its check for that sum to Speer.

8. Speer endorsed the Paolo Ghiberti check to Charlesville National in return for two bank drafts, one in the sum of $1.2 million payable to Fiberco (and amounting to the sum he had embezzled from that company) and the other in the sum of $800,000, payable to Charlesville National to cover debts he owed that bank. In return for payment, Charlesville released stock in Fiberco which Speer's wife, Joan A. Speer, had pledged to it to secure the debt.

9. Speer's check to Paolo Ghiberti bounced because Speer had virtually no funds in his bank account, much less $2 million. Paolo Ghiberti demanded immediate payment, but accepted a 30-day promissory note from Speer for the $2 million Ghiberti had paid him. It took another promissory note for the balance due on the $2.6 stock purchase, that is, $600,000.

10. Speer was unable to pay the note within the thirty days due and Paolo Ghiberti consulted their New York counsel. Their investigation indicates that Speer is insolvent, and that, though Fiberco and Charlesville both have recently had periods in which their accounts dropped below $25,000, their cash position is generally very good and their capital assets are enormous. They accordingly request our opinion about prospects of any recovery under local law.

11. New York counsel indicate that in discussing the matter with Speer's counsel, he contended that Paolo Ghiberti had violated a rule of the New York Stock Exchange which requires brokers to know their customers' basic financial position. New York counsel also tells us that they believe Paolo Ghiberti violated no regulations about financing of stock purchasers.

Please give a complete opinion and full analysis immediately.

Problem 6-5

Xian Corporation v. The Zeller Company

Xian Corporation owned the trademark for Asia House Motels with their faked but famous Pagoda roofline. Xian owned several Asia House Motels outright, but it mainly franchised these motels. A franchisee would be entitled to use the trademark and would receive a number of services from Xian. It would also be subject to a uniform accounting system and to Xian's rules concerning various quality items. The franchisee would pay up-front money to acquire the franchise and would make annual payments, part of which were based on a percentage of gross income.

Xian orally agreed with Janelle Younger that Janelle Younger would become a franchisee for an Asia House Motel in the city of Port West under the usual terms. The contract was to be signed a month later after Janelle Younger had prepared all the necessary papers and bank loans.

The Zeller Company is a competitor to Xian. Zeller franchises the Westward Court motels. After Xian and Janelle Younger made their oral agreement, but before a written contract was executed, Zeller persuaded Janelle Younger not to go through with the Xian Corporation's deal and to join the Zeller chain instead. Zeller offered Janelle Younger somewhat better terms, including less initial capital investment and smaller annual dollar payments.

After Janelle Younger refused to complete the deal with Xian, Xian sued Zeller for interference with contract or with business prospects, not only in the case of Janelle Younger but in 20 other similar situations. The complaint sought all of the following remedies: (1) damages based on

Xian's lost income from the franchisee's up front and annual payments; (2) profits of the defendant Zeller from interference with the contracts or reasonably certain business prospects; (3) punitive damages; (4) an injunction against continued interference with such contracts or prospects. The sole shareholder in Xian joined as a plaintiff to assert a claim for emotional harm to himself resulting from the defendant's interference.

We represent Zeller. Although Zeller may be privileged to compete for mere business prospects, the law of this state imposes liability for interference with existing contracts. The oral agreement may count as such a contract. Assuming that it does, please prepare an assessment of the defense position on the remedial issues. See DOBBS, TEXT §§ 6.6 (1) — 6.6 (5).

Problem 6-6

Ramirez v. Dalton

Dr. Daniel Ramirez operates a clinic which, with Ramirez' own living quarters, occupies all of an old house. The neighborhood is composed of houses that were all once single-family residences. Many houses have been converted to apartments and rental rooms. Some of the houses, like Ramirez', have been converted into professional offices and a few small businesses.

The Ramirez clinic is devoted to medical care for pregnant women. Many of Ramirez' patients are young women who seek abortions. Some are rape victims who wish not to bear the rapist's child. A few want to terminate pregnancy because they have discovered through genetic testing that their fetus suffers serious abnormalities. An even smaller number of women are themselves in danger and need to terminate their pregnancies because they are otherwise at risk of death. The majority of the patients, however, are young women, usually in their upper teens, who are simply not prepared, emotionally, financially, or otherwise to become parents.

Except in emergencies and to save the mother's life, no abortion is performed until the patient has received counseling. Counseling usually consists of a session with a counselor who discusses the patient's reasons for the proposed abortion and discusses alternatives, including adoption. About 5% of the patients decide against abortion after receiving this counseling. In those cases the mother usually gives up the child for adoption, but sometimes keeps the child herself.

Dalton has organized many groups or individuals to oppose abortion and in the last year he has traveled around the country organizing opposition to clinics like Ramirez' clinic. He receives contributions from various sources, but denies that he or any of those who support him are any part of a formal or identifiable group.

For the past ten days, Dalton and his supporters have demonstrated in front of the Ramirez Clinic and maintained round-the-clock vigils there. Demonstrators have repeatedly or regularly (1) carried signs accusing Ramirez of murder, genocide and torture; (2) carried signs accusing Ramirez' patients of the murder and torture of their own children; (3) shouted similar accusations at prospective patients entering or trying to enter the clinic; (4) shouted to children of prospective patients that their mothers were murderers and would burn in hell; and (5) physically blocked entrance to the clinic, preventing some prospective patients from entering.

Some of the demonstrators have been identified individually. These are Kay Williams, Donald Tritsch, and Lyndon Battle. Others appear to be members of a loose-knit group that sometimes goes under the name of STOP. Dalton is not a resident of this state, but seems to be living here temporarily. The others all appear to be local people.

The Allen Firm
From: Peggy Allen

Dr. Ramirez has provided us with the above information, which is true to the best of his knowledge. He claims that the demonstrators have actually and repeatedly trespassed on his property. He says he is not much concerned about technical trespasses, but he wants to stop the demonstrators from actually blocking entrance to his clinic. He wants them entirely removed from the sidewalk in front of the clinic and indeed would like the court to forbid the demonstrations. On that point, he says that the shouting and name-calling has been emotionally harmful to his patients and their children and wants a court order forbidding shouting and name-calling.

Ramirez also says that financially the demonstration has already been a hardship and that since the demonstrations began 10 days ago, his income has dropped by 90%.

Mrs. James Bobbit and Ms. Theresa Fernandez are patients who have tried to enter the clinic and who either have been physically barred by demonstrators or who have suffered emotional problems because of their accusations and physical crowding. They are willing to join as plaintiffs.

Representing Ramirez, Bobbit and Fernandez, we appeared before Judge Steiner in the Superior Court and moved for a temporary restraining order. Judge Steiner issued a TRO last night, forbidding Dalton and those acting for or with him from blocking or impeding the entrance to the clinic. That is all the order said. It was served on Dalton this morning.

Please prepare for a motion for preliminary injunction. Please outline the terms we should seek in the preliminary injunction and prepare for a stiff fight. Dalton is represented by the Zylstra firm.

The Zylstra Firm
From: John Zylstra

Mr. Dalton, along with Kay Williams, Donald Tritsch and Lyndon Battle discussed with us their efforts to close down the Ramirez Clinic and we have agreed to represent them in any action Ramirez or his patients might bring.

Last night, without notice, Judge Steiner issued a TRO, which forbids Dalton and those acting with him or on his behalf from blocking or impeding entrance to the clinic.

The Allen firm represents Ramirez. Please prepare fully to resist and attack the TRO and to resist a preliminary injunction. Do everything you can to resist. We think Dalton is prepared to suffer jail if necessary, but we must try to avoid or pare down any court order and to avoid contempt imprisonment if we can.

Specifically, can we get the TRO dissolved? Can we prevent a preliminary injunction? What obstacles can we raise to a preliminary injunction? Can we limit the terms of either the TRO or the preliminary injunction so much that it won't interfere with Dalton's efforts to close down the Ramirez Clinic?

———

Whichever party you represent, you may wish to review DOBBS, TEXT §
2.11.

Notes

1. Notice that in some instances a demonstrator might actually trespass on
the plaintiff's real property. In that case, the plaintiff could bring this suit as a
trespass case and factually it would fit in the immediately preceding chapter. In
many instances, however, demonstrators accomplish their purpose without entry
upon the plaintiff's land, by blocking or intimidating potential patients. In that
case, the landowner-plaintiff might think of the case as an interference with contract or business prospects. The patient-plaintiffs, on the other hand, might think
of the claim as an invasion of both their economic rights and their civil or personal rights.

2. After you have identified particular legal issues, you will need to consult
other sections. Try to anticipate practical consequences of each potential ruling
and the next possible legal steps.

3. In several somewhat similar cases, federal courts have issued injunctions
against some of the conduct involved in blocking abortion clinics. In *Bray v.
Alexandria Women's Health Clinic*, 113 S.Ct. 753 (1993), the clinics sought injunctive relief on the ground that the protestors, by blocking entrance to the clinics, were in effect conspiring to deprive women of equal protection in violation
of a civil rights statute, 42 U.S.C.A. § 1985. The Supreme Court held that
injunctive relief on that ground was improper because demonstrations against
abortion are not necessarily based on a derogatory view of women as a class.

4. The *Bray* decision does not eliminate any other substantive grounds that
might exist for granting an injunction. Presumably the Allen firm will consider
several substantive possibilities.

5. There are substantive considerations the Zylstra firm will consider as
well. Free speech, as guaranteed by the First Amendment, will surely play a part
in the case. It is well established, for example, that picketing is a form of speech
that is protected from state interference. Social or political boycotts may also be
a form of protected communicative activity. Consider how the free speech issue
will affect the Zylstra firm's remedial arguments.

Problem 6-7

Eldridge v. O'Brien

Judge Steiner issued a TRO and later a preliminary injunction against several named individuals and those acting in concert or active participation with those individuals. The order forbad any entry upon the property of one Dr. Ramirez without the express written permission of Dr. Ramirez or his designates, and further forbad various specified acts such as pushing, shoving, blocking or substantially impeding complete free access to Ramirez' property. The exact wording of the order is not germane to this case.

After the order was issued, it was read over loudspeakers at Dr. Ramirez' clinic and hand delivered to all named individual defendants, including Dalton, who was generally considered to be the chief organizer of the demonstrations. At that point, Dalton asked everyone to leave and to gather in a church in the next block. Everyone did in fact leave and evidence suggests that most if not all of them gathered in the church and discussed the order.

The next day, a group of demonstrators appeared. They included John O'Brien. By pushing, shoving, and blocking one Lucia Lamm, these demonstrators committed acts that would be a violation of the order if the order applied to them. Later, Dalton, who actually had been served, appeared and encouraged them to stop entrance of another prospective patient, Miriam Freeman.

O'Brien asserted that he had never before demonstrated and was not a member of any group or putative group such as STOP! He says he knew of the court order and actually read a copy of it to be sure he was not violating it. Upon further questioning, he admitted that he had attended rallies led by Dalton on several occasions and that he naturally believed in their cause. He added that besides his religious beliefs against abortion, however, he also felt a personal grievance against "abortionists" (his word) because his own daughter had died during or after an abortion.

Dalton has been through this scene a number of times. He has been held in contempt at least 13 times. One time he served a year in jail before the judge finally relented. Dalton himself has never relented or promised to obey the court orders.

Dr. Garry Eldridge bought the clinic from Ramirez, who had had enough of the threats and violence. Eldridge moved to be substituted as plaintiff in the complaint, a motion that was granted as a matter of course. Eldridge then moved to hold Dalton and O'Brien in contempt and served a show-cause order on both of them. The state statute that governs criminal contempt would impose a fine of no more than $100 or a jail sentence of no more than ten days.

The Allen firm represents Eldridge. The Zylstra firm represents Dalton. A third firm, the firm of Skokos & Skokos, represents O'Brien. If you wish you can migrate to the Skokos firm and represent Eldridge. The parties and their attorneys agree that your earlier work for the Allen or Zylstra firm was so limited that representing Eldridge would not violate any professional ethics or disciplinary rules.

Whomever you represent, consult DOBBS, TEXT §§ 2.8 (3) — 2.8 (6).

Problem 6-8

Veatch v. Grissom

Tami and Jess Grissom were sister and brother, aged 55 and 60 respectively. They owned, as joint tenants with right of survivorship, a parcel of land containing 50 acres and on which a substantial house was standing. The parcel was worth about $75,000. In 1970, Tami made a will leaving all her property of every kind to Mary Lou Veatch. In 1971, Jess gave Tami an overdose of sleeping pills from which she died. Jess had one son, Jack, but no other living relatives. Tami had no living relatives. Mary Lou took a small sum in cash under the will, that being Tami's only property other than the joint tenancy. Tami's death was at first considered a suicide, and Jess took title to the land by survivorship. In 1972, Jess sold the land for $80,000 and invested the proceeds in shares of stock in a swamplands housing development. By early 1973, shares for which Jess had paid $80,000 had a market value of $110,000. At this point, Jess sold all the shares and deposited $50,000 of the funds in the First State Savings and Loan Association, $10,000 in the bank, and $50,000 in Jack's bank account.

In the meantime, suspicions about Tami's death deepened. Tami had kept a diary that immediately before her death she had sent to Mary Lou. Mary Lou had been too upset by Tami's death to read it at the time, but on reading it now found Tami's account of Jess's various attempts to kill her. Mary Lou reported this to the district attorney and an investigation established a substantial case against Jess. No criminal prosecution has been brought, but the evidence available would probably be sufficient to get the case to a criminal jury.

Mary Lou has retained the firm of Jordan and Swain to protect her rights under the will. That firm has brought suit against Jess, Jack and the financial institutions in which the monies mentioned above were deposited. The suit asks for a TRO against the financial institutions to freeze all the funds in question and demands a recovery of all the funds on behalf of Mary Lou as devisee and legatee under Tami's will.

This firm represents Jess and Jack. Attorneys for the banks have been in touch with you and strenuously oppose the TRO. They want to cooperate in getting it dissolved and in preventing a preliminary restraining order.

(1) Please prepare a memo in support of our motion to dissolve the TRO and in opposition to a preliminary restraining order, which will certainly be requested.

(2) Please prepare a memorandum on the merits of Veatch's claim, and indicate your recommendations about settlement or defensive posture.

See DOBBS, TEXT § 6.7.

Problem 6-9

Bone v. Sylvania County

Bill Bone has owned the old Faulkner tract, 200 acres of rural, vacant land for over twenty years. He recently decided to try to develop the land. When he conferred with us about developing the land, we discovered that the land was subject to a county zoning ordinance passed about two years ago. That ordinance forbids multifamily housing in most of the county outside city limits. The effect of the ordinance, if enforced, would be to take substantially all of the value of the land, which lies near the city's edge and which is perfect for apartments or condominiums, but which would have little other use.

Unfortunately, Bone did not consider talking to attorneys until he had already used his personal credit to borrow $100,000 from the bank, most of which has been expended in studying financial options, obtaining market surveys and other preliminary matters. We have had a conference with Willa Dean, a real estate appraiser. She has not formally appraised the land, but her offhand estimate is that without the regulation the land would sell for somewhere between $3 and $5 million, depending on the economic situation at the moment. As regulated, the land, which is not particularly attractive for single-family dwellings, is worth no more than $200,000 if Bone could sell it at all. It has no value for commercial development in the foreseeable future.

Our initial assessment is that the zoning regulation is clearly unconstitutional and that we can get a court to enjoin its enforcement.

However, the county might respond by enacting another restrictive ordinance that might not be so clearly unconstitutional or else by delaying the required building and planning permits. One strategy might be to ask the county board to withdraw this provision. We are not optimistic. We think the board passed this provision in an effort to keep the county outside the city as a rich and rural country club and we don't think we can politically induce a change.

The other strategy would be to hit the county where it hurts, with a claim for money. Assume we can get the ordinance declared to be unconstitutional. Can we also collect substantial money damages? If so, what measures of damages and what evidence would we need to have available at trial? One more thing. High voltage lines run adjacent to the property. Some people believe that high voltage lines cause cancer to those living nearby. Would the fact that some people believe that affect our damages?

NOTE ON JOB DISCRIMINATION AND
WRONGFUL DISCHARGE

The substantive law of job discrimination and wrongful discharge is complex and specialized. When employees have no contractual rights to a job — the traditional "at will" employee — the common law permitted the employer to discharge the employee for no reason at all. Many courts have now said that the discharge must not be based on a violation of public policy. For instance, it may be tortious under state law to discharge an employee because he refuses to perjure himself for the employer's benefit.

For more extensive rights, employees must often rely on union or personal contracts, or on statutory protections. Except for civil service legislation, most statutes aim to protect against various forms of discrimination, such as discrimination based on gender, race, or religion. These statutes raise many important remedial issues, but their exact terms differ.

One important federal anti-discrimination statute aimed at private as well as public employers is usually called Title VII.[3] As originally enacted and interpreted, that statute was an economic rights statute only. Its primary remedies in the case of one wrongfully discharged were (a) reinstatement and (b) back pay. Reinstatement was of course an injunction which compelled the employer to take back the employee. This is significant because the traditional equity rule refused to do any such thing. The original statute did not permit ordinary damages, which would have included the potential for punitive and mental anguish awards. Courts interpreted the statute as creating an "equitable" cause of action to be tried without a jury, even though the back pay was a money award and seems to fit exactly within the *Dairy Queen* rule requiring a jury trial.

The 1991 Civil Rights Act added the missing elements of damages, mental anguish and punitive damages, but with restrictions. Those items of damages are recoverable only when the employer is guilty of intentional discrimination; a disparate impact claim alone would not suffice. These recoveries for non-pecuniary loss were also capped with a variable cap, depending on the number of persons employed. The maximum combined recovery of mental anguish and punitive damages against large employers was $300,000.

For the mental anguish and punitive damages claims, but not for the other claims under Title VII, the 1991 Act also required a jury trial. Suppose a plaintiff asserts a claim for (a) back pay, and (b) mental anguish damages. The second claim is clearly a traditional damages claim and the statute itself recognizes a jury trial right. What does *Dairy Queen* require

---

[3] 42 U.S.C.A. § 2000e.

when that claim and the back pay claim are both asserted? How could courts ever have said that back pay was an equitable claim anyway?

Another problem occurs when the plaintiff is reinstated. Suppose that, in violation of the statute, a plaintiff is discharged (or not hired, or not promoted appropriately) on March 1. Suppose that on March 15 the employer hires Newman in the same department. If the court thereafter reinstates the plaintiff, does she get seniority from her original hiring date (or from March 1 if she was never hired)? In other words, will she be senior to Newman? In many industries, seniority has actual cash value. How would you come out on this if you reasoned as courts do in constructive trust cases?

Title VII interposes some procedural conditions on suit; you must first submit your complaint to the Equal Employment Opportunity Commission and you can sue only when that body permits it or delays for a certain period. These limitations have encouraged many plaintiffs to seek redress under other federal statutes where possible, or under state anti-discrimination statutes or state tort law.

For other statutes and other remedial problems, see 2 DAN DOBBS, THE LAW OF REMEDIES §§ 6.10 (1) — 6.10 (11) (2d ed. 1993).

Problem 6-10

United Citrus Workers v. Mecham

The United Citrus Workers is an association of migrant workers who have negotiated with area citrus growers for health coverage. Under the agreement, all area growers withhold a certain amount of money from each worker's wages and contribute a comparable amount themselves, based on a formula tied to annual profits, toward the purchase of health insurance for the workers and their dependents.

The growers jointly hired Chris Mecham to negotiate and purchase group health insurance for all employees of the area growers, as well as to perform other functions for the benefit of all of the growers. After making the arrangements for the initial purchase of group coverage, Mecham made the first several payments due under the agreement with the insurance provider and all went smoothly, with the workers receiving satisfactory health care.

About nine months after the arrangement had been entered into, and just over a month after Mecham's resignation, workers began to be denied medical coverage, and complained to the growers. Upon looking into the problem and discussing it with the insurance carrier, the growers discovered that payments under the plan had been halted over a month before Mecham resigned. Unfortunately, despite several notifications of nonpayment of premiums sent by the insurance carrier to Mecham's attention, the premiums had not been paid and all insurance had been cancelled. By the time the problem came to light, no payments had been made for almost three months.

Upon reviewing the situation more carefully, the growers discovered that there was approximately $30,000.00 missing from the medical premium account that had been set up to pay the insurance premiums. Approximately half of the missing funds had been contributed by the growers and half withheld from the workers' wages.

Last week, one of the representatives of the United Citrus Workers, Lydia Muniz, came into our office to discuss the problem. She related the information provided above, much of which she learned in discussions with one of the grower's representatives. This week, she has given us new information.

Two nights ago, Muniz saw Mecham on television as Mecham accepted $76 million in state lottery winnings. In the interview that followed his introduction as the winner, Mecham told reporters that he had purchased $200 worth of tickets at the 7-Eleven on Orange Grove Road, which is next to the growers' offices. He also told reporters that he bought the tickets the day he quit his job with the growers. Our preliminary investigation reveals that Mecham also purchased a new boat that same day, for which he paid $25000.00 cash.

Ms. Muniz would like to report back to her fellow workers early next week about the possible remedies available to the workers.

CHAPTER 7

CIVIL AND DIGNITARY RIGHTS

Civil rights, civil liberties, and dignitary rights cover broad and diverse territories, linked mainly by the fact that we value these rights less for their pecuniary consequences than for their worth as ends in themselves. We want the right to vote whether the exercise of that right affects our pecuniary interests or not. We want a good reputation even if a bad reputation does not affect our income.

Civil or dignitary rights can be protected by recognizing a substantive cause of action and then affording an appropriate remedy. Those rights can also be recognized by holding that a person who exercises those rights cannot be legally liable for doing so. For instance, a public official cannot recover from a citizen who honestly but mistakenly accuses the official of wrongdoing. That is a way of protecting the citizen's right of free speech. The rule that protects the citizen's right to criticize a public official is of course a substantive rule which gives the citizen a complete defense.

Are there remedial as well as substantive defenses? A defense that bars the action would be a substantive defense. A defense that does not bar the action but limits the remedies available would be a remedial defense. In the personal injury area, comparative negligence would be an example of a remedial defense because it would reduce the plaintiff's damages without barring the plaintiff entirely. "Defense" is the right word with comparative fault because the burden is upon the defendant to assert the defense and persuade the trier that it applies. In other instances, however, "defense" is merely a convenient locution for the idea that the remedy is limited. What role, if any, should these remedial "defenses" or limitations on remedies have in protecting civil or dignitary rights?

Problem 7-1

Sinclair v. The Fort Rouge Record

Sinclair was a medical doctor in Fort Rouge. He attended a public meeting of the county board of supervisors where one of the questions on the agenda was the county's role, if any, in providing AIDS-HIV information, in locating victims, and in providing care or support. When the supervisors called for public comment, Sinclair spoke. He attempted to draw a parallel in what he believed was the treatment of insane persons in times past and AIDS victims. He said, "If I am insane, you throw me in a dungeon and give me no treatment; if I have AIDS, you may not even bother to throw me in the dungeon."

The locution proved to be unfortunate. The reporter for the local newspaper, the *Fort Rouge Record*, understood Sinclair to be admitting that he had AIDS and included a statement to that effect in his story. The result was that the *Fort Rouge Record* published a story, on its front page, headlined "Doctor AIDS Victim Speaks Out." In fact Dr. Sinclair does not have AIDS, is not HIV positive, and did not say or imply anything to the contrary.

That was early this morning. Sinclair immediately consulted us and wants immediate action. What can we do for him? See DOBBS, TEXT §§ 7.2 (1) – 7.2 (6) and § 7.2 (10).

Notes

1. *Restitution.* Suppose a book publisher distributes a book that is pervasively libelous and makes a great deal of money doing so. Could the libel victim recover the publisher's profits as restitution? It is generally thought not. See DOBBS, TEXT § 7.2 (13).

2. *Right-of-reply.* What if a statute gave Dr. Sinclair a right of reply, that is, a right to use the same space in the newspaper to print his own version? This was held unconstitutional as an infringement of the newspaper's free speech and associated rights. See DOBBS, TEXT § 7.2 (14).

3. *Injunction.* A strong tradition, independent of the First Amendment, holds that injunction against speech, including libelous speech, is inappropriate. Suppose your former client, disgruntled and confused, parades in front of your

office every day at noon with a placard announcing that you stole his money, ringing a cow bell to attract attention? No injunctive relief? See *id*.

4. *Declaratory judgment*. Libel suits against media are now big business, with judgments running into the millions and defense costs perhaps as devastating as the judgments themselves. Some proposals on the table would give the plaintiff a choice between a declaratory judgment that the publication was not true and a common law action, but if he chose the common law action, he would be required to prove actual injury by clear and convincing evidence.

Problem 7-2

Eldridge v. O'Brien II

After the decisions on TRO (see *Ramirez v. Dalton*, Problem 6-6 and *Eldridge v. O'Brien*, Problem 6-7), and while the contempt hearing was pending, the trial judge broadened his order. The new order, in response to various confrontations at the Ramirez-Eldridge clinic, was directed to all the demonstrators as a group and many named persons, including O'Brien. The new order contained all the terms of the old one but added an injunction against calling any patient a murderer or any equivalent in the presence of a minor. The point of the order was that the accusations shouted at patients were harming their children, who sometimes accompanied the patient to the clinic.

After the new order was issued, and while the contempt hearing was pending, O'Brien violated the new order by shouting at patients trying to enter the clinic that they were murderers and unfit to have custody of their children. These and worse remarks were made in the presence of children accompanying their mothers to the clinic.

A second show-cause order was prepared and served on O'Brien. O'Brien himself told his counsel he wanted specifically to defend on the ground that the order infringed his free speech rights. Is this a defense?

See DOBBS, TEXT § 2.8 (6).

83

NOTE: ATTORNEY FEES AWARDS UNDER CIVIL RIGHTS AND SIMILAR STATUTES

Reaffirming the American Rule. In *Alyeska Pipeline Service Co. v. Wilderness Society*, 421 U.S. 240, 95 S.Ct. 1612, 44 L.Ed.2d 141 (1975), the Supreme Court re-affirmed the American Rule on attorney fees for federal court cases. The result was that the prevailing party could not collect attorney fees from the losing party unless a statute so provided or one of the traditional exceptions applied.

Federal civil rights statutes. At the time *Alyeska* was decided, Congress had already passed an important statute allowing attorney fee awards to prevailing plaintiffs in Title VII job discrimination cases. *Alyeska* prompted Congress to create further statutory attorney fees claims. The most notable statute was 42 U.S.C.A. § 1988 (b). That statute provided that

> "In any action or proceeding to enforce a provision of sections 1981, 1981a, 1982, 1983, 1985, and 1986 of this title, title IX of Public Law 92-318, or title VI of the Civil Rights Act of 1964, the court, in its discretion, may allow the prevailing party, other than the United States, a reasonable attorney's fee as part of the costs."

Other statutes. Section 1988 was supplemented with other important statutes, for instance, those allowing attorney fee awards to the prevailing plaintiff who recovers under some environmental statutes. In all, there are well over a hundred federal statutes allowing fee awards.

Baseline rules. Several important baseline rules quickly developed for fee awards litigation under the statute. (1) The prevailing plaintiff is routinely awarded a fee in spite of the discretionary language of the statute. (2) The prevailing defendant is routinely denied a fee. (3) The fee is awarded as "costs," not as damages. (4) Only the prevailing plaintiff or her lawyer can recover the fee.

Who is a prevailing plaintiff entitled to recover a fee award? The plaintiff must obtain *some* relief to be counted as a prevailing plaintiff, although the relief may be obtained by settlement in some cases, or even when the defendant unilaterally corrects the civil rights violation. If the plaintiff seeks and obtains an injunction on the merits of a civil rights claim, for example, then the plaintiff is a prevailing party. Even if the plaintiff seeks only a declaratory judgment, that might suffice if the declaration really affects the defendant's behavior toward the plaintiff. What if the plaintiff recovers only nominal damages for violation of a right covered by the fee award statute?

Problem 7-3, *Raskolnikov* and the Supreme Court's decision in *Farrar v. Hobby*, both immediately below, bear on that question. But first, this is a good time to read further about fee measurement and reduction for partial success. On these topics, please see DOBBS, TEXT §§ 3.10 (7) — 3.10 (10).

———————

Problem 7-3

Raskolnikov v. Springdale City School System

In the Springdale City School System, female students in high school have an option to take ballet and no option to take shop. Male students have an option to take shop and no option to take ballet. Last year, as a senior student, Mike Raskolnikov attempted to take ballet but was denied admission to the class on the ground that, as a male, his only option was to take shop or academic courses.

Mike duly graduated and entered college at State, where he majors in engineering. He wants to bring a suit against the Springdale City School System for damages, but he has little or no money. Our firm has listened to his story. We believe from cases we've handled before that both state and federal law prohibit discrimination in schools on the basis of gender; on the surface this looks like discrimination.

We are doing a substantial amount of pro bono work and we really cannot afford to do more. Assuming the school violated state and federal law, can we afford to take this case? What if we recover only $1 as nominal damages?

See DOBBS, TEXT § 7.4 (2).

Notes

1. 20 U.S.C.A. § 1681 (a) (part of Title IX) provides that, with some listed exceptions or qualifications, "No person in the United States shall, on the basis of sex, be excluded from participation in, be denied the benefits of, or be subject-

ed to discrimination under any education program or activity receiving Federal financial assistance . . . ."

    2. In *Franklin v. Gwinnett County Public Schools*, 112 S.Ct. 1028, 117 L.Ed.2d 208 (1992), the complaint alleged in detail that a young woman in high school was repeatedly harassed by a "sports coach," that the school officials knew of it and not only did not put a stop to it but discouraged the student from doing anything about it. The trial court thought that even though the Supreme Court had recognized a private right of action, the remedies did not include a suit for damages. The Supreme Court held otherwise.

FARRAR v. HOBBY[4]
United States Supreme Court, 1992
113 S.Ct. 566, 121 L.Ed.2d 494

[Farrar operated a private school where a student died in 1973. Hobby, a state official, was one of the people involved in seeking and obtaining a closure of the school. Farrar sued, claiming that Hobby and others violated his civil rights. Farrar asked for $17 million in damages. The litigation was long and involved. The jury found that Hobby violated a civil right of the plaintiff's, but that the violation was not the proximate cause of any damages. Farrar was awarded $1 nominal damages. The trial court awarded Farrar $280,000 in attorney fees, $27,932 in expenses, and $9,730 in prejudgment interest. The Court of Appeals reasoned that Farrar was not a "prevailing party" and consequently that no attorney fee could be awarded.]

Justice THOMAS delivered the opinion of the Court.

    We have elaborated on the definition of prevailing party in three recent cases. In Hewitt v. Helms, 482 U.S. 755, 107 S.Ct. 2672, 96 L.Ed.2d 654 (1987), we addressed "the peculiar-sounding question whether a party who litigates to judgment and loses on all of his claims can nonetheless be a 'prevailing party.'" In his § 1983 action against state prison officials for alleged due process violations, respondent Helms obtained no relief. "The most that he obtained was an interlocutory ruling that his

---

    [4] The concurring opinion of Justice O'Connor, and the concurring and dissenting opinion of Justice White are omitted. Footnotes and a number of citations are omitted without textual indication.

complaint should not have been dismissed for failure to state a constitutional claim." Observing that "[r]espect for ordinary language requires that a plaintiff receive at least some relief on the merits of his claim before he can be said to prevail," we held that Helms was not a prevailing party. We required the plaintiff to prove "the settling of some dispute which affects the behavior of the defendant towards the plaintiff."

In Rhodes v. Stewart, 488 U.S. 1, 109 S.Ct. 202, 102 L.Ed.2d 1 (1988) (per curiam), we reversed an award of attorney's fees premised solely on a declaratory judgment that prison officials had violated the plaintiffs' First and Fourteenth Amendment rights. By the time the District Court entered judgment, "one of the plaintiffs had died and the other was no longer in custody." Under these circumstances, we held, neither plaintiff was a prevailing party. We explained that "nothing in [Hewitt] suggested that the entry of [a declaratory] judgment in a party's favor automatically renders that party prevailing under § 1988." We reaffirmed that a judgment — declaratory or otherwise — "will constitute relief, for purposes of § 1988, if, and only if, it affects the behavior of the defendant toward the plaintiff." Whatever "modification of prison policies" the declaratory judgment might have effected "could not in any way have benefitted either plaintiff, one of whom was dead and the other released."

Finally, in Texas State Teachers Assn. v. Garland Independent School Dist., 489 U.S. 782, 109 S.Ct. 1486, 103 L.Ed.2d 866 (1989), we synthesized the teachings of Hewitt and Rhodes. "[T]o be considered a prevailing party within the meaning of § 1988," we held, "the plaintiff must be able to point to a resolution of the dispute which changes the legal relationship between itself and the defendant." We reemphasized that "[t]he touchstone of the prevailing party inquiry must be the material alteration of the legal relationship of the parties." . . . .

Therefore, to qualify as a prevailing party, a civil rights plaintiff must obtain at least some relief on the merits of his claim. The plaintiff must obtain an enforceable judgment against the defendant from whom fees are sought, or comparable relief through a consent decree or settlement. Whatever relief the plaintiff secures must directly benefit him at the time of the judgment or settlement. Otherwise the judgment or settlement cannot be said to "affec[t] the behavior of the defendant toward the plaintiff." Only under these circumstances can civil rights litigation effect "the material alteration of the legal relationship of the parties" and thereby transform the plaintiff into a prevailing party. In short, a plaintiff "prevails" when actual relief on the merits of his claim materially alters the legal relationship between the parties by modifying the defendant's behavior in a way that directly benefits the plaintiff . . . .

We therefore hold that a plaintiff who wins nominal damages is a prevailing party under § 1988. When a court awards nominal damages, it neither enters judgment for defendant on the merits nor declares the defendant's legal immunity to suit . . . . A plaintiff may demand payment for nominal damages no less than he may demand payment for millions of dollars in compensatory damages. A judgment for damages in any amount, whether compensatory or nominal, modifies the defendant's behavior for the plaintiff's benefit by forcing the defendant to pay an amount of money he otherwise would not pay. As a result, the Court of Appeals for the Fifth Circuit erred in holding that petitioners' nominal damages award failed to render them prevailing parties.

We have previously stated that "a technical victory may be so insignificant ... as to be insufficient to support prevailing party status." . . . . Now that we are confronted with the question whether a nominal damages award is the sort of "technical," "insignificant" victory that cannot confer prevailing party status, we hold that the prevailing party inquiry does not turn on the magnitude of the relief obtained. We recognized as much in Garland when we noted that "the degree of the plaintiff's success" does not affect "eligibility for a fee award."

Although the "technical" nature of a nominal damages award or any other judgment does not affect the prevailing party inquiry, it does bear on the propriety of fees awarded under § 1988. Once civil rights litigation materially alters the legal relationship between the parties, "the degree of the plaintiff's overall success goes to the reasonableness" of a fee award under Hensley v. Eckerhart, 461 U.S. 424, 103 S.Ct. 1933, 76 L.Ed.2d 40 (1983) . . . .

In some circumstances, even a plaintiff who formally "prevails" under § 1988 should receive no attorney's fees at all. A plaintiff who seeks compensatory damages but receives no more than nominal damages is often such a prevailing party. As we have held, a nominal damages award does render a plaintiff a prevailing party by allowing him to vindicate his "absolute" right to procedural due process through enforcement of a judgment against the defendant. Carey, 435 U.S., at 266, 98 S.Ct., at 1053. In a civil rights suit for damages, however, the awarding of nominal damages also highlights the plaintiff's failure to prove actual, compensable injury. Whatever the constitutional basis for substantive liability, damages awarded in a § 1983 action "must always be designed 'to compensate injuries caused by the [constitutional] deprivation.'" Memphis Community School Dist. v. Stachura, 477 U.S., at 309, 106 S.Ct., at 2544 (quoting Carey, supra). When a plaintiff recovers only nominal damages because of his failure to prove an essential element of his claim for monetary relief, see Carey, supra, the only reasonable fee is usually no fee at all. In an apparent failure to heed our admonition that fee awards under § 1988 were never intended to "'produce windfalls to attorneys,'" the District Court awarded $280,000 in attorney's fees without "consider[ing] the relationship between the extent of success and the amount of the fee award." Hensley, supra.

[The Court of Appeals "correctly reversed" the District Court. The judgment of the Court of Appeals is affirmed.]

Problem 7-4

Farsjo v. City of Rich Springs

We represented Gene Wallace in a suit against the city for the death of his child due to leukemia caused by electromagnetic fields generated by transformers and/or high voltage lines. [See Wallace v. City of Rich Springs, Problem 3-9.] We settled that claim a few weeks ago and the case has been dismissed. Wallace's civic interests dissipated when a satisfactory monetary settlement became possible, and he was willing to drop the injunction suit as well as the damages claim in return for the settlement. So the entire case was dismissed upon our stipulation as part of the settlement.

The law suit spurred some media and public attention. A protest rally was staged against the city at one point and the topic was discussed repeatedly at city council meetings. However, the city stonewalled and eventually the media interest waned. The city has done nothing about the problem.

We have been approached by a group of prospective clients who wish to bring an injunction suit to compel the city to take steps to reduce the health hazards from high voltage lines and/or transformer stations. Although we are convinced that there really is a danger, there are some obvious problems about such a suit.

First, the scientific literature is all over the ball park. Plenty of reports show some kind of connection between health and electromagnetic fields, but plenty of others cast doubt on any significant connection. Still others say that scientists have not yet asked the right kinds of questions. On the other hand, the city *did* settle the death claim.

Second, assuming we can prove that there is a serious health hazard, none of this EMF is regulated and the city is not in violation of any law or regulation that we have found. So we are a little worried that a judge might not want to issue an injunction on the basis of danger alone. The issue was well-publicized and the voters can speak by voting in city council races or even conceivably by initiating an ordinance.

Some members of the group which consulted with us and which wants to sue are concerned solely about health hazards. However, some members of the group are members of minority populations and they raised a different concern. They say that the health hazards are disproportionately affecting minorities. We looked at a utility map that confirmed their point. High voltage lines are all in relatively poor areas of town and these are, to a very large extent, also areas where the population is mainly composed of minority groups. Transformer stations are scattered, but in fact it looks as if in wealthier, majoritarian areas of town, no residences are close to transformer stations.

So members of minority groups and poorer people are disproportionately subjected to the health danger. Conceivably that might be an independent ground for getting some kind of injunctive relief.

Our firm needs to reach a decision whether to accept any of these clients and if we do, on what basis. Assume that we will be able to develop plausible proof that there is a significant health hazard and that something can be done about it, although that "something" might be very expensive indeed. On that assumption please prepare a simple memo outlining prospects and problems in the injunction claims. On the discrimination branch of the case, assume that we might be able to mount some kind of claim under state or federal law, but that neither law specifically requires an injunction.

Please read DOBBS, TEXT § 7.4 (4). Also consider alternatives that might suit the prospective clients as well.

CHAPTER 8

PERSONAL INJURY

Problem 8-1

Rye v. Trinity Service Co.

Trinity Service Co. is a national company that provides various services to cafes, restaurants, saloons and similar establishments. One of its important services is the provision of music through juke boxes and other devices. A Trinity employee, Max Harlan, picked up a juke box from a customer, the Nowhere Saloon, in a rural part of this state.

Harlan did not adequately secure the juke box. When he hit a pothole in the road, the juke box bounced and fell out the back of the truck. It struck the front of a pick-up truck driven by Susan Rye that was immediately behind him. A corner of the box struck Susan's passenger, William Bonnie, on the head.

Bonnie was taken to the emergency room where the attending physician concluded that he probably had a concussion but nothing worse. Bonnie was a 23-year-old graduate of the Harlan J. Perry School of Law. He made As, was on law review, and turned down all job offers when he graduated several months before. He had no job and was not seeking a job at the time of his injury. He lived with Susan Rye, a 32-year-old social worker, who provided food and shelter.

A few days after the injury, Bonnie consulted a doctor because of headaches. The doctor thought that he only needed rest and that nothing serious was wrong. When the adjuster for Trinity came around, Bonnie apparently acted on the doctor's opinion and signed a release for $10,000.

Thereafter, however, it became increasingly apparent that something was wrong. Bonnie seemed slower both physically and mentally. He made an appointment to see a specialist. However, before seeing the specialist, he lay down one morning, saying he didn't feel well. He went into a coma from which he has never recovered. A number of physicians have examined and tested Bonnie. They all agree that the coma is irreversible.

Susan Rye has consulted our firm about bringing a suit. Bonnie had excellent medical insurance, plus an accident policy that will apparently pay him $100,000 if he is disabled for six months as the result of an accident. Can we avoid the release? If so, what elements of damages can we recover?

If you think we can avoid the release, we would like to have daily medical monitoring of Bonnie's condition in preparation for bringing the suit. That is extremely expensive. Can we force the defendant to pay medical monitoring bills as they accrue before suit, or to deposit a fund?

See DOBBS, TEXT §§ 8.1 (1) – 8.1 (4); 11.9; 8.5; 8.6 and 8.8.

Problem 8-2

In re Franklin & Stephanic Consultation

Franklin & Stephanic is a personal injury law firm. Typically they handle a high volume of small claims, most of them in the range of $5,000 to $25,000. Many of their clients are persons of limited means. As they describe a typical client, he might have a broken leg that prevents work for a couple of weeks, damages to his pickup truck, medical bills, and some pain. The typical client, however, could not survive much delay in payment for his losses. He has no savings or collision insurance, so he cannot repair his truck. If he does not repair it, he has no way to get to work and will be discharged.

Franklin & Stephanic feel that such cases, because of their size and the client's need for early payment, require a quickly negotiated settlement rather than a trial. And that indeed is the Franklin & Stephanic style. They almost never try cases; when they do, they associate experienced trial lawyers in the case. As they see it, this style of practice serves their ends because it permits them to do business on a volume basis. It serves the clients' ends because it gives small-claim clients representation that they might not otherwise get and the relatively speedy payment most of them need.

Because the claims are small and the clients often needy, Franklin &
Stephanic are vulnerable in some ways. For instance, adjusters systematically refuse to pay rental for a substitute vehicle while the client's vehicle
is being repaired. Although this can cause the client to lose a job for lack
of transportation, the claim is seldom sufficiently large to warrant trial.
So the effect is that insurers are generally able to avoid making those payments.

Another difficulty the Franklin firm has arises from medical bills.
Many of their clients have no medical insurance. They consult a doctor
or chiropractor after injury and are billed for the service. Although the
bills are usually under $2,000, insurers almost invariably insist that they
are too high and refuse to pay them unless the bills can be shown to be
reasonable. In fact, the charges of some doctors are much higher than
others, so in that sense the bills are often "unreasonable." However, the
injured clients do not know they are unreasonable. Even if they know,
they are in no position to litigate with the doctor over the bill.

On these two items, rental value and medical bills, the Franklin firm
estimates that its clients as a group are systematically underpaid by several
hundred thousand dollars each year. Since Franklin works on a contingent
fee, this underpayment, if that is what it is, is also costing the Franklin
firm substantial sums.

Although our firm does not handle high-volume claims, the Franklin
firm has retained us to propose strategies for minimizing what they feel is
systematic underpayment. It is a difficult problem, because the traditional
view is that the insurers owe no independent duty to the Franklin clients
at all. They fulfill their duty if they protect their insured from liability and
pay any judgment secured by the injured person. Do you see any steps
that the Franklin firm can take?

Problem 8-3

Peters v. Livingstone

Eileen Peters has four children, all under eight years of age. She
works part time as a waitress, but does not earn much. Her husband, Dan,
has held a variety of jobs, but he is unskilled and his earnings are always
limited and sometimes erratic.

Eileen and Dan concluded that they simply could not support any more children. Their oldest, Lisa, seems to them to be unusually bright and they would like to think she could go to college, although they don't foresee how they could help. Still, if Lisa is not expected to help the family by working in her high school years and after, she might be able to put herself through college.

These are some of the ideas that Eileen and Dan have discussed. They consulted Dr. Livingstone about birth control. He recommended a simple procedure to be performed on Eileen. Eileen agreed, with Dan's support, and the operation was performed. Unfortunately, Eileen became pregnant again just a few months later. She has now given birth to their fifth child, Freddie. Freddie is a normal, healthy child.

Eileen admittedly takes a great deal of joy in Freddie. But times are hard for Eileen, Dan, and the four older children as they make room for Freddie and inevitably give up amenities of a life that is already sparse. Have they a claim against Dr. Livingstone and if so for what damages?

See DOBBS, TEXT § 8.2.

CHAPTER 9

FRAUD AND MISREPRESENTATION

Problem 9-1

Oppenheimer v. Bowles

You represent Richard Oppenheimer. Oppenheimer bought a parcel of land from Maria Gallegos. He was induced to do so because of representations made to him by Sarah Bowles, a real estate broker. Bowles' representations included a statement that the Ferguson Manufacturing Co., a large manufacturer of precision tooled marine frammis screws, had decided to locate in Truman. This was in fact false and known by Bowles to be false.

Bowles further told Oppenheimer that Ferguson had not yet picked a site, but that it would necessarily pick either the Gallegos parcel or one nearby, and that, in either event, the Gallegos land would undoubtedly increase in value. Had these representations been true, the Gallegos land would have been worth no less than $100,000. As it was, the land was worth only about $85,000, but Oppenheimer believed it to be worth much more. The price asked by Gallegos was $90,000. After listening to this carefully and believing Bowles, Oppenheimer agreed orally to purchase for $90,000 and later signed a written contract for purchase at that price.

The contract also provided in part that "no representations of any kind have been made to the purchaser, and the purchaser has relied solely upon his own investigation and judgment in purchasing this property." After a suitable period for financing and title examination, there was a closing and Oppenheimer took title to the land, subject to a mortgage to the Truman Savings & Loan Association in the sum of $50,000. The purchase price was fully paid to Gallegos, except for a commission to Bowles in the amount of $7,500.

Shortly after the closing, Oppenheimer discovered that the Ferguson Manufacturing Company had never even considered moving to Truman and that Bowles had had no reason to say it did. Oppenheimer, who was 70 years old, could not afford to lose his investment, which was intended to produce a quick gain to be invested for retirement income. When he discovered the misrepresentation, Oppenheimer became seriously depressed. During your representation of Oppenheimer, he has regularly seen a therapist for depression and is on medication for that malady. The therapist has said that the fraud deal triggered the depression.

What remedies do you seek and what do you think you can get against Bowles and/or Gallegos? Read DOBBS, TEXT §§ 9.1, 9.2 (1) & 9.2 (5).

Problem 9-2

Schiffer v. Martin

Schiffer leased premises from Martin. Schiffer became unsatisfied and moved out. He brought suit against Martin, claiming rescission and damages because the air conditioning did not work properly. Martin responded by asking the court to compel arbitration. The lease provided for arbitration of all disputes between the landlord and the tenant.

As Schiffer's attorney, you want to resist the demand for arbitration because you believe an arbitration is likely to result in a less satisfactory remedy and because a pending suit pressures the landlord to make a favorable settlement. Schiffer's evidence is that the lease was obtained by fraudulent representations about the air conditioning. Assuming the evidence of intentional misrepresentation is persuasive, does that help you avoid the arbitration?

Problem 9-3

Nancy Westman Associates v. Jefferson-Blair University

We represent Nancy Westman Associates (Westman). After inspection and a series of representations in writing made by Jefferson-Blair University (Jefferson), Westman agreed to purchase a building known to the University as Walter Hall. The purchase price was $4 million. The property consisted mainly of the Walter building and a parking lot.

Ben Cable was president of Jefferson. In negotiations for the sale, he wrote a letter to Westman in response to a number of inquiries. One of the statements in the letter was that "Walter Hall has no termite problems." In fact, as the university's building department knew, the university had repeatedly treated the building for termites and had never been fully successful in the past. Some structural damage had occurred.

Westman took title and possession about six months ago. After they began their renovations they discovered that Walter Hall suffered from another problem of which the university knew nothing. Plumbing began to be a problem after renovations were begun and Westman had a study done which showed that the entire plumbing system would need replacement in the immediate future and that the cost would be high.

We retained an appraiser. His report concluded that (1) If the termite infestation had been known and there were no plumbing problem, market value of Walter Hall would not exceed $3.75 million. (2) If the plumbing condition had been known and there was no termite infestation, market value of Walter Hall would not have exceeded $3.5 million. (3) The total value of the building today is probably somewhat less than $3 million because of the plumbing and termite defects and because the University has almost entirely removed its operations from this area since selling the Walter building to Westman. The area has undergone a definite deterioration in property values in the last six months as the University has shifted its operations east.

Please plan the remedial claim. See DOBBS, TEXT §§ 9.2 (6), 9.6 (3) (1) & 9.6 (3).

Problem 9-4

Nancy Westman Associates v. Jefferson-Blair University

In case it becomes desirable to claim restitution in this case, please consider whether we might be barred by the election of remedies doctrine, either now or on account of anything we might do later.

See DOBBS, TEXT § 9.4.

Problem 9-5

Berreman v. The Providence Foundation

The Providence Foundation wished to acquire a parcel of land owned by Thomas Berreman. Berreman had acquired the land by (1) purchasing 17 acres from Patricia Charise Sparks and (2) inheritance of 8.5 contiguous acres from his uncle. Berreman, Olden Schaffer and McDougald Powell had a contract to develop jointly the smaller tract, which lay along an attractive stream.

Last March the Providence Foundation offered to buy the entire tract of land consisting of both parcels and amounting to 25.5 acres. Berreman refused, but suggested that Providence might want to purchase the 17-acre tract. Providence wanted the entire tract, on which it intended to build a "shelter" for children of abusive parents.

It was important to Providence to acquire the entire tract because certain donors, Bonnard G. Karlen and Jan Olson, had offered a substantial gift to Providence if it acquired a tract of at least 20 acres for the shelter. The gift was to be $500,000 in cash and it would allow Providence to carry out its charitable purposes effectively. Without it, Providence had little hope of providing any substantial shelter for the children.

To qualify for the Karlen-Olson gift, Providence had to acquire 20 acres on an attractive, unpolluted stream and do so within 12 months of the time of the offer. The time was running out for Providence. Its director, Reynolds Smithers, had been unable to find 20 acres on a suitable, unpolluted stream, within the appropriate radius, so the Berreman property was its last best hope.

When Berreman proved adamant in his refusal to sell the 8.5-acre portion, Smithers told him Providence would accept the 17-acres tract instead and they agreed on the price. Smithers suggested that Providence could pay cash by a cashier's check, and that the cost of ordinary closing would be unnecessary. Berreman, who had only to sign a deed and accept the money, was agreeable.

Smithers and Berreman met at Berreman's office and, as agreed, Smithers had prepared a deed for Berreman's signature. He handed Berreman the deed, saying that it covered the deal exactly as agreed. As the description of both tracts was complicated, Berreman did not read the description carefully and failed to note that Smithers had included both the 17-acre and the 8.5-acre tract in the deed. Smithers paid for the property at the price agreed for the 17 acres and immediately recorded the deed.

The next day, with the recorded deed in hand, Smithers presented the deed along with photographs of the stream property to Karlen and Olson, who then jointly executed the promised gift to Providence. Smithers, on Providence's behalf, deposited the sum of money in the Providence account, and then immediately disbursed it to appropriate investments in stocks, bonds, money funds and the like.

A week later, a 21-acre tract on a stream came on the market. This tract was offered by Thurman, for a price much less than the total price for Berreman's 17-acre tract. Smithers immediately sold the Berreman property (25.5) acres to Dr. Phillip Foreman, a doctor Smithers knew well. He acquired the 21-acre tract from Thurman, obtaining Karlen's and Olson's agreement that the 21-acre tract met their approval.

When Berreman, Schaffer, and Powell got ready to proceed with their small development on the 8.5-acre tract, they became aware that title had passed to Providence by virtue of the deed, and that the property had been conveyed to Dr. Foreman. They have asked us to get the property back if possible. They believe that they will make a very good profit on its development and they hope to make their reputation as developers on this tract, so that their credit standing will be high for future developments.

Foreman and Smithers are known to be very close, both professionally and personally. We think Foreman probably knew of Smithers' tactics here, or at least that he was on notice that Smithers was pulling some kind of shady deal. Does that matter? See DOBBS, TEXT §§ 9.5 & 9.6.

Addendum: We don't trust Smithers, although we admire Providence and its goals. We checked with Judge Rogers Noreen and he is available for a short hearing late today if we need it. Should we try to obtain any kind of preliminary relief?

CHAPTER 10

UNCONSCIONABLE CONDUCT

This chapter deals with wrongs that ordinarily do not count as "torts" for which damages can be recovered. Apart from statute, remedies for less-than-tortious wrongdoings are usually restitutionary in nature. Most of the "wrongs" or unconscionable acts in this group are based on the defendant's misuse of some special power over the plaintiff. In duress or economic compulsion cases, the defendant uses physical force or economic power to compel the plaintiff to act as the defendant wishes. In undue influence cases, the defendant uses or misuses the confidence the plaintiff has placed in him to manipulate the plaintiff's will. In many cases, the defendant misuses the power he has as a fiduciary or a person in whom special confidence is reposed, and quite often this involves the misuse of inside information. Duress and economic compulsion cases aside, this chapter largely concerns the law of fiduciary and confidential relationships.

Duress . Suppose defendant threatens to break the plaintiff's arm if the plaintiff does not give the defendant Blackacre. To avoid the broken arm, the plaintiff conveys Blackacre. If the defendant is later jailed, so that his threat becomes less plausible, can the plaintiff recover Blackacre? Yes. Transactions entered into by reason of duress (physical force or threats) can be avoided. Conceivably some such threats would amount to a tort under modern law as well as duress. For example, the plaintiff in this example might recover for intentional infliction of mental distress. Such a tort claim, however, does not seem to address the loss of Blackacre. The duress claim does.

Economic compulsion. By extension of the same idea, a plaintiff may avoid transactions that were entered into under the coercion of economic and other non-physical threats, provided those threats are sufficiently wrongful and coercive. What counts as wrongful and coercive is largely a substantive question. See generally, 2 DAN DOBBS, THE LAW OF REMEDIES §§ 10.2 (1) — (3) (2d ed. 1993).

Undue influence. Unlike duress and economic compulsion, undue influence does not involve coercion. It involves manipulation of another's trust rather than breaking another's will. A dominant person sways the judgment of a more submissive and trusting one. For example, suppose the plaintiff's minister assures her that she can only reach heaven if she makes a substantial donation to the minister. Or suppose a lawyer convinces a trusting client to leave his entire estate to the lawyer. Cases like this suggest undue influence. If the case is extreme enough, the plaintiff (or the estate) will be able to avoid the donation or the gift made by will. See 2 DAN DOBBS, THE LAW OF REMEDIES § 10.3 (2d ed. 1993).

Problem 10-1

Gabaldon v. Harrington

We represent Gabaldon. He was severely injured three years ago and was represented by Emil and Mary Harrington, who procured a settlement for him in the sum of $2 million, of which they deducted 25% as a fee and another $43,000 in expenses, leaving Gabaldon with a net recovery of $1,-457,000. Gabaldon became unhappy about the settlement when he met Sondra Johnson, who was also represented by the Harringtons. Their conversation revealed that Johnson had received a highly favorable settlement for a relatively minor injury.

Gabaldon questioned the Harringtons and obtained a little information but not much. He then checked the clerk's office to find all the Harrington cases pending at the time. Using the information so gained, he located other Harrington clients who had claims in the same time period. Gabaldon talked to each one and eventually concluded that Harrington had represented six different clients, including Gabaldon and Sondra Johnson, with claims against defendants who were insured by American National Federal Insurance Company.

Believing his settlement inadequate, but unsure about what happened, Gabaldon has consulted us about a possible claim against Harrington. He told us he remembered receiving the check for the total of $2 million, with the check made to him and the Harringtons. He endorsed the check and they gave him a check for the net recovery of $1,457,000. He also remembered that there was something about another check, made out to a number of people and the Harrington Clients Trust Account or something like that. The Harringtons told him that this second check was for some other kind of expenses.

When Gabaldon told us that, we had our own suspicions. We located the adjuster, Mike Mattison. Mattison quit working for American National Federal six months ago. He is apparently unaware of any wrongdoing, because he tells this tale freely. He says in the Gabaldon case, he was

101

willing to pay $3 million total, but that in the Sondra Johnson case he was willing to pay only $200,000. There were four other cases, in which he was willing to pay $100,000 each for three of them, and nothing for the fourth, because liability was hotly disputed. The fourth case was a claim by Jean Ibert, who had lost the ends of three fingers in an accident. Ibert was not willing to accept nothing or a nominal sum and the Harringtons probably sensed a losing case as the facts developed, so they wanted to settle. After some negotiation, Mattison agreed to pay a total of $3.5 million for all six cases, to be divided any way that would be acceptable.

Mattison also told us that a week or two after they had reached this agreement, the Harringtons sent a list of the settlement amounts totalling $3.5 million to be divided into seven checks, not six. The seventh check was payable to the Harrington Clients Trust Account. When Mattison said that did not seem right, the Harringtons told him it was an agreement with the clients about how expenses would be paid. When he was still reluctant, they reassured him and said it saved them taxes to handled it this way. They said they'd share the tax saving with him by giving him $10,000, one-third of the taxes they expected to save. So Mattison accepted the $10,000 and arranged for the payment to be made in seven checks.

Mattison remembers that the top check was $2 million to Gabalbon and the Harringtons, that the check to Ibert and the Harringtons was for $100,000, which surprised him, and that the trust account check was for $100,000. The four remaining claimants got checks made to them and the Harringtons totalling $1.3 million.

The pooled settlement is a violation of the disciplinary rule used in this state, DR 5-106. That rule reads:

> A lawyer who represents two or more clients shall not make or participate in the making of an aggregate settlement of the claims of or against his clients, unless each client has consented to the settlement after being advised of the existence and nature of all the claims involved in the proposed settlement, of the total amount of the settlement, and of the participation of each person in the settlement.

The Harringtons appeared to follow the contingent fee practice common in this locality. For cases of the kind involved in all six of these claims, the fee range runs from 40% down to 25%. The 40% charge is common for settlement of cases of $100,000 and under. For cases settled in the range between $100,000 and $500,000, the usual charge is 36%. For settlements over $500,000 but under $1 million, the charge is 33%. For settlements over $1 million, the charge is usually 25%. No rule in this state regulates the amount of the charge except that it must be reasonable.

Our preliminary study of this situation indicates that the $2 million settlement for Gabaldon was low, but not so low that we could establish negligence in accepting such a sum. In other words, although we think the $2 million is low, we fear a judge would hold that a reasonable lawyer might have accepted such a sum if necessary. Still, all of this seems wrong. Can we work up a good case against the Harringtons on Gabaldon's behalf?

See DOBBS, TEXT §§ 10.4 & 10.5 (1).

Problem 10-2

Pauling Dye & Chemical Co. v. Tice

James Allen Tice was a chemist of some note in the industrial world. He worked for several years for a firm known as Newton Brands, Inc., but several years ago he accepted employment with a large, expanding firm, Pauling Dye & Chemical Co.

In substance, Tice agreed to devote his time and energies to Pauling's chemical programs, not to work for any other employer in the same line of chemical work for a period of five years after leaving employment with Pauling, to keep full and accurate records of his work, which would be and remain Pauling's property at all times, along with any formulae that Tice might develop. Tice also agreed to keep his work a secret and that Pauling would be the owner of any patent or trade secrets or useful methods of manufacture that Tice might develop.

Two years ago, Tice was asked to work on a project with Elaine Woods, another high-level employee of Pauling. In the course of this, Woods demonstrated to Tice a process, not patentable, that she was using in the manufacture of a synthetic fiber. Pauling was planning to trademark and market the fiber as "Daffodryl." Tice realized that the chemical process Woods showed him would also be extremely useful in a completely unrelated industry for making synthetic screens and nets of high strength

103

and high conductivity of heat. Pauling has never had anything, even remotely, to do with such a manufacture.

Tice approached the Intercontinental Electronics Corp., suggesting he could tell them of a process for synthetic screens that would save them a great deal of money. After several months of negotiation, IEC agreed with Tice as follows:

> (1) It would pay Tice a flat sum of $50,000 for the process. That sum to be held informally by a banker known to both parties until the process could be tested. (2) IEC would hire Tice as a chemist and general manager of research and development at an annual salary of $100,000, plus fringe benefits, a sliding cost-of-living increase, bonuses, etc.

The information proved satisfactory to IEC. It saved IEC about $50,-000 per year on that process and led IEC to develop two related ideas even more valuable to it. Once IEC was satisfied with the process, it was prepared to hire Tice under the second part of the agreement. At that point, Tice notified Pauling that he was resigning.

Pauling became suspicious, investigated and thinks it can establish the above facts. You represent Pauling. Pauling's house counsel, Julia Storrow, tells you that they are concerned about losing Tice, since his work was excellent and very helpful to Pauling. But they also want to prevent Tice from working for IEC, since, though IEC does not directly compete with Pauling, its subsidiary, Intercontinental Fiber Company, does compete in the production of one kind of synthetic fiber. Because of this close relationship, Pauling feels it would like to force Tice, or IEC, or both, to comply with the contract terms.

Pauling believes, and thinks it can prove, that Tice has already given away to Intercontinental Fiber one of the trade secrets he himself developed and that Intercontinental Fiber is using it in direct competition with Pauling. Storrow therefore asks our firm to develop all possible remedies against Tice, IEC and Fiber. Outline the claims we may make so that a complaint can be drafted with proper remedies in mind. Please evaluate our position on each. See DOBBS, TEXT §§ 10.5 (3) & 10.6.

———————

Problem 10-3

Hoven v. Bok

The Horizon Motion Picture Corporation was a small east-coast company owned principally by about a dozen stockholders. Three years ago this June, the corporation's total assets were about $750,000. There were 1,000 shares of outstanding stock, so that its book value was about $750 per share. There was a small over-the-counter market in this stock. The prices tended to vary within quite narrow limits, with the book value near the center of any variations in price.

At that time, the president of Horizon, August Bok, learned from a close friend in government that a long series of propaganda films would be made by a secret government intelligence agency, and that these would be contracted out to some small film maker. Later in the month, Bok secured a private agreement with some persons in the agency to have the lion's share of these films made by Horizon. There was no open bidding because the films were being made through the offices of the secret agency and classified material was being used in some instances. The film-making was expected to be quite profitable.

Bok did not advise the stockholders of this proposed agreement. Instead he began negotiating to buy up all the stock. The stockholders asked him for the books, which he showed readily. The books did not indicate any new assets (and indeed there were none). Eventually the stockholders sold to Bok.

The sale took place in October. Book value of the stock was about the same as in June, and the price was $750 per share. Two years ago last January, the promised contract came through and the company began performance. Since then, the company has netted gains from this and other similar contracts secured later by Bok, in the sum of $1,500,000. Some of these gains were plowed back into the company, some were taken in increased salaries for Bok, and some paid out in dividends. The stock is now worth $1,000 per share. Bok has been paid salaries of $750,000 more than he received before; about $750,000 has been paid out in dividends or is held in earned surplus accounts.

Hoven, speaking for the other former stockholders, has retained our firm to represent them. He admits that no such film contract would have been entered into had the former stockholders retained control, because

105

they had steadfastly refused to do government film work, which was now the backbone of the great profit increases achieved by Bok. Still, the stockholders feel they should recover.

See DOBBS, TEXT § 10. 5(2).

CHAPTER 11

MISTAKE IN CONTRACTING AND GIFT

TRANSACTIONS

Problem 11-1

Cumberland v. Forrest

Wyrob is an accounting firm. Wyrob negligently audited the Posmer Pickle Company and furnished an audit report showing that Posmer had assets substantially in excess of the assets it in fact held. Forrest was a shareholder in Posmer. As a shareholder, Forrest had a copy of the Wyrob audit. As far as Forrest knew the audit was accurate.

Forrest decided to sell her holdings in Posmer and approached Cumberland as a potential buyer, showing him the Wyrob report. Because the report showed that Posmer had substantial assets, Cumberland purchased Forrest's shares, paying what in fact was market price at $100 per share. The total price was $100,000.

One of the assets listed in the Wyrob audit was a final judgment in Posmer's favor against the International Pickle Company in an antitrust suit, in which Posmer recovered $90 million. Wyrob had misunderstood the meaning of "final judgment." Because International was clearly able to pay the judgement, Wyrob had simply listed the final judgment as an asset of Posmer's. Unfortunately, the judgment was final in the lawyer's sense only. After Cumberland bought the shares in Posmer, the judgment in favor of Posmer and against International was reversed on appeal. The Court of Appeals ordered the case dismissed.

Can you get any relief for Cumberland? See DOBBS, TEXT §§ 11.1–11.3.

Note

In a few states, the tort rule might permit a lender who relies on a negligent audit to recover against the auditor. Most states, however, would allow a tort suit

107

against the auditor only by the person contracting for the audit or by persons in a limited class-to whom the audit was directed.

Problem 11-2

Etrusca Industrial v. Pauling Dye & Chemical Co.

Etrusca sold bulk chemicals. It stored many dry chemicals in large bins. Sometimes customer representatives would be on the premises and place their orders in person. Kaufman, a representative of Pauling Dye & Chemical was on the Etrusca premises when he saw bins of a white chemical powder which appeared to be elemil, a synthetic chemical used by Pauling in the production of certain fibers. The facts are somewhat disputed from this point on, but Kaufman agreed to buy 10 tons and Etrusca agreed to sell 10 tons at $1,500 a ton, for a total price of $15,000. That sum is approximately the market price of elemil on the day the order was placed.

Etrusca delivered a substance to the Pauling bins in the belief it was elemil. Pauling also believed it to be elemil. There were 10 tons of it, and it looked and reacted like elemil. However, Etrusca had delivered, by mistake, a similar substance, one capable of being used wherever elemil is used, but one worth about $2,500 per ton because of other properties. This is the substance known in the trade as milase.

Before the mistake was discovered, Pauling had used five of the 10 tons as elemil. The results were entirely satisfactory because the fibers produced with the milase are actually stronger and longer lasting. In fact, if the fibers produced with the milase could be identified, they might be marketed at a slightly higher price than fibers made with elemil. The production manager at Pauling is trying to identify the bundles made with milase, but so far we can't be sure whether he'll be able to trace the production lots with any reliable certainty.

We still represent Pauling, of course. House counsel Julia Storrow has asked us to give her a memo on where the parties stand. They like Etrusca and want to give them everything they are due, but at the same time, don't intend to be taken on this. What advice?

In addition to earlier readings, see DOBBS, TEXT §§ 11.4 — 11.5.

Problem 11-3

Perfect Printers v. Hidden Hills Mall, Inc.

When a suitable space became vacant in the Hidden Hills Mall, Perfect Printers wanted to rent it. Perfect Printers did a large amount of copy work and short print runs, both heavily dependent on drop-in business and individual contacts, so Hidden Hills, with its large volume of retail buyers, seemed like a good opportunity.

Hidden Hills furnished its form lease. The lease provided in part that the premises would be used for "printing and storage of related items and no other purpose" and that Perfect Printers "shall not use the premises nor permit them to be used for any unlawful business or purpose whatsoever." It also provided: "Lessee shall keep the premises and operate the business therein in a manner which shall be in compliance with all applicable laws, ordinances, rules and regulations of the city, county, state and federal government and any department thereof, will not permit the premises to be used for any unlawful purpose, and will protect the Lessor and save Lessor and the premises harmless from any and all fines and penalties that may result from or be due to any infractions of or non-compliance with such laws, ordinances, rules and regulations."

The lease required Perfect Printers to pay the first month's basic rent, a security deposit for rent, a damage deposit, and an estimated advance on that part of the rent to be calculated as a percentage of gross profits. Perfect Printers complied with all these terms and moved into the leased premises two months ago.

Two weeks ago, as a result of a protest by another Hidden Hills Mall tenant, Perfect and Hidden both discovered for the first time that the entire mall was located in a zone that, under the county zoning ordinance, excluded printshops.

Perfect Printers is in the process of moving out. It incurred substantial expense in making the move in and lost the lease on its former premises in order to make this move. It and the lessor jointly incurred about $5,000 in expenses for remodeling the premises to make them suitable. Perfect Printers would like to recover this, its moving costs, the deposits and rent paid and all other expenses.

The lessor has already found a new tenant, but wants Perfect Printers to pay the lessor's contribution to the expense of remodeling.

Problem 11-4

High Certaldo Corp. v. Boyles

The High Certaldo Corp. owned a large building. The manager, Butterfield, orally agreed to lease the premises to Boyles. The agreement contemplated a rental price to be fixed at 10 cents per square foot per month. Boyles was to measure the building and draw up a lease for Certaldo's signature. Boyles did measure it and inserted in a form lease the figure of $800 per month rental. This was based on the idea that the building contained 8,000 square feet.

Certaldo did not attempt to measure the building personally, but took Boyles' word that this was the correct measure and signed the lease as presented. When Certaldo's accountants saw the first month's rent they expressed the view that it seemed too low. Comparing it with rent from a tenant of an earlier owner, who paid 8 cents per foot, they found a discrepancy. The building was measured by Certaldo's agents as a result of a suggestion by the accountants. It was found to have 16,000 square feet — 8,000 on each of two floors. Certaldo Corp. thereupon called on Boyles to pay $1,600 per month.

Boyles refused, saying, "A deal is a deal." He added that, in any event, the bottom had dropped out of the rental market since the lease was signed. He said he could get 16,000 feet anywhere for less than $800 and that Certaldo should be glad it was getting $800 a month. You represent Certaldo Corporation.

See DOBBS, TEXT §§ 11.6 (1) – 11.6 (3).

Problem 11-5

American National Federal Insurance Co.
v. Charlesville Mercy Hospital

The Wernettes, Bill and Sara, purchased a medical insurance policy covering their family. The policy was issued by American National Federal (ANF). The Wernettes' son, William Robert Jr. became seriously ill. He required hospitalization for several months as well as regular care of physicians. Fortunately, the Charlesville Mercy Hospital was well-equipped and well-staffed to provide care and ANF paid all the major bills without demur.

Under an agreement between the Wernettes and Charlesville, the hospital (and the physicians) would bill directly to ANF, who was authorized by the Wernettes to pay the hospital directly.

ANF's policy expired six months ago. Until the expiration date of the policy, it had processed and paid bills from Charlesville and from private physicians totalling $240,000. By mistake or error, ANF continued to pay bills incurred and submitted after the expiration of the policy. It has paid a total of $316,000 on claims that accrued and were billed *after* the expiration of its policy.

Upon discovery of its error, it notified the Wernettes of the expiration and that it would seek recovery of the money from Charlesville Mercy Hospital. It then asked Charlesville to refund the overpayments. Charlesville has refused.

You represent Charlesville. Upon inquiry, you find that Charlesville has not relied upon the payments in any way. It has not in any way changed its conduct because it received the $316,000 overpayment. Specifically, it would have kept William Robert as a patient even if it had known of the policy's expiration date. It could have inquired about the policy period but it never did so.

See DOBBS, TEXT § 11.8.

CHAPTER 12

BREACH OF CONTRACT

(A) A SURVEY OF BASIC GOALS, REMEDIES, AND MEASUREMENT

(1) Expectancy and Reliance Interests

Problem 12-1

Sabre v. Littleton

Sabre, in need of cash, decided to liquidate his real estate holdings, which consisted of 13 lots in the Mountain View development. Each lot was worth about $50,000 or more sold individually to the ultimate purchaser. A single buyer for all lots, who would expect to resell them, would perhaps pay no more than $25,000 — $35,000 per lot.

Although he was in a hurry to get cash, Sabre also want to maximize the amounts, so he negotiated individual sales for lots. One buyer was Littleton, who, by valid written contract, agreed to purchase lot 141 (adequately described) for a cash price of $51,000. Transfer was to take place on September 1.

In late August, someone discovered that illegal dumping of toxic materials had been carried out by unknown persons within about half a mile of the Mountain View development. Developers were quick to say that the toxins presented no dangers whatever to land or persons in the Mountain View area. Scientists agreed, with some qualifications. Sales diminished, prices in the neighborhood dropped. By September 1 lots were selling for $40,000 to $45,000 instead of $50,000 or more. On September 1, Littleton refused to go through with the deal.

Sabre needs the money. He is afraid that if he does not sue now all the buyers will back out. What can we recover for Sabre? See DOBBS, TEXT §§ 12.1 (1) – 12.1 (2); 12.2 (1).

Notes

1. Land sales contracts will receive more attention later. In general, contract purchasers of land can get specific performance if they so desire; and quite commonly the same remedy is granted to sellers of land. For the moment, concentrate on identifying the basic remedies and the ways expectancy is measured.

2. Should you advise Sabre to renegotiate the price instead of suing? What considerations would be paramount in deciding whether to attempt renegotiation?

3. *Transactional contracts vs. relational contracts.* Most of the problems in this book are simple "transactional" contract problems. But some contracts set up long-term relationships between the parties. A long-term supply contract might require you to think more about remedies that facilitate the relationship and less about the insistent common law remedies that attempt to enforce rights to a particular performance. This idea might be most important when the parties are confronted with unexpected changes of circumstances, problems touched upon in Chapter 13 below. We will be primarily concerned with the "transactional" contracts, and mostly in a business rather than in a consumer setting.

Problem 12-2

Ulmer v. Thomas

Ulmer sells mobile homes or house trailers. In June he owned three trailers which he wanted to sell as soon as possible, first, because he wanted cash to invest in another enterprise and second, because he greatly feared that the local market for trailers would drop enormously with the influx of new models and with the advent of a massive low down payment home sales project. He contracted with Thomas to have Thomas spend no less than one week on the sales lot to sell these trailers. He agreed to pay Thomas a flat sum of $400 plus a commission on each trailer sold.

Ulmer explained to Thomas that it was important to sell these trailers this week because he feared that within a few days a new shipment of trailers would arrive and drive the price down. He also explained to Thomas that he, Ulmer, would advertise extensively and that it was important for Thomas to be present from 3:00 in the afternoon to 10:00 at night (good selling hours in the trade). Thomas agreed to this and Ulmer spent over $200 in local advertising.

Ulmer was out of town during the week in question. He was not aware, therefore, that Thomas had received notice that his father was dying or that Thomas was not present on the lot at any time during the agreed period. Thomas had tried to reach Ulmer, but was unsuccessful in doing so, and had flown to Toronto to be with his father.

No trailer was sold, and, as feared by Ulmer, the next week saw a great influx of competitive trailers, all selling at substantially lower prices. At the same time the low down payment small home sales began. When Ulmer returned, he found that he could not sell his trailers until he reduced the price by $1,000 each. Market value of the trailers during the week Thomas was to have worked on the lot was about $17,000 each. The following week the market value was undoubtedly much less, probably not more than $16,000 each.

Ulmer wants us to represent him if we feel a suit against Thomas is likely to yield a recovery. He says that though Thomas doesn't have much money, he does have a little property worth at least $5,000, and that he "would be good for it" if we got a judgment. He says he might be able to find some persons who would testify that they tried to buy a trailer during the crucial week and that they would have paid the then market price had they found Thomas on the lot. If you think we have a good claim for Ulmer, let me know whether you think this testimony would help. I am a little suspicious of it and really don't think I'd like to use it.

See DOBBS, TEXT §§ 12.2 (1) — 12.2 (3) (expectancy measures); 12.3 (1) (reliance damages).

Note

A glance at the Hadley issue in Ulmer v. Thomas. Later on we'll have readings that deal with the important case of *Hadley v. Baxendale.* Right now we can notice its familiar and basic holding: damages for breach of contract are limited to those elements that were within the "contemplation of the parties." Sometimes the "contemplation of the parties" idea is simplified by saying that damages are limited to types of harm that were "foreseeable" when the contract was made. Some writers interpret *Hadley* in economic terms. However, the Text in this course treats *Hadley* as a rule intended to reflect the parties' bargain, so that the breach victim can recover damages for any harm against which the contract was jointly intended to guarantee, and no others. In this view, general or market damages, based on the market value of the very performance promised, is always recoverable. On the other hand, if the plaintiff wants to recover consequential damages, then they must be damages for the kinds of harm the parties intended to cover.

This is not the same as saying that "foreseeable" damages are recoverable, because many damages are foreseeable that you don't intend to guarantee when you contract. Thomas undoubtedly could "foresee" the type of loss claimed by Ulmer. But he may not have bargained to guarantee Ulmer's loss of sales. What do you think?

Problem 12-3

Esposito v. Stamford

Gerald Esposito locates unusual, one-time wholesale bargains and then retails them in the following manner. He finds a supply of goods that is in popular demand, but available at a special bargain on a onetime basis. He sets up a corporation to retail the goods, buys them in the corporate name, rents a suitable business place for a limited time, and retails the goods in a month or two at "sale" prices, then dismantles the business and moves on to find and sell his next bargain.

In April he located 2,000 automotive tires in Wilhead City that had been levied on and sold to satisfy a judgment. Esposito entered into a contract with Stamford, the purchaser at the sale, to buy the tires for $10,000.

At this point, Esposito intended to follow his usual procedure. He found a warehouse to rent for a month for $1,000, expecting to retail the tires in a month's time at bargain prices. He talked to a sign company and got an estimate of $500 for a sign, and to the painters, who gave him an estimate of $500 for painting the warehouse sales office. Before he expended any monies, however, he learned that Stamford had sold the tires to Pryor for $15,000. The value of the tires sold together was $20,000, but they would have retailed for $40,000. Esposito has asked us to present his breach of contract claim against Stamford, to settle or try the case as we see fit, deduct our fee, and send him the balance, wherever he might be. What is he entitled to recover?

Note

The UCC, § 2-713 provides in part: "[T]he measure of damages for nondelivery or repudiation by the seller is the difference between the market price at the time when the buyer learned of the breach and the contract price, together with any incidental and consequential damages provided in this article, but less expenses saved in consequence of the seller's breach."

115

Problem 12-4

The Native American Store v. Standard Publications, Inc.

Santa Catalina is an romantic old western town noted as a center for exquisite Native American pottery, rugs and jewelry. The rugs rival the best Navajo rugs, the pottery rivals the best found in any pueblo and the jewelry is inventive and well done. Tourists abound, often there to inspect and buy these works of art.

One of the best of the high-quality shops in Santa Catalina is The Native American Store, located in an old adobe building just off the main street of tourist stores. The Native American Store has been in Santa Catalina at that location for twenty years. It is highly successful and respected for its quality. It is often called simply "The Store."

Because The Store is slightly off the main beats of walking tourists, it relies heavily upon advertisement in hotels, motels, and restaurants. It has for many years now advertized in the *Santa Catalina Guide*, an annual publication of Standard Publications, Inc. *The Guide* is a slick book composed of a few short articles and many ads. It is placed in every guest room in all hotels and motels in *Santa Catalina*. Studies have shown that 85% of all tourists staying in one of these rooms will peruse the book at least once and will spend money overwhelmingly at places advertising there.

Eighteen months ago, The Native American Store contracted for its annual full-page advertisement in *The Guide*. It provided the ad copy and a photograph, together with prepayment in the sum of $1,000. When the book was published a year ago, the Native American Store's ad was not in it. No one has ever given a satisfactory explanation, but it is clear that Standard Publications is in breach of contract.

When The Native American Store discovered that its ad was not in the book, it tried distributing flyers at hotels, but met with resistance. Hotel personnel and tourists seemed to have associated the slick *Guide* with quality and to dismiss stores not found in it.

The new book is just out for the coming year and the Native American Store's ad is back in it. However, The Store found that its gross sales dropped last year by a whopping 10%. Because all other major stores in Santa Catalina showed a gain in gross sales last year, The Store believes that all of the reduction of the gross is attributable to the *Guide's* breach of contract. Its reduction in sales alone came to over $100,000. It also failed to make the gains in sales that other stores had. Conceivably, these setbacks in a boom year may have some untoward effect on future sales as well.

The contract breached by Standard Publications contained no clause limiting damages, although the contract for the coming year purports to exclude all liability for lost profit in the event of error in the ad or a failure to publish.

We represent the Quest Corporation, which wishes either to acquire The Store outright or to acquire the rights to franchise similar stores around the country. Quest has asked us to take a look at The Store's potential claim against Standard Publications. We're not sure whether Quest wants this information because it is counting the assets and offering price or because it wants to find some way to induce The Store to sell. Either way, we need to give Quest a clear assessment of the legal position.

See DOBBS, TEXT §§ 12.4 (4) – 12.4 (7).

Problem 12-5

Menon v. Reyna

Reyna contracted to sell 100 shares of stock in the Bavarian Fratchit Company to Menon at the price of $1,000 per share. This agreement was made on March 1, and transfer was to take place as quickly as Reyna could get physical possession of the share certificates and arrange transfer on the company's books.

On March 1, the average price per share in the over-the-counter market in New York was $1,200 per share. The only other substantial market for these shares was located in Munich, Germany. The average price on March 1 in the Munich market was about the same, though expressed in marks. Reyna was unaware that the price had risen so enormously when he agreed to sell. On March 3, he learned that the market price was much higher than his agreed-upon price and he called Menon and told him the deal was off.

On March 3, the average price of these shares was still pegged at $1,200. Menon was unable to reach his lawyer on that date, but he reached her on March 5. The lawyer advised Menon to go on and buy shares in the New York market if he wanted into the Bavarian Fratchit business. On the 6th, Menon attempted to purchase shares and was unable to find any available.

Menon's purpose in attempting to buy BFC shares was to obtain a part ownership in a fratchit company. He wanted to obtain a substantial voice — by way of directorship or merely as a substantial stockholder in a fratchit company — in

117

order to guarantee a suitable supply to his own business (the manufacture of Hoffman Generators). He had decided on the purchase of BFC shares because he estimated that, given BFC's capital structure and its share distribution, he could obtain a substantial voice by a minimal investment of about $100,000-150,000. Had he obtained Reyna's 1,000 shares, he would have satisfied that objective.

When it appeared that there were no shares in the market, Menon returned to Reyna and offered him a premium over the last market price, $1,250 per share. Reyna, now suspicious, refused to sell. Menon then turned to the American National Fratchit Company and purchased 2,000 shares in that company for $200,-000. He estimates that 2,000 ANFC shares gives him about the same voice and the same percentage share in the company as 1,000 shares of the BFC would have given him in that company. This purchase was made on March 7, when BFC stock became available again, and was selling at $1,500.

Fratchit supply was short and Menon's main business, the Abraham Generator Company, had to close down for a month until a supply of fratchits could be purchased for use in the Hoffman Generators it made. This was, of course, the very thing that Menon was seeking to avoid by buying into the fratchit business. Had he gotten into the BFC at the time of the Reyna contract, he would have almost certainly been able to guarantee his company an adequate supply. As a matter of fact, he was able to do this through his ownership in ANFC, but not until much later. Abraham Generator is wholly owned by Menon, and is not incorporated. Because of its closedown, Menon lost a month's profits on the business.

Menon retains another firm for his regular work, but he is not entirely satisfied with their work and he has asked you to bring suit against Reyna. You have a clear impression that, if you do a good job, Menon may become a permanent and most valued client. You therefore use your imagination and energy to develop all possibilities for him. What do you think you can get and why?

Notes

1. *UCC.* Under the UCC sales-of-goods provisions, the time for measuring the *seller's* market-contract differential damages is the time for performance. But the time for measuring the *buyer's* market damages is the time when the buyer learned of the breach. What time should be used when the seller repudiates before performance is due? The common law rule was that the time for performance remained the date for measuring the market-contract differential. As to buyer's damages in anticipatory repudiation cases, the present Code is a shambles of confusion and seeming contradiction.

2. *Cover damages.* The UCC introduced a new concept in damages by allowing the buyer to measure damages by the cost of any reasonable "cover."

This meant that the buyer could buy substitute goods when the seller breached; if he did so, the buyer could then charge the seller with damages for any added cost. The UCC also originated a similar measure of damages for sellers when buyers reneged. The comparable measure for sellers is "resale."

3. *How cover differs*. How does this differ from the market-contract differential? *First*, the buyer might reasonably cover on a different *date* from the date of performance; and if so, the market price might be quite different from the market price used in the market-contract differential. *Second*, the buyer might buy substitute goods that served her purposes but that were not literally identical. The non-identical goods might cost much more than the contract goods. Of course the buyer would not be reasonable in buying expensive substitutes if contract goods were available, but if goods identical to contract goods were not readily available, such a cover might well be commercially reasonable. So for at least two important reasons, the cost of cover might depart quite a bit from the traditional market price.

4. *Minimizing damages*. Cover as a measure of damages is different from cover as a means of minimizing damages. The common law always required minimizing damages when the plaintiff claimed consequential loss. One way of minimizing a loss of profits is to purchase a substitute performance after the promisor reneges.

5. *Cover as an option*. The UCC does not require the plaintiff to cover; she may opt for market-contract differential instead. However, cover might still be required as a means of minimizing consequential damages.

6. *To what transactions do UCC rules apply?* In sales of goods cases, the UCC controls, both as to substantive law and remedy. Apparently, though, the UCC was not meant to cover sales of intangible goods, such as stock shares. Could you argue that courts should use UCC rules, not because the UCC compels it, but because of a purely judicial decision to be guided by the statute? Are there UCC rules that would be of interest to the plaintiff's attorney in this case?

7. An architect prescribes a cheap paneling for a hospital. After the hospital has been built, it is discovered that the panel does not meet building code requirements, as the architect should have known. The hospital is now required to replace the panels with more expensive panels that meet the requirements. Suppose the old panels cost $25,000 to purchase and $10,000 to install, and that it will cost $10,000 to rip out the old panels, plus $100,000 to purchase the new, more valuable panels and $10,000 to install them. Finally, suppose that no prices have changed since the architect originally prescribed the wrong panels. What damages should the hospital recover from the architect?

119

8. In *Lar-Rob Corp. v. Town of Fairfield*, 170 Conn. 397, 365 A. 2d 1086 (1976), the school board contracted with the plaintiff to provide bus service. Most of the buses were to be new, but some older busses were permitted. When the board later decided to reduce services in a budget crunch, the bus company proposed to sell five of the newer buses, but the board insisted that it had to keep the newer buses and sell the older ones if it wished. The parties agreed that this would be done without prejudice to the plaintiff's rights. The courts decided that the plaintiff had the right under the contract to sell the newer buses and hence that the board had breached the contract. Damages were held to be the amount by which

> "the costs of using five of the new buses during the [relevant school years] exceed the costs which the plaintiff would have incurred had it continued to use five older buses . . . . The calculation of the difference in the cost of using the new rather than older buses includes, but is not limited to, any difference in day-to-day operating expenses, maintenance expenses, and finance charges."

In other words, since the plaintiff had the capital value of the new buses, his real complaint on damages cannot be measured in general or capital terms, but must be measured in terms of the costs of maintaining that capital tied up. How would this reasoning apply where the hospital had to replace with more expensive panels, but had their value?

9. In *Baker v. Dennis Brown Realty, Inc.*, 121 N.H. 640, 433 A.2d 1271 (1981), plaintiff had an opportunity to purchase a house for $26,900, but defendant, a broker, interfered with the opportunity and the plaintiff had to buy another, "similar property in the same neighborhood" for $3,100 more. The trial court awarded the plaintiff this $3100. The defendant argued this award was "speculative." Is that the right argument? The Supreme Court of New Hampshire, presented with this argument, held that the plaintiff was entitled to recover the $3100. Is this right?

Problem 12-6

Maryvania Drug Co. v. Killdare Chem. Co.

Defendant Killdare Chemical Company manufactured a chemical used by drug manufacturers. It was known in the trade as Mortid. Defendant contracted to supply Mortid to Maryvania Drug Company, a manufacturer of prescription and other drugs and chemicals. Killdare was to supply 1,000 liters per month for three years at $100 per liter.

Maryvania Drug used about 200 liters a month in its business. The remainder was resold to other drug manufacturers and a few industries that used Mortid. After a few months, Maryvania contracted with two other drug companies to supply them the Mortid purchased from Killdare in excess of Maryvania's requirements at the Killdare price plus 10%, representing Maryvania's costs of handling and shipping and appropriate overhead.

At the end of the first year of the contract between Killdare and Maryvania, the government stepped up its production of certain chemicals used in warfare. As a result, both the cost of manufacture and the price of Mortid itself rose. It finally stabilized around $200 per liter.

Killdare then repudiated its contract with Maryvania and Maryvania sued for specific performance and damages. What relief is available?

Problem 12-7

Hickman v. Jojoba Press International

Hickman, a teacher employed at the Pararie Valley Community College, entered into a contract with Jojoba Press International. Hickman agreed to write, and Jojoba Press International agreed to publish, a book on the left-threaded fratchits, their function and use, primarily for sale in industry and in technical schools.

Hickman regularly had opportunities to teach in summer school sessions, both at Pararie and elsewhere, but turned down several such opportunities in order to write the book. This took two summers and he turned down offers to teach that would have produced a gross salary of $5,000. He completed the manuscript and it reached Jojoba Press, Inc. by the deadline and in the form required by the press.

Due to a recession in technical publishing, Jojoba Press, Inc. decided not to publish the fratchit book. It so notified Hickman. Hickman has brought a suit against Jojoba Press, Inc. for damages, demanding $50,000 in expected royalties. His complaint states that an editor of Jojoba Press, Inc. told him that royalties might run that high over a five-year period, though he admits on deposition that no promises or representations were made to him, and that this was only an estimate.

Our firm represents Jojoba Press, Inc.. Our client admits the breach. Our client also says it can't be sure how much the book would make and that the recession in books of this sort has led them to be skeptical about publishing it, for fear that it would lose money. They also say, however, that the book might be a money maker, and it is all a matter of judgment.

121

Madeline Clarke, the lawyer for Hickman, has made some vague overtures about settlement, but she hasn't set a figure. Our guess is that a jury would find against us on the breach and we should settle if we can get a reasonable sum. What amount would you suggest as a final settlement figure?

See DOBBS, TEXT §§ 12.4 (1) – 12.4 (3) & §§ 12.5 (1) – 12.5 (2).

Problem 12-8

Grace v. Goodin

Grace and Goodin were formerly wife and husband. In a property settlement preceding a divorce, they agreed that Goodin, the husband, would pay the costs of adding a room to the house they owned together and in which Grace was to live. This agreement was eventually incorporated in the divorce decree. Grace built a new room on the house as contemplated, expending $20,000 in materials. However, the labor for the room was donated by construction workers who were members of Grace's church, so that cost her nothing. She demanded $45,000 from Goodin, claiming the labor was worth $25,000. Advise Goodin.

See DOBBS, TEXT § 12.6 (1) for a summary of rules already considered in other contexts. You may wish to consult § 12.6 (4) as well.

---

(2) Restitution

Problem 12-9

Vincent v. Grantham

Vincent agreed to purchase a Gemstone V-16 car from Grantham for $25,000, delivery June 1, time being of the essence. Vincent paid Grantham $5,000 in cash as a down payment. Grantham was not able to produce the car until June 2. Vincent rejected the car. On June 1 the car was selling for only $18,000 because of publicity about the car's propensity to explode into flames on impact.

Vincent demanded return of his downpayment. Grantham refused. You represent Vincent. Grantham's lawyer tells you Grantham won't pay because Vincent suffered no damages.

Problem 12-10

Pfeil v. Fenstermacher

At the beginning of last year, Colby Pfeil, a lawyer, agreed to represent Fenstermacher in a claim against Hardscrabble. Fenstermacher claimed that he had written a computer program that had been "stolen" by Hardscrabble Corporation, a computer software company. Pfeil agreed to a fee of $200 an hour with a top limit for any one year of $10,000.

Pfeil worked hard throughout the year, accruing about $20,000 in fee charges, for which, however, under the ceiling, she could charge only $10,000. At the end of the year Fenstermacher, told Pfeil that he was discharging her and dropping the case to become a monk in Switzerland, in an order that does not speak and does not use computers. Fenstermacher agreed to pay $10,000, but not the $20,-000.

Pfeil tells you she is too close to the case to have any judgment, so she wants you to advise her. Has she a claim against Fenstermacher beyond the $10,000

See DOBBS, TEXT §§ 12.7 (1) & 12.7 (5).

Problem 12-11

Phillips v. Murphy

Phillips owned a Calvert Clay painting, *Flags*, valued at $500,000. Murphy owned a different Clay, *Emblems*, also valued at $500,000. Both were collectors and they knew each other's collection fairly well. They entered into a written contract, drawn by Murphy's lawyer, for a trade of the paintings.

Phillips delivered *Flags* as promised, but Murphy was in the hospital on the day that possession was to be given, and he did not deliver the *Emblems* painting. Phillips was initially unconcerned because Murphy's hospitalization was undoubtedly real. In fact, Phillips visited Murphy in the hospital on the day he transferred *Flags* to Murphy's agent.

After Murphy returned home a month later, however, Murphy told Phillips he'd like to buy *Flags* instead of trading for it. He offered Phillips full market value, $500,000. Phillips refused and demanded the *Emblems* painting. There was a scene of sorts. Phillips persisted for several days by telephone, demanding the *Emblems* painting. He then discovered that Murphy had sold both *Emblems* and *Flags*. The buyer, Count Thurnmill, wanted the pair to hang together and was

123

unwilling to buy either one separately. Count Thurnmill paid a premium for the pair, a total of $1,500,000, a full $500,000 over the value of the two paintings.

Investigation has shown that Thurnmill first made the offer to Murphy after Murphy returned home from the hospital. We have every reason to believe that Thurnmill acted in good faith, believing Murphy to be the owner of both paintings.

Please outline our possible remedies and evaluate them. DOBBS, TEXT § 12.7 (4).

---

(3) Agreed Remedies

Problem 12-12

French v. Lumberton

French was a contractor and an engineer. He contracted with Lumberton, a landowner, that French would draw plans and assist Lumberton in obtaining financing for a large building project. The contract provided that there would be no fee for this work if the landowner hired the contractor for the ultimate work, but that if Lumberton hired another contractor, or didn't do the work, he would pay French the sum of $10,000 for the preliminary plans and assistance in getting financing.

All went smoothly until, at the last minute, Lumberton's brother-in-law went into the contracting business and the contract was awarded to him. You represent French. Can you recover the agreed fee?

See DOBBS, TEXT §§ 12.9 (1) — 12.9 (2) & 12.9 (4).

Problem 12-13

Norman v. Castlewright Co.

Rita Mae Norman is a CPA. She went to work for Castlewright, a large accounting firm. Castlewright accountants work with clients and often build a personal relationship with them. After several years of work with Castlewright, individual accountants sometimes quit work and begin businesses of their own. Frequently, they draw their old clients away from the Castlewright firm. There is nothing to prevent them from notifying these clients that they have set up their own firm and nothing to prevent them from providing services to those clients.

However, Castlewright's employment contract with accountants contains a paragraph devoted to withdrawal. It provides in substance that the employee-accountant is free to withdraw from the firm at any time and to provide services to any of the firm's accounts if clients so wish. However, for any firm account serviced within two years of the withdrawal, the employee-accountant will pay the firm 90% of all fees earned from that client within that period.

In addition to readings covered in the preceding problem, see DOBBS, TEXT §§ 12.9 (5).

Problem 12-14

Alma Processing Co., Inc. v. Good Foods, Inc.

Good Foods, Inc. is a large, nationwide retail grocery chain. It contracts with various suppliers to obtain foods at the best price possible. In the case of national brands, it buys in bulk to obtain price reductions. However, it also contracts with various suppliers to produce goods under the Good Foods or Georgia Flavor label.

Good Foods helped develop the Masterpiece tomato for its superior qualities in canned goods. It wanted several canners in several growing areas to can the Masterpiece under the Georgia Flavor label and provide the canned tomatoes to Good Foods at a favorable price. For this purpose, Good Foods negotiated a deal with Alma, a small canner of spinach and tomatoes grown in the Sasnakra Valley.

It soon became apparent that Alma had insufficient capacity to provide deliveries at the rate Good Foods needed and insufficient capital to expand. Good Foods sensed an opportunity, however, because Alma was in the heart of an important growing district and seemed to have good management. Good Foods suggested the following:

1. Good Foods would enter into a long-time contract to purchase Alma products under the Good Foods or Georgia Flavor label. The contract would call for a very substantial production in excess of Alma's present capacity.

2. Alma would use its contract with Good Foods to establish credit and, on the strength of that contract, would borrow the amount necessary to expand plant capacity.

Alma agreed in principle, but when Alma and Good Foods representatives met with officers of the Alma Bank, they had a setback. The bank wanted assurance

125

that the contract would not be rescinded or breached. The parties discussed the possibility that Good Foods would guarantee the payment to the bank and retain a right to recover from Alma if Alma defaulted. Good Foods rejected that proposal, however.

After some additional discussion, the parties inserted two clauses to induce the bank to proceed. First, the contract provided that in the event of breach by Good Foods, Good Foods would pay liquidated damages in the sum of the balance due on the bank loan to Alma, less 90% of the net appraised value of Alma's facilities after the amounts of all encumbrances were deducted. Second, the contract provided that the obligations of each party under the contract would be subject to specific performance.

Under these arrangements Alma borrowed $1 million from the bank and began expansion. When the expansion was complete, Alma announced that it was ready to begin producing for Good Foods, but Good Foods told Alma that Good Foods would no longer use Masterpiece tomato and that it wanted no production of that item. It suggested that Alma might can the Monte Carlo instead and sell the Monte Carlo at the same price to Good Foods. But the Monte Carlo was not at that time produced in the Sasnakra Valley. Shipping, storing, and other costs of getting the Monte Carlo made this arrangement a loser for Alma.

The bank threatened Alma with suit. Alma demanded the liquidated damages payment. Under the clause in question, Alma borrowed $1 million and spent it entirely on the plant. However, the plant was subject to an old first mortgage in favor of the Arkola Bank for more than it was worth, so its value minus encumbrances was zero. That meant that the liquidated damages clause came to $1 million.

Good Foods is in breach, but says Alma has no damages whatever, for the following reasons: (1) Alma's plant expansion has increased in value by $1.10 for every dollar borrowed and spent on the expansion, so that even after it repays the bank, it will be better off. (2) Alma would not have profited by more than $50,-000 over the entire life of the contract.

Our firm represents Alma. It needs help if it is to survive as a going business. Can we get the liquidated damages? In addition to readings covered in the preceding problems, see DOBBS, TEXT § 12.9 (6) & § 12.8 (3).

(B) PARTICULAR SETTINGS

(1) Land

Problem 12-15

Oakes v. Fullbright

Oakes was the owner of Lone Pine Farm. He agreed by a contract in writing to convey the farm to Fullbright for $300,000 and to give Fullbright immediate possession. Fullbright agreed in the same writing to pay the purchase price in three installments.

Fullbright was allowed to move onto the land before the first installment was paid and while the title was still being searched. He remained on the land from March 1 until December 20, when he moved off. He never paid the first install-ment, though it was due in April. He has stated that he would not go through with the deal.

Oakes never made any conveyance and the contract was not recorded. Ac-cordingly he was able to re-sell the property very shortly thereafter. He sold to Ms. Patricia Schuyler for $50,000, which at all times material has been the market value as appraised by the local appraiser. Ms. Schuyler paid cash and the property has been conveyed.

Fullbright lived on the land a period of approximately eight months. He was never asked to leave, though payment was repeatedly demanded. Our client, Oakes, wishes to sue. Has he any claim?

See DOBBS, TEXT §§ 12.12 (1) & 12.12 (2).

Notes

1. *Comparison case:* In *Vines v. Orchard Hills, Inc.*, 181 Conn. 501, 435 A.2d 1022 (1980) the plaintiff deposited $7880 on a purchase price of $78,800, then reneged because he moved to another city. He sued to recover the deposit.

In the proceedings below, the purchasers established that the value of the condominium that they had agreed to buy for $78,800 in 1973 had, by the time of the trial in 1979, a fair market value of $160,000. The trial court relied on this figure to conclude that, because the seller had gained what it characterized as a windfall of approximately $80,000, the purchasers were entitled to recover their down payment of $7880. Neither the purchasers nor the seller proffered any evidence at the trial to show the market value of the condominium at the time of the pur-

chasers' breach of their contract or the damages sustained by the seller
as a result of that breach."

Justice Peters thought the purchaser could recover if the seller had no damages
at all, but that this proof did not suffice to show that. The purchaser would need
to use the breach date and prove "that the condominium could, at the time of their
breach, have been resold at a price sufficiently higher than their contract price
to obviate any loss of profits and to compensate the seller for any incidental and
consequential damages."

2. *Comparison case (2):* In *Carpenter v. United States*, 17 Wall. (84 U.S.)
489, 21 L.Ed. 680 (1873) the government agreed to buy land from the landowner
and was allowed to go into possession. The government then discovered that it
had no authority to purchase and the purchase was not consummated as planned.
However, the government eventually secured authority and bought the land as
originally agreed. The vendor claimed rental value for the government's pre-
purchase occupancy. The Supreme Court held that he could not recover because
the express contract showed the parties intended a sale, not a lease.

3. Consider what additional information you might need to develop your
remedial options.

Problem 12-16

Sitwell Industries v. Roth

On August 9, Heidi Roth contracted to sell an irregularly shaped 20-acre
parcel of land she had originally purchased along with other lands from the Rendleman family. The contract purchaser was Sitwell Industries. Closing was to
take place as soon as possible after 60 days.

The parcel was described by metes and bounds, with reference to natural
landmarks, including a river. On August 19, Roth executed a conveyance of land
to Vincent d'Antonio. The d'Antonio conveyance actually described 50 acres,
including all of the 20-acre Rendleman parcel. D'Antonio conveyed the 50-acre
tract to The Rowe Corporation on September 12.

On October 5, Sitwell's lawyers discovered the conveyance out from Roth.
Discussions indicated that Roth had not been aware that she was conveying the
Rendleman parcel to d'Antonio. It seems clear that Roth was mistaken about
something, either about what she was obliged to sell to d'Antonio or what she was
describing in the conveyance to him. Either way, she seems to have been honest
and never intended to mislead Sitwell.

The contract called for Sitwell to pay the purchase price in cash at the closing. The price was to have been $220,000. Just before Sitwell's lawyers discov-
ered the conveyance to d'Antonio, Sitwell, a contract purchaser, was offered
$250,000 for the parcel by another company that wanted the land for industrial
purposes. At this time, it does not seem likely that the Rendleman parcel can be
recovered, certainly not without litigation. Sitwell has invested about $20,000 in
legal fees, planning costs, and other expenses of preparing to take title and erect
a plant on the land.

Our firm represents Sitwell Industries. What can we do about this situation?
See DOBBS, TEXT § 12.11 (1).

Problem 12-17

Carey v. Williams

Williams owned a tract of land along Lee's Creek, lying south of the village
of Dutch Dam and north of the confluence of the creek and Big River. Williams
honestly and reasonably believed that the tract contained 1,000 acres. (It contained
only 900, as the parties later discovered.) Williams validly contracted to sell his
land to Carey at a total price of $2,000,000.

The figure was bargained for at some length, and during some of the bargain-
ing the price was discussed in terms of $2,000 per acre. The contract called for
the conveyance of a tract, adequately described, which was said to contain "1,000
acres, more or less." According to all the appraisers, a tract of 1,000 acres located along Lee's Creek south of Dutch Dam would be worth $2,500,000. Apprais-
ers also agree that the 900-acre tract was worth only about $2,000,000.

Williams's original contract was made in good faith, but when he discovered
he did not have 1,000 acres, he told Carey he would not convey the 900 unless
Carey was willing to pay $2,000,000 for the smaller tract. The reason, he said,
was that he needed to raise $2,000,000 and if he could not do so, he would rather
sell off some other holdings.

To what remedy or remedies is Carey entitled? See DOBBS, TEXT § 12.11 (3).

Problem 12-18

Eastman v. Tyler

Our client Mary Eastman, a businesswoman, was approached by a representative of Bill Tyler, a builder and developer. She was shown lots in the Tyler development. After some negotiation she and Tyler executed a written contract in

which (a) Eastman was to purchase three designated lots, ##248, 249 and 250, for $50,000 each, and Tyler was to build a house on lot #250 for a total price of $80,000. The house was to be like one of the model homes already built and was designated on plans as "Colonial Ranchome" style. Eastman paid an earnest money deposit of $1,000 for each lot, for a total of $3,000, and was to close, with financing by Mountain Valley Savings & Loan Association on May 1. Mountain Valley issued a letter of commitment. In April, while Eastman was out of town, Tyler sold two lots, ## 248, 249 and some others to a purchaser named Mercy Edwards. Edwards paid $85,000 each for these two lots, though the financing arrangement was somewhat different with Edwards. Eastman had not filed a copy of her purchase contract anywhere, and, as far as we know, Edwards knew nothing of it. After hearing of these developments, Eastman talked to Tyler who at that time told her that he would not build the house called for, though she could still go through with the purchase of lot # 250. He said that costs had gone up enormously and that he would build the house now only at a total price of $110,000.

Eastman immediately got a credit report on Tyler and found that the Pollock Corporation holds a judgment against him for $150,000, that his general assets are in excess of $1 million, but that his debts, including the judgment debt, total about the same. There may be obligations the credit agency did not uncover.

Please assess Eastman's situation and recommend a course of action, with reasons for each recommendation. DOBBS, TEXT § 12.11 (2).

Problem 12-19

Hazen v. Van Dyke

Hazen purchased an option to buy Van Dyke's property, which included a four story office building. The option will expire two weeks from today. The purchase price stipulated in the option was $2 million. Hazen paid Van Dyke $16,500 for the option. Van Dyke covenanted to keep fire insurance paid up during the option period. If the option were exercised before it expired, he agreed to keep fire insurance paid up until title and possession were transferred or until the parties agreed otherwise.

Ten days ago, the Van Dyke building burned to the ground. There were no suspicious circumstances and arson has been completely ruled out. Two days later, Hazen learned of the fire; he notified Van Dyke that he was exercising his option to purchase and demanded a credit equal to the reduction in the land's value because of the fire or equal to the insurance paid, whichever was greater.

After that date the parties established that the land's value was reduced to $ 1 million and that the insurance policy would pay $800,000.

Van Dyke does not view Hazen's notification as an exercise of the option because it expressly refuses to pay the option price. Van Dyke says that he will recognize an exercise of the option if Hazen is prepared to respect the terms of the contract by paying $2 million as the purchase price. He also says that if Hazen does not properly exercise the option at full price within two weeks, the option will expire and Van Dyke will not accept any offer from Hazen after that.

See DOBBS, TEXT § 12.14.

Problem 12-20

George v. Hecht

In June, the plaintiff, Pamela George, contracted to buy a certain parcel of land from Hecht and made a $50,000 deposit. This contract was conditioned on Hecht's ability to secure certain zoning changes from the city. It provided that if the changes were not secured within six months, George could rescind and recover her deposit.

Hecht did not own the land at the time, but had an oral agreement for a contract to purchase it from Trini Montoya. Hecht was in financial difficulty. He used the $50,000 deposit from George to make his deposit with Montoya. Montoya thereupon signed the written contract to convey the land to Hecht in July.

The zoning change never went through. After the six months was up, George demanded return of the funds. Hecht is in worse financial condition than ever.

We represent George. Hecht is undoubtedly required to make restitution, but seems to have insufficient assets and may be in bankruptcy soon. Our client should have arranged some security for the return of her $50,000, but she did not. We have heard that Hecht is brewing a deal to assign his interest in the Hecht-Montoya contract to Italian Villas Inc. Maybe that will provide Hecht with some funds to help pay off George, but we can't count on it. Is there anything we should do?

In addition to any relevant earlier readings, see DOBBS, TEXT § 12.11 (4).

131

Problem 12-21

Opp v. Adkins

Adkins was 70 years of age and retiring, but uncomfortable and worried about retirement income. Opp suggested a plan. Opp would buy Adkins' land, some 220 acres, for $2,200,000. But payments would be made (a) $100,000 on closing, (b) $10,000 per month for five years, and (c) a final payment of $1.5 million at the end of five years. Opp would take immediate title and have the right to terminate the contract without further liability at any time up until the final payment, but in that event would be obliged to reconvey the land by warranty deed and without encumbrances.

As Adkins saw it, this arrangement assured him of more that adequate income during the five-year period, even allowing for runaway inflation that could eat up his fixed retirement income.

The written contract was dated September 8. Closing was to take place within 60 days, that is, by November 8. Adkins recorded the contract in the recorder's office, so that it appeared in the chain of title.

The contract price was favorable to Opp because the land's value in the period between September 8 and November 8 was probably a little more than $10,000 per acre. In fact, Opp probably could have made an immediate 10% or even a 20% profit if he could have sold the land immediately.

As Opp knew when the parties first began discussions about the land, Adkins's land was subject to some small encumbrances. In addition, it was perhaps arguable that Adkins' children had some small interest in the land. So part of the contract was that Adkins would clear the title by satisfying all liens and by getting warranty deeds from all his children to make sure title was absolutely clean. When it appeared that he could not complete these tasks before November 8, Opp told him to keep trying and that they would put off the closing.

Adkins was ready to close by January 8, but Opp put him off. Opp announced readiness to close on March 8, but in the meantime Adkins had received advice from his children. He refused to sell and Opp brought suit for specific performance.

We represent Adkins. Can we successfully defend this suit? See DOBBS, TEXT § 12.8 (4).

---

(2) Leases

Problem 12-22

Snebley v. Leister

Richard Snebley leased premises from the owner, Inge Vlassis. The premises consisted of a building used as a fast-food restaurant and some equipment in it. Snebley's lease ran five years from February 1. His rental was $800 per month. On February 1, one year later, he subleased the premises to Leister for the remaining four years of the lease. Leister was to operate the business as a fast-food restaurant, just as Vlassis and Snebley had. Leister's rental was $2,000 per month. After a year of unsuccessful operation, Leister appeared in Snebley's office, threw the keys on Snebley's desk, declared he was quitting, and left.

Snebley inspected the premises and found the equipment damaged. He was paying $800 per month to Vlassis and had insufficient funds to repair the equipment. Feeling he could not get another tenant without making repairs, and feeling financially insecure about making the repair himself while paying Vlassis, he negotiated a surrender of the prime lease to Vlassis, effective July 1. At this time the sublease to Leister had 30 months left to run. Leister had paid only 12 months' rent out of the total 48 months.

The damage to the equipment, for which there is no doubt that Leister is responsible, comes to $6,000 and Leister will stipulate that he owes this sum.

Our firm represents Snebley. The original lease period has almost 30 months to run at this point. What can Snebley reasonably expect to recover from Leister?

DOBBS, TEXT § 12.15 (3).

---

(3) Goods, Services, and Business Interests

(Including contracts that may affect third persons)

Problem 12-23

Lobdill v. Ramsey

Lobdill owned a year-old Mercer-Benson auto, top of the line. It was stolen two weeks ago by an unknown person. Before any insurance was paid, police located the car by happenstance. It was in a foreign-car garage undergoing some repairs and additions. The garage was owned and operated by Ramsey, who said the car had been brought in by a man who claimed to be the owner and who gave his name as Bill Ataf. He had ordered the repairs and additions to the car, then had come back and taken the tires, saying he had some new experimental tires he wanted to put on instead. However, the man never came back after that. Ramsey had done $2,000 in work on the car as requested by the ostensible owner. Ramsey does not want to let the car go until Lobdill pays the $2,000. Lobdill does not want to pay. You represent Lobdill. What do you do? See DOBBS, TEXT § 4.9 (5).

Note

Compare or contrast the following: Mr. Smith opens a charge account at a department store on the basis of his own credit. He signs a document stating that he agrees to pay all charges and another one that permits the store to charge items to his account when they are purchased by his wife. A year later, Mr. Smith unceremoniously leaves Mrs. Smith and his two children, providing no support for any of them. Mrs. Smith charges items on Mr. Smith's charge account. The store is having difficulty collecting the debt from Mr. Smith and Mrs. Smith and the children are having even more difficulty collecting any support. Mrs. Smith received the goods charged to Mr. Smith's account. Can the store collect from her?

Problem 12-24

Landers Lumber, Inc. v. Eisengrim

Eisengrim and Jensen owned a parcel of vacant land as joint tenants with right of survivorship. They built a small dwelling house on the land and lived in it. Jensen then got a job with Landers Lumber and became eligible to take advantage of the company policy of supplying employees lumber on credit. With the lumber and other building supplies obtained on credit from Landers, Jensen built a large home on the Jensen-Eisengrim land. He paid cash for some labor and some of it was donated by fellow employees in exchange for Jensen's labor on similar occasions when they built homes. When the house was completed Jensen had taken a total of $44,000 in lumber and supplies on credit from Landers and he executed a note for this in accord with the company policy.

Jensen and Eisengrim lived in the house for several months. Jensen then quit his job and left for Atlanta. There was some negotiation between Jensen and Eisengrim about the house and Eisengrim eventually purchased Jensen's "half" for $50,000. The house and land at that time was probably worth about $110,000, the land alone being worth (at that time) about $30,000.

Landers has discovered that Jensen has no assets and lives on unemployment checks. What he did with the $50,000 paid him by Eisengrim is not known. Landers has for this reason brought suit against Eisengrim for the amount owing, or one-half of the value of the lumber and materials supplied, or one-half the value of the house, whichever is greater.

You represent Eisengrim and have moved for summary judgment. Counsel for Landers have filed an opposition to the motion and memorandum of law in support of their complaint. In this they state their claim is grounded on unjust enrichment of Eisengrim, since he was enriched by at least one-half the value of the house or the lumber. You will file a memorandum of law in support of your motion. What are the arguments?

See DOBBS, TEXT § 12.20 (3).

Problem 12-25

Finney v. Smilgas

Contract and breach. Lucy Milanich, a builder, contracted to construct a house on Smilgas land, following specifications provided. The total price was $150,000, payments to be made periodically as work was satisfactorily completed. Milanich completed about three-fourths of the work on about December 16. Milanich and Smilgas had constant disagreements, however, and on that date Smilgas breached the contract by refusing to permit Milanich to continue work on the house.

Completed house and its value. Smilgas hired another contractor who completed the work. The labor and materials furnished by Milanich through December 16 were worth a total of $150,000. It would have cost Milanich another $50,000 to complete the house to specifications. The house was completed by Three Brothers Construction Co. for a total cost of $50,000. The completed house adds to the value of the land by the sum of $225,000.

Milanich's work, value and payments. On December 16, when Smilgas breached, he had paid Milanich $100,000. Actual value of all the work done and materials incorporated by Milanich was $150,000, but the contract price for the work and labor to that date was only $120,000. Smilgas admittedly owed her $20,000 for work satisfactorily completed, representing payments withheld pending completion.

135

Subcontractors. Milanich in turn owed plumbing, electrical and roofing subcontractors a total of $35,000 for work done on the house. She also owed $15,000 to Landers Lumber Co. for lumber supplied and incorporated in the house.

We represent Finney, the roofing subcontractor. Under Milanich's contract with Finney, he is still owed $25,000 for work he completed about November 1. He says he thinks the electrical work was done by Truman Electric Co. and believes Truman to be an unlicensed contractor. Truman's claim is $5,000. Plumbing was done by Flash Plumbers, and their claim is for $10,000. Milanich herself has quit the building business and now works as a construction worker. She appears to have no ready assets.

Summary of Figures in Finney

Total completed value	$250,000
Contract price	150,000
Payment made to Milanich	100,000
Payments made to Three Bros. (Cost of completion)	50,000
Payments owed to Milanich under withholding clause	20,000
Value of Milanich work	150,000
Third party claims	50,000
Finney's claim	25,000

Statutes in Effect

§ 981 (A) *Lien against owner for improvements.* Except as provided in §§ 1002 and 1003, every person who labors or furnishes professional services, materials, machinery, fixtures or tools in the construction, alteration or repair of any building, or other structure or improvement whatever, shall have a lien on such building, structure or improvement for the work or labor done or professional services, materials, machinery, fixtures or tools furnished, whether the work was done or articles furnished at the instance of the owner of the building, structure or improvement, or the owner's agent.

(B) *Owner's liability to those with whom he has no contract.* Every contractor, subcontractor, architect, builder or other person having charge or control of the construction, alteration or repair, either wholly or in part, of any building, structure or improvement is the agent of the owner for the purposes of this article,

---

---

and the owner shall be liable for the reasonable value of labor or materials furnished to the agent.

(C) *Unlicensed contractors excluded from protection.* A person who is required to be licensed as a contractor but who does not hold a valid license as a contractor shall not have the lien rights provided for in this section.

(D) *Notice required to claim protection.* A person required to give preliminary twenty day notice pursuant to § 992 is entitled to enforce the lien rights provided for in this section only if such notice has been given and proof of service made.

§ 992. *Preliminary Notice of Lien.* Except for a person performing actual labor for wages, every person who furnishes labor, professional services, materials, machinery, fixtures or tools for which a lien otherwise may be claimed under this article shall, as a necessary prerequisite to the validity of any claim of lien, serve the owner or reputed owner, the original contractor or reputed contractor and the construction lender, if any, or reputed construction lender, if any, with a written preliminary twenty day notice as prescribed by this section.

The preliminary twenty day notice referred to herein shall be given not later than twenty days after the claimant has first furnished labor, professional services, materials, machinery, fixtures or tools to the jobsite.

§ 1002. *Owner-occupants exempted.* No lien provided for in this article shall be allowed or recorded by the person claiming a lien against the dwelling of a person who became an owner-occupant prior to the construction, alteration, repair or improvement, except by a person having executed in writing a contract directly with the owner-occupant.

See Dobbs, Text § 12.20 (3).

Notes

1. A lien against land is often the real property equivalent of an injunction that freezes funds. Don't overlook its strategic value.

2. Apart from a lien, might Finney have an ordinary unsecured claim against Smilgas?

3. How can the landowner get protection against subcontractor's or laborer's claims? After all, the landowner intends to pay the agreed price to the contractor, not the agreed price plus an unknown amount in claims of subcontractors.

4. A lien against government property might be undesirable. State and federal statutes avoid the lien by substituting a bond for the land. They require

137

contractors to post a bond to guarantee payment of workers, subcontractors, and materials suppliers. See 40 U.S.C.A. §§ 270a—270d (The Miller Act). One effect of the bond is to draw into federal court the claims of subcontractors on the bond.

Problem 12-26

Egret v. Harron Development Corp.

Egret is now 32-years-old. He was 29-years- old when he last worked for Harron Development Corporation. He had worked there for five years and had achieved a position of department head. The company's policy manual stated that department heads and those higher would not be discharged except for good cause.

Egret was discharged in June three years ago, supposedly because of a reduction in force. In fact, Egret knows that his immediate supervisor hired the supervisor's close friend to fill a position that has been given a different title but that seems otherwise identical to Egret's former job. Egret had a sterling record. He was well-liked and his employment record showed no complaints against him.

Egret could find no employment at a similar level. He had taken the LSAT the preceding spring but had not applied anywhere. After a month looking for jobs, he went to the University, presented his LSAT scores and got on a waiting list. He continued to seek jobs. In mid-August the University admitted him and he entered law school.

Egret has done very well but not spectacularly in law school; he has about a B average. So far he has found no prospective employment except for occasional clerking jobs on a project basis. He is about to graduate and the statute of limitations is about to run on any contract claim he might make against Harron. He approached Harron about a settlement, and Harron has referred the claim to us. Please assess the claim's potential for recovery. See DOBBS, TEXT § 12.21 (2).

Problem 12-27

Bugout, Inc. v. MJF Corp.

A local businesswoman, Mary Jane Forman, formed a corporation, MJF, to take the franchise for Bugout, a well-known company which uses chemicals to eliminate or control bugs, termites, spiders and pests.

The agreement between Bugout, Inc. and MJF is, in substance, as follows: MJF will use Bugout's name, trademarks, and advertising; MJF will also follow the rules in a package of operations materials. Some of these materials give instructions about the "Bugout Plans," the payment arrangements with customers, and the mechanics of spraying. Other parts of the packs give considerable guidance on accounting and other aspects of operating a business. MJF is to use only Bugout's trademarks, slogans and chemicals. MJF agrees to pay $100,000 for the franchise which is to last 20 years. MJF paid $20,000 upon signing the agreement.

MJF was obliged to pay the remainder of the debt by paying a $1 per gallon surcharge on the price charged by Bugout for chemicals. In addition, MJF was to accept and to pay cash for at least 1,000 gallons a month at a price fixed in schedules and subject to certain changes. The $1 surcharge, however, was to remain constant until the balance of $80,000 was paid. Payment of this balance did not affect MJF's obligation to accept Bugout chemicals and other supplies at the regular (non-surcharged) prices during the balance of the 20-year term. If Bugout canceled the contract for breach by MJF, MJF still owed the purchase price, less credits for sums already paid.

MJF operated this franchise successfully for two years. It paid in surcharge fees at the $1 per gallon rate some $63,000 of the $80,000 due. MJF then began buying some of its chemicals elsewhere and at a considerably cheaper price. When Bugout discovered this, it canceled the franchise, as it clearly had a right to do under the provisions of the contract. MJF, however, has continued to use the Bugout trademark and some of the Bugout supplies it had in inventory.

We represent Bugout. Plan for legal action and anticipate responses that MJF might make.

———————

CHAPTER 13

UNENFORCEABLE CONTRACTS

(Adjustment of Miscarried Transactions)

Transactions between parties to a bargain miscarry in a wide variety of ways. We have examined two ways in the preceding chapters — breach of contract (not necessarily by reason of anyone's fault) and "fraud" (often the result of fault). In the present chapter, the bargain miscarries without breach and without wrongdoing. For instance, the transaction is marred by mistake of the parties, or their purposes are frustrated by an unexpected turn of events; or it turns out that one party was a minor incapable of forming a valid contract; or the statute of frauds offers one party an escape. Even where the contract miscarries because it turns out to be illegal, the parties may not be conscious wrongdoers; in any event their wrong is a wrong to the public, not to each other.

When any of these reasons causes a transaction between parties to miscarry, the courts have two kinds of problems. One is the substantive problem — should we enforce the expectancies of the parties under normal contract rules, or should we somehow make an adjustment in their obligations, for instance, by "rescinding" the contract for mistake? If the court is willing to make adjustments, the second problem arises. How are adjustments to be made and how is the relief to be shaped and measured? This latter is, of course, the remedial problem.

As always, the remedy should carry out the substantive policy, and the substantive decision should be made in the light of the remedies that can be used to effectuate that decision. Although detailed substantive discussions are not required, some substantive material is necessary if one is to make sound remedial decisions.

In most of these cases, neither a damages remedy nor a coercive remedy is available. Courts are unwinding an arrangement, not enforcing it, and for this reason the remedy cannot be either damages or injunction. That seems to leave restitution, and indeed that is what courts and writers call it. If a contract is to be avoided for mistake, frustration, or incapacity of the parties, courts will order "restitution." Each party will give back what he got and get back what he gave. The main problem, then, is the problem, not of selecting among several possible remedies, but the problem of measuring the one remedy available, restitution.

Over the years, courts have perhaps become more willing to unwind unsuccessful transactions where neither party is especially at fault. Have they also become more flexible in making the necessary economic adjustments? Are they really simply awarding restitution or are they adjusting economic relations between the parties on a more pragmatic and ad hoc basis? Is there really a remedy here that is neither damages nor restitution, but some third thing — a compromise that may give more or less than restitution out of recognition of hardships and economic situations? Will courts ever simply force the parties to split the losses or gains when a transaction has unexpected and unintended developments?

Problem 13-1

Edwards v. Franz

Edwards and Franz were partners in a large and successful enterprise, but seven years ago they decided to dissolve the partnership. Edwards was to buy out Franz's interests and to continue the business as a sole proprietorship. The partnership had purchased insurance policies on the life of each partner. The partnership paid annual premiums of $5,000 each year on Franz's policy and the beneficiary was named as the surviving partner, Edwards.

Upon the dissolution of the partnership, the parties agreed that the policy would be assigned to Franz's wife, Anita M. Franz. There was no written agreement about it, but, as both Edwards and Franz now agree, they understood quite clearly that the partnership no longer existed and that Edwards had no intention of paying premiums on the policy. The dissolution took place without incident and Franz was paid a total of over $500,000 for his interest. Ms. Franz was given the policy on Franz's life and the assignment duly made on notice to the insurer.

For the past seven years, however, the disbursing officer of the business continued to make payments to the insurer, since no one had told him to stop. Only now has the error been discovered. Payments since dissolution have totaled some $35,000.

The Franzes are financially strapped. To repay Edwards they would have to cash in the policy. However, if they could wait a year or two, the policy's cash value will increase dramatically and they could draw on cash value, pay Edwards, and still keep some insurance on Franz's life.

Business is slow for Edwards. He wants the money now. You are clerking for Judge Flower. The judge wants a complete explanation of the options. Start with a review DOBBS, TEXT § 11.1 — 11.3 & 11.7, all subsections.

Notes

1. If Edwards is given back the premium money he paid after dissolution, he will be getting exactly what the contract called for. This is thus not a case of unwinding a contract. But, if relief is given, it is a case of unwinding a mistake or the mess made by a mistake.

141

2. If relief is given, will it be "restitution"? Can you think of different forms that relief might take here, whether it is called restitution or "adjustment?" The problem does not state whether Ms. Franz is solvent or has assets other than the cash surrender value of the policy. Suppose she has no other assets. Would that matter?

Problem 13-2

Schwartz v. Pauling Dye & Chemical Co.

Eliot Schwartz, a successful independent inventor and electrical engineer, entered into a contract with Pauling Dye & Chemical Co. under which Schwartz, as an independent contractor, would undertake to develop a cheap process for yelectrically bonding a certain compound. If it could be bonded properly to certain materials, it would possess excellent properties and great sales potential. Schwartz was to use $100,000 supplied by Pauling to purchase equipment. If he needed additional equipment, he would be obliged to furnish it himself. He would devote his best energies to full time development for the next two years and be paid at a contract rate of $150,000 a year. In addition, Pauling would pay certain expenses of assistants, technicians, and operations. If Schwartz achieved success in less than the two year period, he would receive a bonus proportioned to the time saved. However, the contract price would be reduced by any amount of time he did not actually work.

Schwartz had just begun working on the project about two months — having invested about $5,000 of his own money — when Pauling, probably through a trade secret leakage from another company, came up with a satisfactory process. They notified Schwartz to stop work immediately. Schwartz threatened suit, saying that his good name and opportunity for professional achievement, as well as the money, were important to him. He then consulted us. Pauling takes the position that the whole purpose of the contract has been defeated and that it is not liable for anything. Has Schwartz any claim for any remedy against Pauling? How much? Check DOBBS, TEXT § 13.3 (1) – 13.3 (3).

Note

Chicken or egg: Right and remedy should be commensurate with one another. Do we adjust the remedy to fit the right, or adjust the right to fit the limits of the remedy? Your attitude as a judge about the issue of frustration or impossibility in a given case might depend, don't you think, on what you think you can do, remedially speaking?

Problem 13-3

Ashton v. Devine Milling Co.

Richardson orally agreed to hire Ashton for five years as a sales manager for wholesale distribution of Murg at an annual salary of not less than $10,000 guaranteed, with a certain commission schedule. Ashton went to work heartily, but the dropping price of Murg returned him very few commissions and eventually Richardson sold the Murg business to the Devine Milling Company, which operated it as a small sideline to keep its corporate foot in the organic food door. Devine assumed Richardson's liabilities.

Richardson, before selling to Devine, told Ashton he was out of a job. It was clear, and Richardson doesn't deny it, that his motive was economics — that is, business was bad and Ashton could not produce enough business for him to make it worthwhile. However, it is clear that this state (and others whose law might conceivably govern this case) all have a statute of frauds with a one-year performance provision and that Richardson might have relied upon that had he chosen to do so. Nothing in the case makes it improper for Devine to rely on that provision. Ashton worked a total of five months and sold Murg that produced commissions of about $2,000. Richardson paid him the commissions, but not the guaranteed wage. Ashton was not able to find other suitable work as a salesman for three months. Since then he has earned at an annual rate of about $8,000 for several months, and, more recently, at an annual rate of about $12,000. To what, if anything, is he entitled to recover from Devine?

See DOBBS, TEXT § 13.2 (1) – 13.2 (5).

Problem 13-4

Wing v. Balantine

Wing was born on the Chinese mainland and lived there until the age of 23 when he paid smugglers to bring him illegally into this country. He endured the passage with little food, water, or air, but eventually Wing was smuggled into the country. At first, the smugglers helped him find work, but he soon realized that they were grossly underpaying him because they could threaten to expose him.

Wing left his original work and sought work as a gardener in affluent suburbs. He was eventually given a full-time position by a well-to-do family that was itself an immigrant family, the Balantine family. The Balantines agreed to provide a room for Wing and two meals a day. They were to pay him minimum wage (although he was a skilled gardener). However, the cash was not to be delivered to

143

Wing until he had worked two years or the cash balance had accumulated in a sum sufficient to permit him to enter an American college.

Wing's status was discovered and the INS threatened him with deportation. He claimed political asylum, thereby delaying deportation. The Balantines, fearful of their reputation, did not want to be known as a family harboring illegal aliens, so they refused to have anything further to do with Wing.

Wing has no money and does not know what to do. His English is limited. He is sent to you as part of your regular pro bono work. You've found another lawyer who knows more about immigration law to help on that side, but you want to consider the possibility that Wing could recover the promised wage, or even the value of his services. Take a look at DOBBS, TEXT § 13.6.

Problem 13-5

Evans v. Kelley

You are law clerk to The Honorable Leslie Stevens, Judge of the Superior Court, an elected position. A case has been filed that your judge considers to be a sensitive one politically. Judge Stevens has told you privately that this case must be decided "by the rules of law, the principles of equity, the tenets of natural justice, the commands of the Bible and the will of the people. It must accord with the Wisdom of Solomon, Socrates, and Confucius and the self-awareness of Buddha. In other words, no mistakes on this one." The facts below can be gleaned from depositions on file.

Cross motions for summary judgment are pending. There is also a jury trial demand in the event the motion for summary judgment is denied. Should either motion be granted, in whole or in part? If not, what issues are likely to be developed at trial, and what ruling should be made on the jury trial demand?

About ten years ago, Nanette Jordan Evans, then 22 years of age and a sophomore at Northern University, met Harold Chapman Kelley, then 30 years old and an instructor in a small college in New England. Kelley was at Northern giving a lecture. He met Evans at the reception afterwards and they became acquainted. He spent most of his time with her on that occasion and when he had to go back to his teaching post, asked her to go live with him. She did so.

During the remainder of the year and through the spring of the next year, she lived with him and kept house, cooked, did laundry and other home chores. The following fall, she went to work full time as a waitress and they lived on her income and a small amount of savings while Kelley finished writing his dissertation for a Ph.D. Degree. This was completed the next year, and Kelley went back to teaching. Having finished his degree, Kelley then obtained a more prestigious and remunerative position in a large middle-western university. Evans quit work when he finished his dissertation and returned to the household chores, which Kelley had taken care of when she worked. In their new location, they were dissatisfied with housing they could rent and Kelley saved some of his salary toward a downpayment.

After they had been living together two and a half or three years, Evans went to work for six months and contributed her earnings to a vacation which otherwise would have been impossible because of Kelley's effort to save for a house. The following year, Evans worked for four months and contributed $1,000 of her earnings toward the downpayment, which, with closing costs, came to $7,000. The house was purchased during their fourth year together. It was valued at $75,000 at the time it was purchased. Evans did not work outside the home after that, but stayed at home and did house chores and pursued her own interests. She occasionally entertained when Kelley would ask her to do so, but they never presented themselves as a married couple. Evans did not wear a ring, nor did Kelley. They used their own names.

After eight years of living together, Kelley and Evans had a serious conversation. Kelley told Evans he felt it was time to split. He asked her to take her things and leave as soon as she could. He said he was taking a week's vacation and hoped she would be gone by the time he got back. Evans has now brought an action against Kelley claiming she is entitled to

(1) one-half the equity in the house. It is now worth $100,000 in a quickly rising market, and the indebtedness against it is $50,000, leaving an equity of approximately $50,000;

(2) the reasonable value of her time and work in the eight years they lived together, including the value of her work in the house and her companionship and affection; and

(3) the expense of relocating and completing her college degree.

Evans testified in substance on deposition: (1) Kelley told her he did not believe in marriage as it destroyed individuality and genuine respect, but that he loved her and they would be married in every way that counted, just without a ritual and without the interference of an unjust state. (2) Kelley also explicitly promised her one-half of everything. (3) Evans gave up finishing college and her hoped-for career as an editor and writer. (4) Evans did not believe herself to be married, nor did she ever present herself as married, not even when the Department's Chairperson came to dinner with the Chairperson's spouse.

Kelley testified in substance in his deposition that (1) He never made any promises or representations about sharing his income, except that it was understood he would provide support while they lived together. (2) There was no understanding of permanent relationship. (3) He never asked Evans to work as he believed in everyone doing his or her own thing and Nanette did what she wanted. (4) There were never any discussions about money except that they would talk about whether they could have a vacation or the cost of a downpayment; she would sometimes on her own initiative go to work and say, in effect, "here's money for a vacation." It was her idea to work while he finished his dissertation. He could have finished it anyway, but it would have taken him another year, maybe two at the outside. (5) She kept house, did the meals and laundry, mended clothes, did some minor repairs around the house, did errands and a very small amount of professional entertaining. He had no complaints about her management of the household. (6) In her "spare" time he was not sure what all she did; she had some friends and they did things together at times. She also wrote some short stories and poems, but she had told him they were rejected by publishers. He had the impression she had quit writing, but he did not really know as he never asked.

See DOBBS, TEXT § 13.6.

Notes

1. *The Marvin case.* The older view that agreements to live together is a kind of prostitution, or at least illegal, has largely dissolved in practice and even in the courts. A leading case is *Marvin v. Marvin*, 18 Cal. 3d 660, 557 P.2d 106, 134 Cal. Rptr. 815 (1976). A woman there claimed that there was an oral contract dealing with their respective rights in earnings and property. As against an illegality contention, the California Court said in part:

> [W]e base our opinion on the principle that adults who voluntarily live together and engage in sexual relations are nonetheless as competent as any other persons to contract respecting their earnings and property rights. Of course, they cannot lawfully contract to pay for the performance of sexual services, for such a contract is, in essence, an agreement for prostitution and unlawful . . . But they may agree to pool their earnings and to hold all property acquired during the relationship in accord with the law governing community property . . . So long as the agreement does not rest upon illicit meretricious consideration, the parties may order their economic affairs as they choose, and no policy precludes the courts from enforcing such agreements.

557 P.2d at 116.

2. *Legitimate "express" promises.* Under *Marvin*, an express promise of one cohabitant to another would be enforceable in the absence of a statute of frauds problem, so long as the promise is not founded, in the words of the New Jersey Court, "explicitly and inseparably" on sexual services. This means that if M promises F "I'll take care of you," F will have an ordinary contract action for breach. In *Kozlowski v. Kozlowski*, 80 N.J. 378, 403 A.2d 902 (1979), the court awarded support based on a "take care of you" promise. This raises difficult problems, since it is usually not very clear exactly how pillow talk should be translated or quantified. However, it is at least clear in principle that a promise and the reasonable expectations it creates are being enforced.

3. *Implied contract claims.* Where there is no promise or tacit understanding what is the basis for liability? In *Marvin* the California Court suggested that one of the partners might "recover in quantum meruit for the reasonable value of household services rendered less the reasonable value of support received if he can show that he rendered services with the expectation of monetary reward."

4. *Rejecting implied promise claims.* Some courts have rejected claims based on a pure restitution or implied contract basis in the cohabitation situation. The New York Court of Appeals, denying recovery on this basis in *Monrone v. Monrone*, 50 N.Y.2d 481, 413 N.E.2d 1154 (1980), commented:

> "Historically, we have required the explicit and structured understanding of an express contract and have declined to recognize a contract which is implied from the rendition and acceptance of services. [ ]. The major difficulty with implying a contract from the rendition of services for one another by persons living together is that it is not reasonable to infer an agreement to pay for the services rendered when the relationship of the parties makes it natural that the services were rendered gratuitously."

The New York Court also thought there was a risk of "emotionally laden afterthought." A similar result was reached in *Tapley v. Tapley*, 449 A.2d 1218 (N.H. 1982), where the court also required an express contract, observing that by rejecting marriage, the parties indicated they did not want the rights and responsibilities imposed by the state.

5. *Rule or law or proof?* Ms. Lawrence lived with Mr. Cline for 14 years, part of those years in property she rented, part of them in property he purchased. She spent some of her money in rent and groceries. Cline died without a will. Ms. Lawrence sued for the reasonable value of her services. Should recovery be allowed under the *Marvin* rule? What must Lawrence prove besides the services and their value? *Lawrence v. Ladd*, 280 Or. 181, 570 P.2d 638 (1977). The New York rule would call for dismissal of the case. What about treating the

question as one of proof whether the plaintiff expected payment? Who should have the burden of proof?

6. *People who believe they are married.* How does winding up a relationship based on mistake differ? Suppose M and F believe themselves to be married, for example, because they believe they have procured valid divorces or because they believe their former spouses are dead. If they are mistaken in this belief should their affairs be wound up differently?

7. *Dissolution and annulment.* Dissolution of a marriage may provide little analogy since the expectations of the parties — or at least justified expectations — are ordinarily different in degree if not kind. What about annulment, however? In *American Surety Co. v. Conner*, 251 N.Y. 1, 166 N.E. 783, 65 A.L.R. 244 (1929), a woman promised to marry Conner if he would provide her certain property. He did provide the property and she did marry him, but a short time thereafter he was convicted of embezzlement and imprisoned. She obtained an annulment. The surety company paid off the victim of the embezzlement and then sought to reach Conner's assets for indemnity. It claimed that one of his equitable assets was his right to recover back property given to his putative spouse, since annulment of the marriage was assimilated to rescission and since, on rescission, he would be entitled to have the consideration restored. Cardozo commented:

> "Gains there had been, and losses beyond the process of appraisal. The man had enjoyed the society of a woman . . . . The woman had given herself to the society of a man . . . ."

The Court held that Conner and his surety would not be entitled to recover the property. Does this imply that there was something of a quid pro quo? If so, does that tend to undermine claims for "quantum meruit" in cases like *Evans v. Kelley*? In *Matter of Hanna*, 575 P.2d 1024 (Or.App. 1978), the marriage lasted only four days before it was annulled. The putative husband had given his putative wife about $3,000, which she used to pay off a lien on her home. The court substituted the husband as a lienor, although the annulment resulted from the fact that the husband had an undisclosed criminal record.

8. In the case of services in and out of the home there is an element of quid pro quo, as Cardozo's comments perhaps suggest. Are property and money to be treated differently from services?

9. In some cases, M and F live together in spite of the fact that one or both are already married and have children. In *Kozlowski*, supra n. 2, each party knew the other was married and had children. In other cases one party does not know of the other's married status. In *Reen v. Berton*, 115 N.H. 424, 342 A.2d 650

(1975), Robert was married to Phyllis and had children. He apparently told Jane he was divorced and went through a form of marriage with her. When she discovered the facts, she sued him in tort for fraudulently inducing a spurious marriage and settled for $35,000, with an agreement that Robert would set aside a conveyance he had earlier made to Phyllis. Jane sued to set aside this conveyance and the trial court found it was a fraudulent conveyance, but refused to set it aside. Although Jane's hands were unclean, this was thought to be insufficient ground for denying her relief. But since the conveyance was made to support the family, which was innocent, the court refused to set it aside.

What if Jane had provided money or property to Robert and were seeking restitution of that from the donee wife? Does the answer reinforce the suggestion that there might be a difference between money and property on the one hand and services on the other?

10. *Value of services rendered?* If services furnish a basis for a restitutionary recovery — or some other kind of recovery — how should their value be measured in a case like *Evans v. Kelley?*

Problem 13-6

McGraw v. Patton

McGraw and Patton lived together in terms of sexual intimacy. McGraw became pregnant. Up until this point there had been no promises or arrangements of any kinds, except that it was expected that McGraw live in Patton's house during the existence of their intimacy. When McGraw became pregnant there were a number of discussions about the whole situation. McGraw took two strong positions: first, she would not have an abortion, and second, she expected Patton to support the child and would bring an action if need be. Patton would have been liable for at least some support of the child under the laws of the state.

As negotiation proceeded, with fluctuating good will, matters gradually resumed proportion. Patton suggested the solution would be to continue as before, with the understanding that Patton would support the child as a member of the household as long as the relationship continued but that if he and McGraw parted company Patton would provide for the child by leaving his entire estate to the child in his will. Patton at that time held a large amount of realty, which he told McGraw was worth at least a million dollars. He also held a few shares of stock and some other assets and earned a very good income as an accountant.

At that time, Patton was 50 years of age and McGraw 28. Neither had been married. McGraw agreed to Patton's proposal after a four-way discussion with

149

Patton, McGraw, McGraw's brother, and a friend, Jim Tinney, who happened to be a counselor at a college. They all shook hands on the agreement and had a drink. Thereafter McGraw and Patton lived together as contemplated.

The baby was born in due course and named Erin Kathleen McGraw. When Erin Kathleen was six, Patton suffered a disabling heart attack and a few months later died of a second attack. There was no will, and by inheritance laws Patton's mother, who was 84, would take his entire estate, which is now valued, before tax and lawyers, at about $1,250,000. There is no memorandum in writing about the agreement between Patton and McGraw. The "dead man's statute" does not prevent proof of that agreement, however, if it is admissible on any ground. Is there a claim on behalf of Erin Kathleen?

Notes

1. When *Marvin v. Marvin* removed the bar of "illegality," it only revealed the more serious problems involved in winding down domestic relationships. One of these problems centers on the statute of frauds. Is this a problem in *McGraw v. Patton?*

2. In *Bramlett v. Selman*, 268 Ark. 457, 597 S.W.2d 80 (1980), the plaintiff, a man, was married and had children. He became involved in a homosexual relationship with defendant. He left his wife and children and lived with defendant. Plaintiff put $7,000 in a bank account in defendant's name. This money was later used to purchase a residence where they both lived. Plaintiff put the money in defendant's name in order to prevent his wife from reaching these funds. Defendant orally agreed he would convey the house to plaintiff once the divorce was completed.

Later, the plaintiff repented his mistreatment of his wife and paid her for her interest in the fund and/or property that it was used to purchase. The chancellor imposed a constructive trust, ordering the defendant to convey to the plaintiff. On appeal, this order was affirmed over three dissents. The oral character of the promise was thought to be no bar to relief if the defendant acted fraudulently or in abuse of a confidential relationship. Though the court was unwilling to say that all homosexual relationships involved "confidential relationships," the chancellor could find such a relationship here and the plaintiff should not be denied relief merely because he is a homosexual. As to the plaintiff's purpose to defraud his wife, he had repented of this and "abated the fraud," so this would not be a bar to recovery.

3. *Third persons — rights of first spouse against the second.* Another problem concerns the rights of third persons, to whom no direct promise was made. Is this a part of the problem in *McGraw v. Patton?*

In *Simonds v. Simonds*, 45 N.Y.2d 233, 380 N.E.2d 189, 408 N.Y.S.2d 359 (1978), Frederick Simonds had been married to Mary. They executed a separation agreement in which Frederick agreed to maintain $7,000 of life insurance in existing or substituted policies, with Mary as beneficiary. After their divorce, Frederick married Reva Simonds and they had a daughter, Gayle. In violation of the contract with his first wife, Frederick permitted the insurance to lapse. Thereafter he purchased new policies naming Reva and Gayle as beneficiaries. These new policies, issued by three different insurance companies, provided for a total payment of about $56,000. Frederick died and Reva and Gayle seem to have taken the benefits provided for them. Frederick's estate is insolvent.

The New York Court of Appeals, in an opinion by Judge Breitel, concluded that the promise in the separation agreement "vested in the first wife an equitable interest in the insurance policies then in force," and that this interest was "superior to that of a named beneficiary who has given no consideration . . . ." Consider how a court could reach such conclusions.

Given the conclusions Judge Breitel came to, would a constructive trust on the policy benefits and in favor of the first wife be appropriate? Consider the tracing rules.

PART II

SUPPLEMENTARY PROBLEMS

In this Part we pose problems that are not identified by subject matter or issue and that furnish no references. The problems are presented in no particular order. The idea is to permit one working with these problems to identify issues and research appropriate readings in the same way a practicing lawyer would be required to do.

Problem 1

Cranmer Fibers v. Western Fidelity and Bonding

The City of Velde planned a new police station. It accepted the bid of Contractors General Corporation as the general contractor. Pursuant to statute, Contractors General provided a bond guaranteeing payment of all subcontractors and suppliers of materials for the building. The bond was issued by Western Fidelity and Bonding. The total bid price, which including certain fixtures such as lockers, special weapons rooms, and property rooms, was $5 million. The bond was in this sum.

Contractors General used a number of subcontractors for completion of the building. One subcontractor was the Safety Locker Co., which had supplied and installed the lockers. Another was Cranmer Fibers, which had provided roofing material and had installed the roof. When construction was substantially completed, Contractors General still owed Safety $200,000 for its work and supplies, and still owed Cranmer Fibers $300,000 for its work. (In both cases, some payments had been made to subcontractors earlier.) At this point the City of Velde owed Contractors General the sum of $200,000 in payments it had withheld pending approval of the project. Contractors General appeared to be in shaky financial condition. Both Safety and Cranmer notified the city of the unpaid claims against Contractors General and stated that they were entitled to recover against the funds held by the city for payment to Contractors General. The city responded to these claims by filing an interpleader suit in the Superior Court. Both Safety and Cranmer were made parties defendant.

In an independent action, Safety filed a suit against Western, claiming on the bond. This case quickly went to judgment and Western paid Safety the full $200,000. Western then intervened in the interpleader suit, claiming a right to

152

recover against the fund held by the city. Cranmer opposed the Western claim and also filed a separate suit against Western on the bond. However, the statute of limitations had run on the bond claim by this time and Cranmer's suit on the bond was dismissed.

That leaves the interpleader action, in which the city had deposited $200,000. The only real contestants in that action are Cranmer and Western. Cranmer discharged its original attorney and asked us to represent it. Can we salvage anything for Cranmer?

Problem 2

Presson v. Dacia

Dacia negligently ran down Presson, a pedestrian. Presson was seriously injured and was in the hospital for three weeks. He incurred medical bills in excess of $1,000, and there is every reason to think that he will incur medical bills in the future in an equal amount. He has had much pain and suffering and will have pain and suffering in the future. He is undergoing psychiatric treatment for the considerable emotional problem he has had because he knows that the injury has shortened his life expectancy by ten years. He is also having a hard time adjusting to the fact that his hand is deformed as a result of the injury and that he can no longer carve figurines, which had been a passionate hobby.

Presson had not been employed regularly, and lived mainly on a small pension. However, before the accident, he was capable of working, and when he worked, he was able to earn about $400 a week. His incapacity to work lasted over a period of five weeks in the past, though he seems to have fully recuperated now. What elements of harm will the jury be permitted to allow damages for? Will Presson be fully compensated? Will he be more than "compensated"?

Problem 3

Daniels v. Schuppe

Daniels and 20 other members of the Truman Choral Society booked passage at a group rate of $40,000, on the ship *Susan Ehringhaus* departing from New York to Copenhagen on June 12. The sum was paid to Schuppe, the owner and operator of the line, on May 1. The price included a return on the ship *York* departing from a French port in late August. The group was scheduled to give a number of concert appearances in music festivals in Europe during the summer.

The group arrived in New York on June 10 and immediately discovered that Schuppe had canceled their passage and had devoted the entire *Susan Ehringhaus* to another and larger group whose passage was somewhat more profitable.

Schuppe told Daniels and his group that they could be accommodated on another ship leaving one day later. The second ship did not suit Daniels as well and the group arranged to travel on the vessel *Katherine Roan*, which sailed June 12. The substitute travel plans had identical costs but there were slight differences in ports of call, services on board ship, and other minor matters. One difference was that the new plans allowed the group an extra day in Europe, and they were able at the last minute to schedule a concert in Paris and to earn an extra $2,000 as a result.

Daniels has asked us to file suit against Schuppe, on behalf of all the group. For what relief should we ask? What can we get?

Problem 4

Jastrow v. Durbin

Durbin owned and operated a large farm of 30,000 acres on the Raleigh River, where he maintained docks and a large 30-foot yacht. On September 10, after an unusually dry month, lightning struck a tree near a storage shed where Durbin kept a good deal of gasoline and oil for the mechanized equipment. These supplies exploded and a large conflagration was set off, endangering crops, barns, cattle and various buildings and supplies.

A number of people pitched in to halt the spread of the fire. Some were neighbors, some were volunteer firemen from the South Raleigh County Volunteer Fire Department. Jerome Jastrow was a resident of another state, but was driving by on the highway overlooking the farm and saw the fire. Jastrow was not trained in any way concerning fire-fighting, but he was a construction engineer. From his vantage point, he immediately perceived that there were several strategic steps that could be taken to minimize the fire. For one thing, he realized that the prevailing wind was shooting down a natural "trough" formed by a small canyon or ditch and that its effects would be devastating unless something was done. He drove down to the farm and immediately began directing the efforts. He worked through the afternoon with all the men and women fighting the fire. About 4:00 p.m., he realized that his strategy had worked and that the fire was now redirected to the river, which was wide enough to prevent any further spread. However, the yacht belonging to Durbin was moored there and was endangered by the redirected blaze. He ran to the docks and cast the yacht off.

It drifted to the far side of the river and came to rest with minor damage when it struck a twenty-foot fallen tree a mile down river.

Shortly after this, Jastrow fainted from exhaustion and had to be hospitalized. A number of years ago he retained our firm for a modest annual retainer and we have advised him mostly about business deals. He has called to ask us whether he can legally claim anything for his hospital bills, his time and effort or anything else from Durbin. Please give me a memo.

Problem 5

Singleton v. Shore Vista Corporation

Shore Vista is a corporation formed under the laws of Lancaster to develop lots for sale on Shore Island, Lancaster. It mailed out brochures to selected prospects, inviting them to visit Shore Island, accept free gifts when they arrived, and see for themselves how easy it would be to own a vacation lot.

Ed and Jean Singleton, husband and wife, received such a brochure. Ed and Jean are African-Americans living in a mostly white neighborhood. They were interested in a vacation lot where they could camp and later build a cottage, but only if other African-Americans would also own lots in the area. They went to Shore Island and talked with a salesman named Bill Edmonds who took them to a lot marked 169 and tried to interest them in its qualities. The Singletons liked the lot, but there were several problems on their minds. First, they wanted to know whether any lots had been sold to other African-Americans and, if so, whether they were being "pushed off in one corner." Edmonds assured them that several African-Americans had bought lots and that there was absolutely no discrimination.

Edmonds was in error about these purchases. He honestly thought several African-Americans had purchased lots and had good reason so to believe, but he was in fact mistaken. Reassured by Edmonds' responses, the Singletons wanted to know about financing. Edmonds made some inquiries of the Singletons as to financial status and then promised them financing would be no problem. They could put $500 down and the bank would finance the remaining $2,000 of their down payment; after that, it was all a matter of monthly payments. Edmonds took them to the Atlantic National Bank on the mainland (a five minute drive) where the whole thing was arranged through a bank officer named Preston. The Singletons signed a purchase agreement in the bank, along with notes to the bank and to Shore Vista Corporation. The Singletons were given an "owner's package" simultaneously with or just before signing.

155

When they arrived back home several hours later they put away the owner's package without opening it. Four or five days later, both of them were beginning to doubt the wisdom of their purchase. Ed Singleton got out the notes and computed the interest and realized that, while it was not usurious, it was very high. He then checked and found they could have borrowed the $2,000 much more cheaply at their bank in Charlesville. He also discovered, buried in the mass of figures in these papers, an added finance charge payable to the Shore Vista Company as a fee for "guaranteeing" his note to the Atlantic National Bank.

Singleton looked further into the "owner's package," and found it contained (1) the property report required by the Interstate Land Sales Full Disclosure Act, 15 U.S.C.A. § 1701 et seq. and (2) the land sales contract. The contract provided that a purchaser who had inspected the lot and who had read the property report in advance, and who acknowledges by his signature that he has made such inspection and understood such report, had no power to revoke the contract. The contract stated, just above the signatures of the Singletons, that they had been shown the property report, read it, and understood it, as well as the contract.

On further checking, Singleton found that no African-Americans have purchased lots on Shore Island, but that quite a few of his white friends had done so under circumstances similar to his own. Most of them had decided that they had been high-pressured into an unwise decision. Singleton called a meeting to discuss the matter. Over fifty disgruntled buyers eventually decided to pool their resources and consult an attorney. They formed an executive committee, headed by Singleton, for dealing with attorneys, and the committee has consulted us.

Fuel shortage has interrupted ferry service to the island in the past month and all lot sales have stopped. A check with an appraiser informally suggests that the value of lots there has dropped from about $10,000 each to about $7,500 each, and probably won't rise again until a permanent bridge is built and a lot of sales effort is made.

What remedies can we pursue? Should we consider a class action on behalf of all purchasers? The Interstate Land Sales Full Disclosure Act applies to Shore Vista.

Notes

1. *The Interstate Land Sales Full Disclosure Act.* The Interstate Land Sales Full Disclosure Act, 15 U.S.C.A. § 1701 et seq. requires developers who use the mails or other instruments of commerce to file a "statement of record" with the Secretary of Housing and Urban Development. This is to contain a number of items of information specified in the statute. The developer-vendor or lessor must also give the purchaser, before purchase, a property report containing most of the same information,

and including such items as standard sales prices, statement of roads and access, details about future plans for buildings and recreation areas, and so on.

2. *Unlawful acts under the Act.* Subject to certain exemptions, §1703 (a) (1) makes it unlawful for such developer or agent   (A) to sell or lease any lot unless a statement of record with respect to such lot is in effect in accordance with section 1706 of this title; (B) to sell or lease any lot unless a printed property report, meeting the requirements of section 1707 of this title, has been furnished to the purchaser or lessee in advance of the signing of any contract or agreement by such purchaser or lessee; (C) to sell or lease any lot where any part of the statement of record or the property report contained an untrue statement of a material fact or omitted to state a material fact required to be stated therein pursuant to sections 1704 through 1707 of this title or any regulations thereunder; or (D) to display or deliver to prospective purchasers or lessees advertising and promotional material which is inconsistent with information required to be disclosed in the property report . . . .

Also subject to certain exemptions, § 1703 (b) makes it unlawful (A) to employ any device, scheme, or artifice to defraud; (B) to obtain money or property by means of any untrue statement of a material fact, or any omission to state a material fact necessary in order to make the statements made (in light of the circumstances in which they were made and within the context of the overall offer and sale or lease) not misleading, with respect to any information pertinent to the lot or subdivision; (C) to engage in any transaction, practice, or course of business which operates or would operate as a fraud or deceit upon a purchaser; or (D) to represent that roads, sewers, water, gas, or electric service, or recreational amenities will be provided or completed by the developer without stipulating in the contract of sale or lease that such services or amenities will be provided or completed.

3. *Revocation provisions.* Section 1703 sets up a number of provisions for revocation of the contract. Exempt transactions aside, the purchaser is entitled to revoke any covered purchase within seven days, or later if state law so provides. (§ 1703(b)). In addition, if a property report is required and not supplied in advance of the purchaser's signing the agreement, the purchaser may revoke within two years. (§ 1703(c)). The same section provides additional grounds for revocation.

4. *Enforcement provisions.* Section 1709 makes these provisions for remedies: (a) A purchaser or lessee may bring an action at law or in equity against a developer or agent if the sale or lease was made in violation of section 1703(a) of this title. In a suit authorized by this subsection, the court may order damages, specific performance, or such other relief as the court deems fair, just, and equitable. In determining such relief the court may take into account, but not be limited to, the following factors: the contract price of the lot or leasehold; the amount the purchaser or lessee actually paid; the cost of any improvements to the lot; the fair market value of the lot or leasehold at the time relief is determined; and the fair market value of the lot or leasehold at the time such lot was purchased or leased. (b) A purchaser or lessee may bring an action at law or in equity against the seller or lessor (or successor

thereof) to enforce any right under subsection (b), (c), (d), or (e) of section 1703 of this title. (c) The amount recoverable in a suit authorized by this section may include, in addition to matters specified in subsections (a) and (b) of this section, interest, court costs, and reasonable amounts for attorneys' fees, independent appraisers' fees, and travel to and from the lot.

Problem 6

Verkuil v. Mar-Lou Mfg. Co.

We represent Mar-Lou Manufacturing Company. Mrs. Joan Verkuil has filed a suit against Mar-Lou asking for an injunction against an alleged nuisance and for a preliminary injunction. The hearing on that is tomorrow. The complaint also alleges severe personal injuries with permanent injury and future expenses. The basic facts are:

1. Mar-Lou has had a factory here in Charlesville for about 40 years in the same location. The area is a mixed one, with some stores and some homes in the $150,000 range. There has never been any complaint from either the storeowners or the homeowners.

2. About a month ago, Mar-Lou geared up to manufacture a new synthetic fiber on which they'd spent about 20 years in research and development. They are going to call it "Twied." It is a synthetic wool-cotton that breathes like natural fibers when woven into cloth but that holds a press like many synthetics. Unlike most synthetics, it is virtually independent of petro-chemistry. It will not consume petroleum products nor present problems of waste disposal.

3. Immediately after production started, Mar-Lou began getting complaints from storeowners and homeowners in the neighborhood. Almost everyone around complained of foul odors. A smaller number complained they had skin rashes and breathing problems. Mar-Lou's plant manager paid very little attention to these complaints, thinking people would adjust to the new smells.

4. Nine days ago, however, a complaint was served on Mar-Lou on behalf of one of the neighbors, Ms. Joan Verkuil. The Verkuil complaint prays for an injunction against further discharge of noxious gases that began about a month ago, claiming a nuisance. The complaint asks a preliminary injunction, and there is a hearing scheduled on that tomorrow afternoon. The complaint alleges severe blistering rashes and serious interference with Ms. Verkuil' respiratory tract. It asks damages for the personal injury thus caused, which is alleged to be permanent in some respects, though not all.

5. John Gibson, Verkuil's attorney, tells me his client's doctor was alarmed by her condition and demanded that she move out of the neighborhood. According to Gibson, Verkuil really was deathly ill and she didn't require much urging. She sold her house for $150,000, which Gibson claims is probably about $10,000 below its market value immediately before the alleged nuisance. Gibson also says Verkuil had to pay about $185,000 for another house of comparable size, though not in so industrialized a neighborhood. Verkuil is not happy with the new arrangement, either, because when she goes back to work — assuming she recovers sufficiently — she'll have to drive ten miles a day instead of walking a short distance as she did in the past. Gibson tells me he will get an amendment to the complaint as soon as possible, but as a courtesy to us, wanted to let us know before tomorrow's hearing so we wouldn't think he pulled a fast one.

Where do we stand on all this? What should be our posture at the hearing tomorrow? What about after that?

Problem 7

Green v. Lorca

Green, who owned a parcel of land, contracted with Lorca to provide a building on the land according to certain specifications. The total price was $50,000, which was pre-paid in full. Completion date was to be no later than August 1. There was a clause providing for $500 per day liquidated damages against Lorca for every day after August 1 in which the building remained incomplete. After working a few weeks on the building, Lorca notified Green that he was quitting the job and that it could not be reasonably completed. The cost and the reasonable value of Lorca's services and materials during this period was $20,000.

The building was intended as a small movie theatre, but was entirely too small for its purpose and the location was unsuitable. In its present condition, substantially vacant, the land is worth $50,000. If the building is completed, the land and building together would be worth about $75,000. Cost of completing the building would be about $40,000. What are Green's remedies?

Problem 8

Burbage v. Ephron

Burbage owned a valuable collection of rare stamps, worth at least $50,000. Ephron convinced Burbage that he, Ephron, was promoting a grand philatelic exhibition in Washington, in which some very famous collections would be exhib-

159

ited to the public under armed guard. Burbage's town pride was appealed to and he ultimately agreed to let Ephron have the collection for exhibition.

Ephron picked up the Burbage collection with armed guards at his side. This convinced Burbage that Ephron was reliable. As he was leaving the house, Ephron asked Burbage to sign the standard form agreement reflecting permission to exhibit the collection. Ephron explained that he needed this protection in case anyone questioned his right to be have possession of the stamps. The form was printed and, as Burbage now remembers it, it had a symbol at the top, which he thought was the symbol or logotype of the Philatelic Exhibition. He signed the document without reading it in detail.

The document was in fact a bill of sale which described the Burbage collection in detail. After leaving Burbage, Ephron wrote under the signature, in handwriting similar to Burbage's, "telephone." He wrote a phone number, which was the number, not of Burbage, but of Ephron's confederate and cousin, Buffet.

Ephron then took the stamp collection to a dealer in New York City, who knew of the Burbage collection by name. Ephron showed him the bill of sale, gave him references, and suggested he call Burbage if he had any doubts. The dealer, Carolyn Branson, called the number on the bill of sale. Buffet was waiting. He impersonated Burbage, and assured Branson that Ephron was indeed authorized to sell the collection and that the bill of sale was indeed genuine. Thus assured, Branson conducted a serious appraisal, and after a week, offered Ephron $40,000. After some dickering, Ephron accepted a bid of $45,000, took a cashier's check, left the stamps with Branson, and took up quarters in the Mayflower Hotel in Washington, D. C. under the name of Don Malouf. He endorsed the cashier's check in his own name and with it opened an account in the name of Don Malouf at the Urban National Bank of Washington.

During the first two weeks, he withdrew $5,000 in cash from this account. He then wrote a check in the sum of $20,000 to a stock broker named Martin. Investigations conducted later showed that this was payment for a purchase of stock in the Chesterton Corporation. During the ensuing weeks, more cash withdrawals totalling $10,000 took place. The Chesterton stock dropped, and eventually Ephron sold it for $10,000, which he redeposited in the Don Malouf account. This left him with $20,000 in the account. He withdrew all of this sum and purchased stock in the Janus Corporation with it. This stock rose in value to the sum of $50,000. This is its present price and "Don Malouf," alias Ephron, holds it.

Our firm represents Burbage who has just discovered all this. We need an immediate answer to this question: Can we get hold of the stock, have it held, or prevent its sale in order to reach the assets? Ephron is in town today and we can serve him today or tomorrow. Please give immediate attention to this prob-lem.

Second, we need a longer view. What are our ultimate remedies? Can we reach Branson, assuming she still has the stamps? If she sold them, can we reach the proceeds and profits of the sale?

Problem 9

City of Truman v. Bonney

Mark F. Bonney was in the business of manufacturing and selling highway and street signs, usually made of metal and lettered with material that glowed. He wished to sell the City of Truman a new set of signs for all streets as well as new directional signs. The city operated under a state statute requiring bidding procedures and an award of any contract over $250 to the lowest bidder. Bonney's competitors, if bidding, would be likely though not certain, to underbid him.

Bonney began lobbying the city council about the need for signs. At this point, Ed Meriwether, the chief engineer in the city's street department, suggested privately that he could draw the specifications on the sign contract so as to virtually eliminate the bidding from Bonney's competitors, whose products would not meet specifications. Meriwether asked for $1,000 in return and Bonney agreed. The city decided to go ahead with the project, which in fact was much needed. It ordered the street department to prepare specifications and to call for bids. Meriwether drew the specifications. They neatly, though not obviously, required characteristics that most of Bonney's competitors' products would not have. Bonney was the only bidder and eventually took the job at a contract price of $237,500.

Bonney paid Meriwether in cash and began manufacturing the signs and delivering them to the city. Most of the signs had already been delivered and installed by city street crews when, due to some internal politics in the street department, Meriwether was investigated. Other graft was pinned on him and he eventually confessed to the deal with Bonney as well.

You are the assistant city attorney and you've been asked to attend an executive session of the city council to explain all the possible rights and liabilities the city might have. Be prepared to answer questions and to deal with various contingencies the council members may raise.

161

Problem 10

Watney v. Guiness

Sam Watney, 28 years old, owned a 40-acre farm on which he had a small house or cottage. He wanted to acquire a larger place, but was short of funds. Guiness, an older farmer of the neighborhood, wanted to retire to a small place where he could fish and raise a few vegetables. He wanted to sell his larger place. Guiness put his place on the market, but it did not sell. Eventually he and Watney discussed their respective problems and decided to work a trade, with Watney to pay annual cash payments in addition to transferring his farm. When the payments were completed, Guiness would give Watney a deed to the Guiness farm, and Watney would deed his farm to Guiness. In the meantime, the parties would go ahead and trade possession of the respective farms.

However, Guiness insisted on one thing before the trade: Watney would have to construct a good pond on his place so Guiness would have a place to fish. This was all agreed upon orally and Watney set about to fulfill his side of the bargain. He himself was no fisherman and knew nothing of ponds, but he read up on the subject, got a bulldozer to his farm and constructed the pond as required. By spring it was full and the Wildlife Commission provided stock for it. The parties traded the farms in time to begin spring plowing, Watney moving into possession of the larger place, Guiness leaving the larger farm and moving into Watney's place.

About six weeks later, Guiness announced he was homesick, could not stand the small place, and wanted to call the deal off. Watney protested that he had plowed and planted the larger farm, built the pond for Guiness, and could not move off without disastrous loss, especially since it would be too late to get a full crop on the smaller plot. Guiness insisted.

Watney consulted a lawyer, who explained the statute of frauds to him, along with the summary ejectment statute. They decided that Watney should move off and do the best he could with plantings on the smaller place (the Watney land), and bring suit against Guiness to see what he could get. Watney did this, returning to his own land. Watney says he would have made a good profit the first year on the Guiness land, simply because it was larger and he could plant more. In addition, he lost some of the profit he would have made had he been on his own land all spring, because he could not get as many crops out of it, starting late as he did. He says he spent, cash, about $1,000 to build the pond, and put in labor worth at least twice that much, as he figures it. He says old man Guiness is not farming the Guiness farm, even though Watney had plowed and planted it. Should we bring suit on behalf of Watney? What can we recover?

162

Problem 11

La Foret v. Elias

Bill Felix, 42, was struck by a car driven by James Elias as Felix was in a pedestrian crosswalk. Elias, a stranger in town, was confused and thought Felix would not walk out in front of him; Felix evidently thought Elias would stop in deference to a "Stop for Pedestrian" sign placed in the walk. Felix suffered a great deal of internal injury, to kidneys principally, and after ten days in the hospital, died. La Foret is his administrator, and under the statute is the proper party to bring any action for wrongful death. We represent La Foret. There is not much question that we could get to the jury on the issues of liability.

Felix was earning about $50,000 a year and was contributing substantially to his aged and crippled father, Harold Felix. Mr. Harold is 78 years old and quite infirm. Most of the time he stayed in Mr. Bill's small house. In his worse periods he stayed in a nursing home at Mr. Bill's expense. The house was not owned by Mr. Bill Felix, but was leased. Mr. Harold will have to vacate it shortly. Bill Felix had been a widower for several years. He has one grown son, Elbert, who is 23, married and self-supporting. Elbert lives about 1,000 miles from here in a climate unsuited to Mr. Harold's condition. Mr. Bill had not contributed anything to Elbert for about 5 years, though they were on warm terms and wrote to each other often. We'll be in the negotiating stage soon. Would you outline the elements of damages we can recover and indicate the kind of factual information you think we need to have to prove maximum damages?

Problem 12

Schaeffer v. Crawford

Schaeffer was a building contractor. He contracted with Crawford to erect a $ 3 million building on Crawford's land according to plans and specifications furnished. The contract was a long and involved one and required a substantial amount of time to complete. The parties anticipated various difficulties would occur and provided that any disputes would be arbitrated in accordance with the rules of the American Arbitration Association. In the event of any dispute, either party could ask the AAA to appoint an arbitrator to resolve the dispute as quickly as possible to permit work without any delays or friction.

A number of disputes did arise between the parties which they resolved on an ad hoc basis as they went along without any arbitration. However, in August, Schaeffer notified Crawford that, due to Crawford's failure to have a portion of the land graded and ready for work as required by the contract, as well as for

163

other breaches, Schaeffer was quitting the work and "rescinding." He had warned Crawford that he would feel compelled to do this if Crawford could not perform his side of the bargain. Schaeffer moved his machinery and workers off the job immediately.

Crawford responded by demanding arbitration and asking the AAA to appoint an arbitrator. One was appointed and Crawford asked the arbitrator (a) to require specific performance of the contract by Schaeffer, and (b) to award damages for delay occasioned by Schaeffer's breach in leaving the job. Schaeffer's attorneys notified the arbitrator of Schaeffer's contention that this dispute was not subject to arbitration because of Crawford's breach and that only disputes that occurred while work was going on were subject to arbitration. Thereupon, Schaeffer's attorneys immediately filed suit in a court of law demanding damages for Crawford's alleged breach equal to the net profit he would have made on the job had Crawford not breached.

It is not clear at this stage who is in breach, if anyone. Such contracts are complicated and a number of minor departures have occurred on both sides. For instance, Crawford's position is that, while he did not have the land graded as called for by the contract, this was partly due to Schaeffer's delay in doing another portion of the job, which in turn had tied up a subcontractor who was to have done the grading. This is mentioned merely to make it clear that the question of breach remains to be settled.

You represent Crawford. He wants arbitration and specific performance. Outline your legal position and plan the strategies both in the arbitration proceeding and the court proceeding. Be sure you understand and anticipate Schaeffer's moves on this and make a realistic assessment of your case.

Problem 13

Perry v. Nicholas

(1) Perry is owner in fee simple of a large tract of land. Several years ago, a man named Snopes opened negotiations for the right to cut hardwood timber from the land. Snopes offered $100 per thousand board feet for the right to cut. Snopes explained that cutting costs and transportation, clean-up and land repair after cutting, would run a total of around $50 per thousand, and that the ultimate sale price would be around $185 delivered at the buyer's furniture factory in the town of Stick. Perry thought this was a fair offer but wanted to consider the possibility that he might mount a lumbering operation himself, and he refused the offer.

(2) Perry did not live on the land and seldom inspected it, but knew he had some good hardwoods there. Last summer, a hardwood shortage arose and there was great competition among furniture manufacturers for good wood. Prices increased up to nearly $200 per thousand. The Stickler Manufacturing Company of Stick contracted with a logger named Nicholas to by all of Nicholas's hardwood. The contract provided that Nicholas would keep his regular crews working full time and would produce as much as feasible. Nicholas was to be paid at the rate of $220 per thousand, a $20 per thousand advance over the market. However, this payment was based upon the agreement that Nicholas would produce a large and steady supply (specified in detail in the contract). The contract further provided that, in the event Nicholas failed to produce a large and steady supply at a given minimal rate, or failed to produce a total amount, Nicholas would become immediately liable to repay the $20 per thousand premium he had been paid and that all prices in the future would be at the market rate.

(3) Operating under this contract, Nicholas produced a steady supply well over the minimal levels for some weeks. However, one source of supply he intended to use was burned over, and he was outbid for another. He began to run short after he had produced around one million feet. At this point he had been paid, pursuant to the contract provision, the regular $200 market price per thousand, plus the agreed upon $20 per thousand premium for steady supply. If he failed to produce at this point, he would be obliged, therefore, to return some $20,000. In addition, he would fail to make the additional profit represented by the $20 premium in future deliveries to Stickler.

(4) Nicholas knew that Perry would refuse to permit logging on Blackacre, which was adjacent to lands Nicholas was cutting. Sometime during last fall, Nicholas began cutting on Blackacre. He cut approximately 500,000 board feet. The market value for this timber in and near Stick, (the only viable market) was right about $200 per thousand, or a total of $100,000. Cutting, transportation, clean-up and related business costs for producing this timber ran about $50 per thousand. Nicholas sold it for $220 per thousand to Stickler. At this point, Perry discovered Nicholas's activities. At least four or five million feet remain on Perry's land, worth around $1 million gross, at present market prices.

(5) The market value of Blackacre at this point is approximately $600,000. Market value has been diminished by Nicholas's cutting by about $50,000. If all timber were stripped, the land would be worth around $250,000, because it is favorably located for current development of suburban housing. Obviously, the timber rights represent the bulk of its present value; but once the timber is gone, the housing developer's interests will be increased.

165

(6) The state has a statute providing that any person cutting timber on another's land, unless he acts in a bona fide belief that he is the owner or has a good legal right to cut, is liable for double damages.

(7) The lumber from Perry's land is identifiable because it has all been stored in a separate lot for the Stickler Company, which, so far, has not used any of the Perry wood in its manufacturing. There are other furniture manufacturing companies in the immediate vicinity.

(8) We represent Perry. He has asked for advice about what to do. Please give me your opinion as to the remedies we should seek what we might expect.

Problem 14

Nguyen v. Nielsen

In March, a group of citizens sought the town's blessing on a proposed new shopping center to be called Clintwood. They displayed an architect's drawing showing a mall and shopping plaza, parking and the other usual accouterments of a shopping center. The town council, pursuant to law, re-zoned the area in question. There is no question here about the propriety of that act.

Nguyen, who owned a bakery and deli, happened to be at the meeting and saw the drawing. About 3 months later, he saw that the first building was being constructed. He stopped by a finished portion of the building where a sign said "Now leasing." After some discussion, he signed a lease for the corner of the building being constructed. He moved in when it was completed about a month later. Two other small businesses have moved in the remaining portions of the building. However, no further development has taken place, except that a small parking lot has been constructed. The mall and giant parking lot, and the remaining several buildings shown in the proposal have not been constructed. (The proposal to the city and the city's approval did not in any legal sense require a building of the proposed shopping center.)

Nguyen's bakery is making a good deal less than it was in its old location. Nguyen feels that this is due to the lack of traffic and custom in the area. There was no promise to develop the shopping center contained in the lease contract and he concedes that none was made orally. However, he says it was "understood" that such a center would be built. Has he a claim for damages against the lessor-developer, Nielsen, assuming he can show lost profits with reasonable certainty?

166

Problem 15

Ikeda v. Overholt

Sarah Ikeda owned a painting by the famous medieval master, Giocomo Jones. In June, she had it valued by art experts, who placed its value at $20,000. In July, it disappeared. In August, it was discovered that, by means unclear, it had come into the hands of Overholt, a reputable art dealer who had obtained the painting in the honest belief that the man who sold it to him had the right to do so. Overholt sold the painting to a rather fatuous art collector, who, to prevent a competing collector from purchasing it, offered and paid $40,000 for it. The purchasing art collector, one Perce, admits he paid twice its value, but does not mind since beat out the only other collector with a comparable collection of medieval paintings.

The firm of Donaldson & Phipps has filed suit against Overholt, on behalf of Ikeda. You represent Overholt. The suit demands $40,000. Overholt tells you that such instances are a recognized danger of his business and he wants to pay whatever the law requires, preferably without suit. However, he does not want to pay more than the law requires. What is your advice to him?

Problem 16

Thornton v. Darrow

Thornton found some plans for an eight-sided house in a magazine. He sketched a few changes he wanted and showed the plans to a contractor, who agreed to build the house for a total price of $200,000. Thornton was living in another state at the time, but planning to move to Chapelapolis where the house was being built on a lovely, high wooded lot.

About the time the house was begun, Thornton contracted a serious disease and was flat on his back in a hospital for 90 days. When he sufficiently recovered, he visited the house site, only to find that the house had inexplicably been modified and was a six-sided rather than an eight-sided house. The area of the whole house remained the same, but different rooms were, naturally, changed considerably and the interior was nothing like that planned by Thornton. The total value of the house was probably no different from the total value of the eight-sided house. It probably cost about the same to build and was worth about the same amount on the market. It is vastly different from the house Thornton designed. The contractor has no explanation, admits that the original plans were eight-sided, doesn't know exactly when redrawings changed the plans or why.

You represent Thornton. Is the contractor liable? For how much, if anything?

Problem 17

Sail Beach Corporation v. Hillerman

Walter F. Hillerman inherited the southern one-half of a sandy island off the coast. Hoping to make improvements and exploit the island commercially, he formed the Hillerman Corporation, of which he was the sole stockholder. However, he soon found two problems in development. First, sewage disposal in the southern portions of the island was difficult or impossible because of shellfish beds nearby. Currents around the southern portion of the island swept offshore pollution into these beds, which were protected from such pollution by state law. It would be possible to pipe sewage north, if an easement could be gained, but Hillerman found this expensive. His other problem was that there were unpredictably shifting channels cutting through the island. Hillerman's engineers advised it would take years of study and restructuring of the island to be able to say with surety where buildings ought to be located on the southern part because of these shifting inlets and channels.

As a result of these difficulties, Hillerman turned his attention to other matters and never developed the southern half except to build a vacation cottage of his own there.

The northern part of the island was owned by Mary C. Dobbs until she sold all her interest to the Sail Beach Corporation. Sail developed its ownings, consisting of everything not owned by Hillerman, namely all the northern half of the island. The northern half had none of the problems the southern half had. Sail put in rental cottages, a restaurant, and a motel. It decided to expand if possible, and opened discussions with Hillerman about purchasing his portion of the island. During these discussions, Ben Higuchi, the president of Sail, states that Hillerman made two representations at various times and in various words, sometimes indirectly, sometimes directly, but in each case, the substance being: (1) there are no sewage disposal problems on the southern half, and (2) there are no problems with shifting channels on the island. Apparently Hillerman will deny making these statements, but Higuchi's testimony is very detailed and factual.

As a result of these discussions, the parties came to an agreement for the purchase and sale of the southern portion of the island, usually called South Sail. The price was $2 million. Before the agreement was reached, the Sail Corporation had appraisers and others look over the land. No one mentioned to Sail any potential problem about sewage disposal or channel shifts.

The final closing took place in February or March. Months later, the two problems were discovered. Sail immediately notified Hillerman that it would hold him responsible. However, Sail did not see us as its lawyers at this point. Instead it attempted to install a sewer line from South Sail to North Sail. For various technical reasons, this proved unexpectedly expensive, and in fact Sail might not have attempted it had it known the final cost, which ran double the first estimates. Total cost for the installation of a basic, working sewage system for South Sail was $100,000.

In addition to this, qualified appraisers indicate that South Sail would have been worth $2.5 million had neither of these problems existed but that, given these problems of sewage and shifts, the South portion was not worth more than $1.75 million.

When Sail gained possession of the south portion, it contracted with various interested persons and companies for their use of the south portion the following season. It contracted with the Pearl Island Motel Corporation to sell it an area of land, to be served by streets and sewers to be built by Sail. As a result of the delay concerning the sewer system and the problems with shifts, this promise could not be met. Pearl Island sued Sail on the contract. Sail defended this suit on grounds of frustration and impracticability, and paid out attorney's fees of $10,000. It also lost the suit, and paid damages of $25,000 assessed in the case. Sail had also taken reservations for one of its own motels that it had intended to erect on South Sail but could not because of the delays mentioned. It refunded deposits where they had been made, and where not, did not accept any payments, since the motel could not be built until sewer lines were installed. Gross income lost here was about $5,000.

Sail wants to keep the south portion of the island, but wants to recover damages. Our firm has already reviewed the substantive law on the point and concluded we have a good chance of winning. What damages can we recover?

Problem 18

Arbuckle v. Lowell

Gerald Arbuckle negligently drove his truck into a panel delivery truck owned and operated by Howard Lowell. The Lowell delivery truck was seriously damaged as a result. Arbuckle and his insurer at first denied liability for the collision. Lowell took the truck to a repair shop and ordered repairs. However, the repair shop, a reputable one, was unable to get needed parts for some weeks. After three weeks, the truck was repaired, but by this time, Lowell was unable to pay the repair charges.

During the preceding three weeks, he had tried to rent a substitute vehicle to carry on his delivery business but was unable to find one. He had tried to use a car, but it could not accommodate large materials. His customers ceased to hire him. As a result, he had little or no income during the three weeks following the accident, and he was unable to pay the repair charges. The repair shop, Wallers Auto Repairs, refused to let him have the panel truck until they were paid. It was two more weeks before Lowell could borrow enough money to get his delivery truck.

His business picked up again at its past level. The depreciation in the value of the truck was $1350.00, though the cost of repairing the truck was only $987.00. The cost of renting a substitute, had one been available, would have been approximately $225.00 per week. (This is an estimate based on average mileage.) The profits lost during the period Lowell was without a car amounted to about $300 per week. Lowell has brought suit demanding these sums. The insurer for Arbuckle has retained you as counsel pursuant to its obligation under the liability policy. You have reviewed the file and have concluded that Arbuckle was negligent, that Lowell was not contributorily negligent, and that the company is obliged to pay on behalf of Arbuckle all legal damages suffered by Lowell. What sums would you advise the company to pay and why?

Problem 19

Hutchins v. O'Neal's Garage

O'Neal owned and operated a garage in Chapelapolis for the repair of motor vehicles. In connection with this business, he often bought and sold used cars, sometimes on a retail, sometimes on a wholesale basis. In September, O'Neal purchased three used cars from Gonzales in Ellensborough, for a total price of $9,000.

170

One of the cars was intended by O'Neal for his own use as a second car in his family. The other two were intended for resale, either on his own lot or to a retailer. The cars were to be made into a "lot" and shipped at one time by truck. Consequently shipment was not made until October, when the entire lot was put together.

O'Neal was purchasing from Gonzales at "wholesale," and the price paid Gonzales was a good reflection of the wholesale used car market at Gonzales' place of business. Retail market at Gonzales' place of business would have been about $12,000-$13,000 for the lot.

During the delay period, while O'Neal was waiting for shipment, the used car market in Chapelapolis dropped considerably due to several factors, including an influx of a large volume used car dealer, and the onset of what looked like a long term strike at a major factory. Anticipating difficulty in selling, O'Neal decided to cut his losses. He was able to contract with Hutchins, a used car dealer, for a sale to Hutchins of two of the cars at $2,500 each. The two cars to be sold to Hutchins under this contract were a Dodge and an Oldsmobile, identified by proper motor and serial numbers.

The cars were loaded at Ellensborough, Gonzales' place of business, in October. The carrier truck went off the road on a mountain two miles away and overturned. The Dodge was destroyed and so was the Ford that O'Neal had intended for his own use. The Oldsmobile was damaged, but capable of being repaired. It was eventually shipped on to O'Neal, who repaired it in his own shop and proceeded with the sale to Hutchins at the originally agreed on price. After two days, O'Neal was able to find a substitute car to replace the Ford he had intended for his own use. He paid $3200 retail, no wholesale cars being available to him in Chapelapolis. It was a Ford with approximately the same retail value as the one destroyed.

The repair of the Oldsmobile was done in spare time by mechanics and repairmen already working for O'Neal. He paid a total of $70.18 in wages, fringe benefits and social security taxes for this job. His shop manager was on salary and was paid no more for supervising this job. The same was true for his bookkeeper and other personnel peripherally involved in the work.

O'Neal had been renting a second car while awaiting the shipment from Gonzales. He continued to rent the car for one day after the shipment overturned. While looking for a replacement, however, he managed without having a second car, though he spent an entire day's time looking for the replacement which, as indicated above, he ultimately bought.

The driver of the car carrier was negligent. His name was Svensen and he worked for Carrier's Red Top Car Top, Inc. Carrier's was insured by the Pure Casualty Ins. Co., and Pure had admitted liability for damages resulting from the overturned shipment.

You represent Pure and its adjuster asks you what damages, or elements of damages, should be paid and to whom. After a brief look, you decide the answer is not simple and you phone Pure. Pure authorizes you to prepare a memo on the whole subject for future guidance of its adjusters.

———————

Problem 20

Hensen v. Valentine

Catherine Hensen and Hans Valentine submitted a dispute to arbitration. The arbitrators had before them a question of damages resulting to Hensen when Valentine used some inferior materials in house construction. Hensen claimed $13,188 and Valentine said he owed only $500. Under the legal rule that was probably applicable — the diminution in value rule — Hensen might have recovered as much as $5,000 on the basis of testimony she offered. Under the cost of repair rule, which almost certainly would not have been used by a law court, she might have recovered $13,188, provided, again, that the testimony most favorable to her was accepted. Valentine's testimony on both rules was more favorable to his side. Under that testimony, if accepted, Hensen probably would not have recovered more than $500 under the diminution rule, or $1,118 under the cost of repair rule. The arbitrators are not bound by either rule, but are permitted to "do equity" in assessing damages.

For quite some time the arbitrators kept the submission without making an award. For financial reasons Valentine wished to get the matter out of the way and he offered Hensen $2,500, on the morning of March 1. Neither party was aware that the evening before, February 28, the arbitrators had met and decided in favor of Hensen in the amount of $10,000. Not knowing this, Hensen accepted the settlement offer and endorsed and deposited Valentine's check. She executed a release. Two days later, the award of the arbitrators arrived in the mail. Hensen immediately offered a bank draft to Valentine in the amount of $2500.84, representing the amount paid plus interest at 6%; in addition, Hensen offered to make good any expenses of the settlement transaction. She therefore demanded recision of the settlement. When Valentine refused, Hensen hired your firm to bring suit. What results do you expect and why?

———————

Problem 21

Grenfell v. Bernal

Our firm represents Bernal, a resident of this state who operates a business across the state line in Lancaster. He has dumped some very large boulders on land belonging to Grenfell, over in Lancaster. He has also built a small building on Grenfell's land there. According to Bernal, all this was done with Grenfell's permission, though Grenfell denies this. Bernal says he needed a place to dump the boulders as he removed them from a nearby construction site on which he was erecting a major building. It is not feasible to move them because there is no place to put them in the city. The area around Grenfell's land is so built up, he hesitates to dynamite the boulders; Grenfell objects to this and has blocked access to the land in any event. Now Grenfell has brought a suit here in our state to compel removal of the boulders and the building on the land in Lancaster. Bernal says if Grenfell succeeds, the effect on him, Bernal, will be very serious. What defenses can we urge and what is the chance of success?

Problem 22

Vogel v. Gabaldon

Gabaldon began worrying about nourishment problems when she opened a natural foods restaurant. She became increasingly concerned about diet and especially about the plight of many poor people in the county. Last year, she located some land in the county that was vacant — in fact, an abandoned farm. She organized a group of volunteers to farm the land first to demonstrate that it was feasible to grow "natural" food, without the use of artificial fertilizers and poison sprays and second, to provide the food so grown to undernourished families in the county.

A sizeable group of persons worked on the farm, from about March 15 through September. None of the group lived on the farm. Following Gabaldon's directions, they all materially contributed compost, natural fertilizers and a great deal of effort. They raised food to the value of no less than about $15,000.

The products of the farm were disposed of in two ways. Most were given without charge directly to persons deemed to be in need (not including any of the workers on the farm) or were given without charge to the local food bank. Some of the food, about $5,000 worth, was sold at wholesale to natural food retail stores or restaurants.

173

In October, Vogel, the owner of the land, which had been lying fallow for over ten years, noticed activity on it, investigated and discovered the facts outlined above. He brought suit against Gabaldon demanding (1) the value of the food so produced, $15,000 or more; (2) in the alternative, whatever relief to which the facts might show he was entitled.

Represent the client you'd prefer to represent and prepare to forward his or her interests on the remedies issues.

Problem 23

Perryman v. Blair

We represent Mr. Charles S. Perryman, who is in the business of putting together blocks of acreage and developing the land for homesite purposes or selling it to other developers. On April 15, Mr. Perryman — without consulting us — executed a contract to purchase the Blair farm, consisting, according to the contract, of 300 acres more or less, with farm house, barn, deep well, working sewage disposal apparatus, and a 10-acre pond built on a small clean-water stream, suitable for watering cattle, or swimming, or both. At that time he paid $10,000 towards the purchase price.

Mr. Blair was to convey no later than June 1, and could convey as early as May 1. The delay was intended to give Blair time to dispose of his cattle at the best price possible, to hold auctions on his equipment, and generally to wind up the farm. The contract also provided that Mr. Perryman could enter and make improvements and take possession of any portions of the farm not used for living purposes or for winding up the farm. Perryman did some grading for streets and a little paving of streets and walks on land bordering Highway 94.

On May 15, Blair announced he had completed selling off his equipment and cattle and was ready to convey but had discovered that he owns only 250 acres and, further, that the pond dam had broken and the water escaped. This created swampy conditions on lower ground. The area could not be graded for several weeks. The dam would have to be rebuilt after grading became possible. The cost of repair, apparently, will run several thousand dollars if not more. Mr. Perryman told Blair on that date to hold up until they could decide what to do about the dam. He then consulted us.

Mr. Perryman says he would like to get out of the contract because the package of acreage he had hoped to put together has fallen through. He cannot get any commercial zoning on his side of the highway. Though the opposite side has now been zoned commercial, the land over there belongs to a competing developer. The Blair farm may be valuable someday, but it might be hard to sell for development purposes right now and Mr. Perryman doesn't want to tie up his capital or credit. Mr. Perryman doesn't really care about the pond except that it provides, he hopes, an excuse to get out of the contract. He might utilize it in the development as an attraction if he does indeed develop the place. Of that he is unsure at the moment.

Can we claim a rescission here or what? Are we under any time pressure?

Problem 24

Dietman v. Charles

Professor Jo Dietman, a scholar working with manuscript materials of Sir Isaac Newton, discovered a paper that she believed to be a Newton manuscript. It was for sale, along with a lot of junk, in an antiquarian's shop owned and operated by Frederick Charles in Cambridge, England. Charles obviously did not recognize the manuscript as even potentially valuable and he sold it mostly as a decorative specimen of old fashioned writing for the sum of $15.00. Professor Dietman purchased it and took it home to the United States. After considerable study and examination she found it to be the "missing link" in a chain of important manuscripts. Its value to collectors or universities would probably be about $10,000. Professor Dietman wrote up her find in a scholarly journal and there was a substantial stir about it in the press. Charles came to her house after reading press accounts and asked to examine the manuscript. Professor Dietman showed it to him and he insisted that it was rightfully his and that she had defrauded him. Professor Dietman denied any fraud. Charles became angry and left -with the manuscript in hand. Professor Dietman called the police and asked them to retrieve the property, but Charles had left town.

Professor Dietman thinks he is now in New York at another shop in which he owns an interest, but she fears he will leave the country in a day or two and take the manuscript with him. If so, she is sure she'll never get it back. She says this is professionally and personally a major find that she's never likely to duplicate. Private collectors might buy it secretly, even if they knew her title to it was good. I asked her about customs declarations on leaving England, with the idea that the English might have some "national treasure" law that would have forbidden taking this out of the country. I don't know whether they do or not, but she made no declarations or disclosures of any kind to any of the English authorities. Our main problem now is to stop Charles from leaving the country with the manuscript. What can we do?

175

Problem 25

Wagner v. Flora

Geraldine Flora built a small office building on her land. By error, about seven inches of the building — most of the thickness of one wall — was actually over the property line and on Wagner's adjacent property. Flora's lot was small, about 50 feet wide and slightly tapering toward the rear. This permitted very little leeway in office design. The total width of the building was seven inches wider than it could have been had Flora stayed within the property line. The depth of the building was less than the depth of the lot — about 100 feet.

After the building was complete, a town survey made for other purposes revealed the mistake. There is no question that it was a mistake, not an intentional error. Flora has had tenants in the building regularly since it was built and most of them have leases of several years. To remove the wall would be costly to Flora, would reduce the office space and disrupt tenants on that side — possibly enough that they could claim a constructive or actual eviction.

The paved parking lot for tenants in the back of the building is, due to irregularity of the lot line, almost entirely on Wagner's land. Wagner has access to it for his own use and that of his tenants. Wagner has brought suit seeking (1) removal of the encroaching building wall, (2) injunction against further trespass by use of the parking lot, and (3) any other relief to which he may be entitled in law or equity. We represent Flora. What is the range of her maximum and minimum liability? Have we any negotiating strengths?

Problem 26

Millar Mfg. Co. v. The Taylor Co.

Our firm represents Millar Mfg. Co., which is largely owned by Bob Millar, who operates it. Millar manufactures a patented part used widely in many industries and known as a Millar, or, when made of aluminum, as an "Alco-Millar." Millar uses steel or aluminum fang-screws in manufacturing the Millar and Alco-Millar. He has purchased most of these from Taylor Co. in large lots. Millar entered into a contract with Taylor by written order, accepted by Taylor in November, for the purchase of 100,000 fang-screws to be delivered at Millar's plant in Charlesville between January 1 and January 15. Terms were $20,000 prepayment, which was made, and the balance of $80,000 within ten days of delivery.

Millar used fang-screws in two ways. Primarily he used them in manufacturing the Millar, which of course was patented. But fang-screws are not themselves

176

patented or patentable and Millar kept a supply of fang-screws to sell separately on a wholesale and a retail basis to his "Millar" customers who required them for repair or replacement.

When the order was placed with and accepted by Taylor, market reports show that the price of fang-screws was $1 each, bought in wholesale lots, and this was in fact the contract price. By December the wholesale price was up to $1.10. Retail prices were maintained at about $2 each in November and December.

On December 20, a registered letter from Taylor arrived at the Millar plant and was signed for by a plant foreman. Millar was out of town at the time and his secretary was ill. The letter was placed on his desk. Millar arrived back in town on Christmas Eve but did not go to his office. He spent Christmas Eve with his family and also Christmas morning. At 1:00 p.m. on Christmas day, he went to his office and opened the Taylor letter. It stated that Taylor would not honor its contract to provide the fang-screws in January and was going to re-tool to manufacture a more profitable line of industrial equipment. The letter stated that the shift had to be made immediately and that the Taylor Company was confident its customers could find replacements in the market without inconvenience.

There were no markets for fang-screws open on December 25, though Millar tried to reach plant managers of several plants who manufactured such items. On December 26, Millar reached a number of plants, but found that Taylor, the world's largest fang-screw manufacturer, left a vacuum in the market. Most of the other manufacturers were swamped with back orders that began rolling in before Christmas. The price had risen to $1.50 per fang-screw in wholesale lots. Millar also found that he could not get delivery until February or March.

For several days Millar tried to devise some substitute part for the fang-screw but he was unable to do so. He then ordered 100,000 from the American Aluminum Foundry Co. of Seattle, Washington. By this time the price had risen to $1.60 and delivery was guaranteed for no sooner than March 15.

Millar ran out of fang-screws on February 1 and was unable to produce any further "Millars" for this reason. His normal net profit on Millars in the current market would have run about $15,000 for the six-week period between February 1 when he had to stop production and March 15 when he was able to begin again. He kept his plant open during this period, paying all fixed overhead expenses, such as rental on the factory, executive salaries and so on, for the total sum of $20,000. In addition, he paid the salaries of a few nonexecutive employees as a matter of keeping their loyalty and good will. This additional sum amounted to $6,000 for the six-week period.

Millar is not sure whether he will ultimately lose customers as a result of the stoppage or not. Some of his customers or potential customers undoubtedly turned to manufacturers who produced competing substitute items (not "Millars;" he has licensed no other manufacture of these items).

What items can we support as elements of damages against Taylor?

Problem 27

Craft Construction Co. v. The Sampson Corporation

The Sampson Corporation entered into a valid agreement under which Craft Construction Company would grade and pave a parking lot and erect a small attendant's building thereon. The total price was to be $25,000. Craft paid $400 to an engineer to provide some drawings and figures for the project. It also paid $1,000 for asphalt, binders and other supplies. At this point Craft received a call from Sampson, who said the deal was off, because Sampson had decided not to build the parking lot after all. We represent Sampson, which admits the breach. They have been given a demand from Craft's attorney for $5,000 in damages, but we can produce evidence if necessary that materials and labor costs are rising and that Craft probably would not have made much, if any profit on the deal. What should we offer in settlement?

Problem 28

Morrel v. Dallem

By valid contract dated June 1, Morrel promised to sell and Dallem promised to buy certain premises, hereinafter called "Whiteacre." The property was business property, vacant, but suited to development of business buildings in a city. Morrel was to deliver a valid warranty deed to the property no later than August 1. The purchase price was $75,000. Dallem paid $10,000 of this to Morrel at the time the contract was signed.

Unknown to Morrel, Dallem had already negotiated with Ratner to sell the property to Ratner for $100,000. Ratner was unaware that Dallem had no title at the time.

On August 1 Morrel notified Dallem that he decided not to sell and intended to build on the land himself. Dallem offered him more money, but Morrel remained adamant. Dallem said she'd have to sue, but Morrel still refused to sell. Dallem then approached you asking to get specific performance, but you checked and found that Morrel had already sold the land to Casey, for $100,000. As nearly as you can determine, Casey was not aware of the contract between Morrel and Dallem.

At Dallem's direction, you notified Ratner that the Dallem-Ratner contract could not be carried out. Dallem now wishes to sue Morrel for damages. She is pretty sure also that Ratner will sue her. Prepare to handle both cases by thorough analysis of the remedial opportunities and limits. The market value of the land on August 1 was, according to every appraiser in the city, not more than $75,000.

Problem 29

Burch v. Kanakakis

Thomas Kanakakis owned and operated a large food supply house for restaurants. He baked and prepared various kinds of breads which were supplied wholesale, fresh and frozen, to restaurants over a multi-state area.

Burch manufactured commercial kitchens and bakery goods, such as ovens, automatic dough kneading machines, and various expensive items used in such kitchens and bakeries. Kanakakis was in need of some new equipment, priced in the Burch Catalog at approximately $100,000. Kanakakis suggested to Burch that Burch could take some of Kanakakis' old equipment on trade and Burch agreed that it was possible. A Burch engineer surveyed Kanakakis' place of business and found a number of items Burch would be willing to accept, including three old ovens built into a brick wall. The parties finally agreed as follows:

Burch would deliver the desired equipment to Kanakakis for a total cash price of $100,000, less a "trade-in allowance" on the ovens and other equipment specified, in the amount of $20,000. Some of the equipment was of a line and model not handled by Burch and required repair. It was agreed that Kanakakis would remove the ovens from their brick walls and repair certain other items to be traded in.

The actual value of the trade-in items, as repaired, would have been about $10,000, though the "allowance" was $20,000. Kanakakis began removal of the ovens and repairs on the other items in time to have these items ready on the delivery date agreed upon. The ovens proved to have an unexpectedly complicated position in the walls and it cost Kanakakis $8,000 to have the walls removed and rebuilt to get the ovens out. Repairs to other equipment cost about $3,000.

179

On the date Burch was required to deliver the new ovens and the other equipment two things happened. Kanakakis' truck drivers, who delivered the food and bread to restaurants, went out on strike. Next, Burch called saying he could not deliver on the contract at all because the manufacturer of the equipment had closed down.

Kanakakis lost a considerable amount of normal business during the next two months because he had no ovens operating and because he could not deliver either bread or food supplies to his restaurant customers. He was operating at about 20% capacity. He saved about $8,000 in wages for the two month period, but his fixed overhead, such as rent which ran to $1,000 per month, remained constant during this period. Kanakakis eventually re-installed the ovens at a cost of $2,-000.

You represent Kanakakis. To what damages is he entitled?

Problem 30

Kerr v. Spiller, Inc.

Kerr agreed to sell, and Spiller, Inc. agreed to purchase a certain city lot. The date for the transfer of title was February 1, and the purchase price was to be paid in cash in the amount of $100,000. On February 1, Spiller, Inc. refused to accept the property or to pay the price. On that date, the value of the lot was $100,000, but Spiller, which had intended the lot for a business building, decided on moving its business in different directions as a result of a stormy stockholders' meeting, in which a large number of stockholders protested certain activities of the corporation as anti-environmental.

During February, the value of property in this general area of the city and of this general description remained constant, but in March property values downtown began to fall steadily. The lot, as of June 1, was valued at no more than $90,000.

Kerr has now consulted us about a suit against Spiller, Inc. Breach is clear. What remedies can we assert?

Problem 31

Craig v. Pure Life Insurance Co.

Pure Life Ins. Co. issued a life policy in the amount of $100,000 on the life of Samuel Craig. His wife, Mary Ann, was named as beneficiary. She later divorced Craig and married Robert Durham. They moved to California and she became a citizen of California. Thereafter, Durham was transferred to Singapore. They are now residing there, but are still U.S. citizens and return to visit from time to time.

Craig married Janice Love. At the time of Craig's death earlier this year, Janice Love Craig had separated from Craig and was residing in Italy, though she, like Mrs. Durham, remained a U.S. citizen.

Following Craig's death, Mary Ann Durham brought suit against Pure in Texas, where her brother is a lawyer. She sued on the policy as the named beneficiary. About the same time, Janice Love Craig brought suit in New York. She sued, alleging that the policy had been validly assigned to her. Both women have pleaded substantial cases. Pure is willing to pay either and has no claim of its own.

You are employed in the office of Pure's General Counsel. He asks you to prepare, very quickly, a memo outlining the proper strategy for Pure, so that local attorneys in Texas and New York can be advised and all proper steps can be taken to protect Pure's interests. He wants reasons for all your recommendations as well as indications why you reject any alternatives available. He tells you that, all other things being equal, Pure would by far prefer to have the matter tried in or near New York. What is your advice to him and to local counsel?

Problem 32

Carroll v. Pure Ins. Co.

Pure issued an accident policy to Dwight B. Carroll. The policy contained agreements to pay certain accident benefits, but excluded from coverage any accident subject in whole or in part to workers' compensation coverage. On July 4, Carroll was injured at a picnic. The picnic was composed mostly of employees of Clark-Robinwell Corporation and their families. The picnic had been organized more or less spontaneously by employees, and the company manager and vice-president had attended briefly. The company, upon some importuning, had agreed to provide a certain, but insufficient, quantity of beer. Pure's claims supervisor approved payment to Carroll of various sums resulting from an injury at the picnic, in the belief that workers' compensation could not possibly cover the case. Carroll, however, applied for compensation. An affiliate of Pure, the Pure Employers Casualty Company, carried the workers' compensation insurance. It urged that Carroll had made an election to use his private insurance. It argued that, in any event, he was not within the course and scope of employment when injured. These contentions were rejected and Carroll recovered compensation. Pure Insurance Company now sues to recover all payments it has made to Carroll, in the sum of $2,118.32. You represent Carroll. What defenses? What is your prognostication?

Problem 33

Higuchi v. Brown

Brown and Higuchi were partners. On a Friday afternoon late, knowing he had a sure thing at the Saturday afternoon races, Brown took the firm's night deposit bag containing $1,000 in cash, saying he would deposit it. In fact, he took the money and bet it all on a horse in the first race. The horse won and paid 10 to one. Brown pocketed $10,000. Higuchi heard of the winning from a mutual friend who had seen Brown collect. Higuchi became suspicious and questioned Brown, who admitted the whole deal. Higuchi demanded the entire $10,000 for the partnership. What rights has the firm in this sum or any part of it?

Problem 34

Image Nation, Inc. v. Buyer's Five and Dime, Inc.

Image Nation, Inc. is a manufacturer of TV sets marketed principally to cooperatives and to discount stores for sale under house brands.

Image Nation contracted with Buyer's Five and Dime to sell a total of 500 sets to Buyer's for re-sale by Buyer's at various localities. Sets were to be shipped within a one-month period beginning in November to various local destinations named in the contract. Buyer's was to pay freight, which was to be billed separately later. The total price of the sets was $75,000. Normal re-sale price would be double this or more.

Image Nation built only on order because it had limited marketing facilities. As a result of Buyer's order, it acquired raw materials and parts needed to make 500 sets. However, Buyer's repudiated the contract during the summer before any work had begun. Image Nation at that time finished manufacturing for the orders on hand and, because of Buyer's repudiation, closed up the plant until further orders arrived. The plant was closed about a month before Christmas

182

orders began arriving. It reopened during that period. It was able to use some of the parts and raw materials it had ordered for Buyer's production, but not all of them.

The normal cost of manufacture for 500 sets, exclusive of fixed overhead, was about $30,000. This represented parts, royalties on patented items, labor, fuel used in operations, and other expenses directly attributable to manufacture of the sets. On this basis, the profit expected on the Buyer's production would have been about $45,000.

Fixed overhead for Image Nation was relatively high. It manufactured about 2,000 sets a year (about 1500 on the year in question, because of the breach by Buyer). Total fixed charges such as executive salaries, amortized cost of plant and equipment, minimum guaranteed royalties on patented parts, and the like was $150,000. Of this sum, approximately $80,000 was paid in executive salaries, $40,000 to the president and general manager, Joe D'Imagio, and $20,000 to two younger brothers, one who was active in the business and one who was only a figurehead.

Buyer's has now conceded that it is liable for breach of contract, but takes the position that Image Nation should have little or no net damages. You represent Image Nation. What is your assessment of the probable recovery against Buyer's?

Problem 35

Thornton v. Darrow

Additional facts have come to hand as a result of further investigation in this case. (See supra, Problem 16).

We have discovered that the contractor's original cost estimates show an expected cost of $150,000 to build the house. Actual cost, in spite of some slight rise in prices of materials, was only about $125,000. There is reason to believe that the lower cost was a result of the changes made in the plans.

Darrow made a good impression when we took his deposition and he is likely to impress the jury favorably. There is a strong likelihood that the jury will accept his story that he honestly did not intend any change. There are some plans widely published that seem similar to those used by him here and it is possible that working plans simply got mixed up.

The appraisers have done a thorough job in reporting on the values involved. They believe that the house as originally planned would have improved the Thornton lot by about $225,000, giving a total lot and house value of about $275,000. They say that the house actually built, though it cost less, apparently because it was more efficiently designed from the builder's point of view, has improved the lot by about the same amount. They say it might be just a shade less, but not substantially so. Both types of house plans have gained some popularity in recent years and buyers have not substantially distinguished the two, at least not to the extent that it reflects in price.

With this additional information, what is our position on recovery?

Problem 36

CLIENT FILE: **(A) 93-625(13) Everstone Corporation**
                     (B) 93-112(3) Simco, Inc.

FROM: DRB

Everstone Corporation and Simco are both valued clients of long standing. As the file numbers indicate, we do considerable business for Everstone. We do less for Simco, but it is an older client. We may have a conflict of interest in representing these clients, resulting from the following facts.

Everstone manufactures a product by the same name. Over the years it has sold this product to various users, including large quantities to Simco, which uses a great deal of Everstone or similar products. Three years ago, Simco stopped buying Everstone and began buying a competing product, Durock, manufactured by the Dura Mfg. Co. This was a serious loss to Everstone, which had been making profits from Simco sales of about $20,000 per year.

Everstone attempted to recapture this market by talking with Simco purchasing agent, John Silver Long. Long gave various reasons why he had switched to Durock, but did not convince Everstone. Simco paid the same for the Durock as it paid for Everstone. As a result of doubts, Everstone hired a private detective specializing in corporate information, trade secrets and the like, to investigate. The detective, Pride, concluded that Simco switched to Durock because Durock had paid Long, the Simco purchasing agent, some $3,000 each year.

Armed with this information, Everstone went to see Simco President, Arly L. Simpson. Both Simpson, and Everstone President Crofton A. Goldman, have just left a joint interview with me. Both wish to assert their interests to the fullest. I have advised them that there may be a conflict of interest and that it may be that we can only represent one of them. I have also advised that we would not represent either of them if information furnished would prejudice the other. It is therefore essential to decide (1) the rights of each and (2) whether these may come into conflict that would require us to withdraw our representation of one or both.

Simpson believes that Long is quite well off. The Dura Mfg. Co. certainly has ample assets to cover any claims.

Be sure to indicate to me, as quickly as possible, the maximum claims each of our clients can make. Please make a recommendation on the conflict of interest problem as well.

Notes

1. How are the following two situations and the questions they pose related to the *Everstone* problem?

(a) A wishes to sell Blackacre. A contracts with B, a Broker, to sell it at a 7% commission for at least $10,000. B locates C, who wishes the South one-half of Blackacre. B induces C to pay $10,000 for this. B then reports to A that Blackacre has been sold to D (a confederate of B's) for $10,000 and asks for a deed. A makes a deed to D. D, pursuant to an agreement with B, conveys the north half of Blackacre to B and the south half to C. Shortly thereafter, both A and C discover they have been duped. What are their remedies? What is the substantive wrong involved? If either party is entitled to "restitution," is it restitution in kind or substitutionary?

(b) M, an employer engaged in technical work, employs S, a skilled technician, to work on secret processes that are not, however, patented. S does work on them, learns much, and then quits her job upon being offered a higher paying job with M's competitor, MM. The new job involves working on a process similar, though not identical, to M's process. MM is somewhat behind in developing this process, which is commercially important. Any remedies against S or MM? What if S admits she intends to use all her skill and knowledge about the M process? What if she has already done so?

2. As indicated in the other problems and in the Text § 9.2, when a misrepresentation is intended to deceive, strong remedies may be warranted; when it is an unintended misstatement, sometimes the remedy is limited to rescission or some relief more or less the equivalent of rescission. What remedies would you expect when the wrongdoing is hard to define or attenuated in some other sense? Consider the following examples:

(a) Clifford employed Murphy to build a house for him for the sum of $40,-000. Payments were to be made as work progressed, with the final payment of $10,-

000 when work was complete. Clifford paid $30,000 when it was due. Murphy, pressed by other obligations, needed the final payment to finance other work. If he did not begin and complete work for Scott very shortly, he would be subjected to a serious loss because of a liquidated damages clause in the Scott-Murphy contract. Murphy, therefore, hurriedly, but properly, finished the Clifford job so he could get the final payment. Clifford knew or suspected all of this. When Murphy presented the architect's certificate of satisfactory completion, Clifford offered Murphy a final settlement of $7500 instead of $10,000. Murphy was eventually forced to accept this so he could get the needed working capital to begin the Scott job. Clifford insisted he would pay nothing unless Murphy accepted the $7500 in full settlement and signed a release. Murphy did this. He then sued for the balance. Clifford pleaded the release. Who will win? Why? What about a suit in tort for damages instead. Who would win that one? Why?

(b) Max Van Buren, a lawyer, represented an old woman named Ellie Sue Finken. Miss Finken was 80 years old. She was apparently of sound mind. Shortly before her death, she conveyed Whiteacre to Max Van Buren. The consideration recited was "payment of debts owed the said Max Van Buren for services rendered." Van Buren had been Miss Finken's legal advisor for 30 years and he had advised her on many occasions. He does not have complete records of conferences, phone calls, various wills and other work he has done, but it seems substantial. His income records are intact and they show that Miss Finken paid him an annual retainer of $100 per year and no other sums, even though she had had a relatively high volume of work. Whiteacre is worth $85,000. The Finken heirs are excited about the conveyance and want it for themselves. Can they get it? How about a suit for damages against Van Buren? What is the substantive wrong involved?

(c) Grabben leases a small office in an area of the city occupied mostly by persons on welfare, persons with low incomes, and persons periodically laid off work. The office is covered with various full color advertisements for items such as refrigerators, stoves, freezers. Two employees "work" the neighborhood, door to door, and get potential customers into the office where these ads and small models are used to "sell" them. The selling price is invariably about three times the usual retail price for the goods, and in addition there are finance charges. There are no price ceilings in effect under state or federal law. There is no misrepresentation, though of course Grabben does not tell his customers that the same quality goods can be purchased more cheaply downtown. Many of the area residents probably do not feel "at home" in downtown retail stores, where customers and even employees are well dressed, where there are carpets on the floor and so on. Except for this kind of pressure, and normal sales talk, there is no reason why customers of Grabben cannot discover cheaper prices elsewhere by simple comparison shopping. However, they do not in fact do so, and Grabben sells a sufficient number of high-priced items each month to stay in business. He sold a refrigerator-freezer to Mr. and Mrs. Herman Wolcroft, both 68-year-old pensioners living on social security. He charged $1500, plus financing. The same quality goods are sold elsewhere for about $500. The Wolcrofts had paid $600 on the goods, plus interest and finance charges, when they went to the legal aid office where you put in one night a week. What can you do for them?

UCC § 2-302 provides in part "(1) If the court as a matter of law finds the contract or any clause of the contract to have been unconscionable at the time it was made the court may refuse to enforce the contract, or it may enforce the remainder of the contract without the unconscionable clause, or it may so limit the application of any unconscionable clause as to avoid any unconscionable result."

Duress, undue influence and unconscionability are discussed in the Text §§ 10.2, 10.3 and 10.7 respectively.

3. California courts have developed an "implied covenant of good faith and fair dealing" on the part of contracting parties. In *Gruenberg v. Aetna Ins. Co.*, 9 Cal. 3d 566, 108 Cal. Rptr. 480, 510 P.2d 1032 (1973), the plaintiff owned a restaurant and lounge. It was covered by fire insurance by defendants. Plaintiff's business burned and he went to the scene, where he had an argument with officers. An adjuster for the insurers told officers that the plaintiff had too much insurance. Perhaps because of these two things, the plaintiff was charged with arson. While the criminal charge was pending, the insurers, through attorneys, demanded that the plaintiff submit to questioning under oath as to his claim. The insurers would ordinarily have a right to demand answers on oath. However, the plaintiff refused to submit to questioning for fear of prejudicing his defense to the criminal charge. About a month later the criminal charge was dismissed for lack of probable cause and the plaintiff then offered to submit to questioning. The insurers took the position that his coverage was canceled for noncooperation and that they had no liability. The plaintiff then sued, alleging the insurers, through the adjuster's comments to officers and through the attorneys' insistence on questioning, had breached the "good faith" duty imposed by California law on contracting parties. He claimed damages for "severe emotional upset and distress," economic and special damages, and punitive damages. The California Supreme Court held he had stated a good claim on these facts, even though ordinarily the insurers would be entitled to demand cooperation of the insured and to avoid liability if that cooperation were not forthcoming.

Notice that the claim is for damages. Is there an element of economic compulsion here? Might the case also be regarded as simply establishing a rule of conscionability for performance of contracts that closely parallels the UCC rule for conscionability in formation of contracts? Would restitution furnish a better result here than damages? Is there any way to get "restitution"?

187

Problem 37

Nance v. Mueller

Elsa Mueller purchased a lot in Charlesville in November for $10,000. This was approximately the market value of the lot at the time and at all times since then.

The following January she entered into a contract — against the advice of her friends — under which Nance was to construct a house on the lot. The house was large and imposing and the contract price was $150,000. It was, however, much too nice for the general neighborhood. Casual appraisals by friends at the time were that the house and lot would be worth only $125,000 when the house was completed because, though it sat on a nice hill, the surrounding houses were much, much cheaper. Professional appraisal since then has come up with about the same figures.

The contract called for beginning work in the summer. Nance contracted in January to secure materials needed in the summer at January prices. He began work in June, but at this point there was a massive strike in the materials and transport industries. Nance found that all his contracts contained strike and "Act of God" clauses and all were canceled. When the strike was over in August, Nance was forced to negotiate new contracts at substantially higher prices. His cost estimates in September indicated he would stand to lose, on completion, about $10,000. About halfway through the work, in September, Mueller became dissatisfied with the work and told Nance she was "canceling" the contract. Nance had spent about $50,000 and no payments had been made by Mueller. The unfinished house, as it stands, adds nothing to the value of the lot. If it is finished on its present foundations and within the present framing, costs will run about another $125,000 at current prices. Value of the house and lot if the house is complete will be about $125,000. Mueller was in breach. We represent Nance. Can we recover anything?

Problem 38

Freund v. Freund

Leb Freund, an old man of 80, asked his great nephew, Hammond Freund, to stay with him and care for him. Leb did not want to go to "an old folks' home." After considerable discussion, Leb agreed with Hammond on the following terms: Leb would immediately give Hammond a deed to a small farm Leb owned, and Leb would make a will leaving the house he lived in to Hammond, together with other items of value. Hammond, in turn, would live in the house, sleep there at night, prepare meals, and see to medical needs. It was contemplated that Hammond would continue in his job in a hardware store, but that he would come home in event of emergency, leave food prepared for lunch on Leb's "bad days," and make other adjustments. Specifically, it was contemplated that Hammond would regularly sleep in the house and be available at night.

The arrangement worked well for several months but eventually broke down. Leb made more demands on Hammond than he had expected and Hammond was unwilling to stay home from 5:30 until bedtime every evening. Lately Hammond has been spending weekends and some nights out at "his" farm, improving it and doing a little farming there. Leb has been in worse shape physically than ever before and he wants Hammond to stay home. He has called us and I have interviewed Leb, and there is not much doubt that we can prove a breach if Leb's understanding is accepted by the trier of fact. What can we do for him?

Problem 39

Dempsey v. Swensen

When Marissa Dempsey planned to marry, she decided to follow several traditions of her family, one of which was to wear in the wedding ceremony an elaborately embroidered shawl depicting her face and that of her husband, along with their names and various other decorations. Marissa's mother had followed this tradition as had her grandmother. Each of the elder women had kept the wedding shawl mounted and framed in their homes. Marissa designed her shawl and, with her mother and father, entered into a contract with Swensen under which Swensen was to provide the shawl in accord with the design. He was to procure and sew the cloth, do the drawing and embroidery and furnish the shawl no later than ten days before the wedding. Swensen understood the purpose and the background and inspected the wedding shawls of the elder women in the family. The Dempseys made it clear that time was of the essence and that the shawl, though decorative and beautiful, would have little value unless it was actually used in the wedding and became a memento of the event.

Swensen, without any wilful intent, nevertheless failed to have the shawl ready, or even substantially ready, for the wedding. Marissa was extremely upset, as were members of the family, but the wedding was held in spite of this because of out-of-town guests and other arrangements difficult to cancel. Marissa underwent a difficult time and consulted a psychiatrist for some period immediately after her marriage, mostly as a result of her distress. The shawl was eventually furnished and the Dempseys paid Swensen, with the understanding that this was not to prejudice any claim they might have. The shawl itself is an excellent piece of work and has been appraised as having a value at least equal to the amount

189

paid for it ($500). The Dempseys are nevertheless outraged and have brought suit against Swensen, demanding damages. We represent Swensen. It seems clear that Swensen was in breach. But is he liable for anything, and, if so, for what?

Problem 40

John P. Pryor File 976-1

National Honey, Inc. is a national franchising company that franchises local "Honey Bear" quick food shops. John P. Pryor executed a contract in standard form with National, in which Pryor's operation is referred to as "Local."

The contract provides in substance that Local will provide $20,000 in cash and will pay a percentage of gross profits to National. Local agrees to operate continuously along lines spelled out in detail and to use certain products and processes bought from National. National in return supplies (1) national advertising at minimum specified rates for various media; (2) dollar-matching local advertising; (3) a local advertising "kit," containing mats and other paraphernalia for advertising and public relations; (4) an exclusive right to use the Honey Bear trademarks and trade names and sell its products in a specified area — Carr Harbour and Chapelapolis in this case; (5) certain discounts on food and supplies not trademarked by National but purchased by it with national buying power. The contract also provides that if Local does not have $20,000 in cash, National will aid it in getting a part of the cash on loan and it did so in this case. Pryor provided National with $10,000 in cash of his own, and, on National's guarantee of his credit to the 42d Street City-Bank of New York, borrowed the additional $10,000 from that institution. National added a $200 "guarantor's charge" for this service. Local did not know it, but National also took "brokerage" from the bank at the rate of 1% of all monies loaned to customers provided through National.

After Pryor had been operating as a Local franchise for four months he discovered the brokerage mentioned above. He also discovered that advertising by National was substantially less than promised during the previous six months. He is beginning to make money in the business now and feels it will get better and better. But he is also uncertain about National and wants to consider the possibilities open to him. He cautions us that he is afraid National might terminate his franchise — there are rumors among franchisees that National has done so at the first sign of any Local backbone — and he wants nothing said to National at this point.

Please consider the remedies available to him and the scope and measure of each, as well as defenses and tactical considerations. What do you recommend?

Problem 41

Williams v. Pure Life Ins. Co.

When Williams was 18 years old, he purchased a policy of insurance from Pure Life Ins. Company. The policy as issued provided for payments of $100 per month in the event of total disability incurred while the policy was paid up and a waiver of any further premiums due during a period of total disability. When Williams was 48 years old, he became totally disabled within the meaning of the policy. Upon proof of this, Pure began making monthly payments. Pure paid out $200 a month until last year, computing this by doubling the $100 per month payment promised in the written policy. The doubling was done by a clerk, who mistakenly read the double indemnity portion of the policy to apply on disability coverage as well as death benefit coverage. Pure discovered this error and wrote Williams, requesting a return of the mistaken payments and interest. This amounted to the principal sum of $10,200.

Williams wrote back saying that the original understanding was that the policy would pay $200, that was the deal he had with the agent. He had some old letters and receipts photographically reproduced and sent them to Pure to show his original agreement. It was true that the original agreement, if these documents were indicative, was probably for a $200 monthly disability payment. (However, the premiums had been set at a level appropriate only to the $100 level. Had he paid premiums at a level appropriate to the $200 disability payment, these would have amounted to the sum of $2 per month more than he paid.)

Pure responded by denying any such agreement and renewed its demand for back payment. Williams wrote once more, reiterating his earlier statements and adding, "I don't have the money anyway. What do you think I'm living on?" To this letter Pure responded with a threat to cut off further monthly payments as a means of collecting the debt. Williams has called you and you have called at his home to hear everything first hand.

You are now considering tactics as well as substantive and procedural problems. You are considering, among other things, whether to bring an action against Pure or whether to await its actions. The statute of limitations provides a three-year limitation "for relief on the ground of fraud or mistake; the cause of action, in such cases, shall not be deemed to have accrued until the discovery by the aggrieved party of the facts constituting the fraud or mistake."

What are your ideas on tactics and procedure? How do you rate your chances?

191

Problem 42

Yancy v. Landers

Landers owned a large tract of land in Lancaster. By contract dated April 1, he agreed to sell, and Young R. Yancy agreed to buy, some 250 acres of this land at a price of $2,000 per acre, for a total of $500,000. Yancy and Landers walked over the land and Yancy understood that the purchase was to cover, within the 250 acres, a substantial tract of land lying on a hill with a beautiful view. This was important to him because he intended to build an exclusive residential area and it was obvious that the hillside and top were the most desirable parts of the acreage. It later turned out that the deed description included none of the hillside or hilltop land. Yancy contends that the agreement reached when they were walking on the land clearly was to cover the hill; Landers denies this and says the deed accurately describes the land agreed upon.

Before the mistake was discovered by either party, Yancy began doing some grading on the hilltop, preparatory to building some houses. Landers discovered this and demanded that he stop, since in Landers's view, the land belonged to Landers and grading destroyed the natural beauty of the land, which he wanted to keep and to leave to his grandchildren.

Yancy refused to stop and Landers secured a TRO in state court against Yancy. Representing Yancy, we appeared on his behalf and urged that the TRO be dissolved because he was owner, and asked for reformation of the deed, since a survey has now shown that the hill is clearly not included in the deed description. Alternatively we have prayed for an award based upon the value of Yancy's work on the land. He estimates that his labor, machinery rental, etc. would be valued at no less than $10,000. He also says the land is improved by the grading, since whoever owns the land will be better prepared to build on it now. He estimates that the value of the land is improved by at least $5,000. Landers filed a response to this answer, (1) demanding a jury trial on the ground that title is in issue and saying that the court should keep the injunction in effect until a separate jury trial on the title can be held; (2) denying any improvement in value of the land, saying that the grading had marred its scenic and natural beauty and demanding $5,000 damages to be assessed in the jury trial (if there is one) for the cost of replacing soil and forestalling erosion; (3) denying that there were grounds for reformation and demanding a rescission of the whole deal.

We represent Yancy. Please prepare a memo on the status of his claims and of Landers's claim against him.

———————————

Problem 43

Urbino Mall, Inc. v. Winborne Stores, Inc.

Urbino Mall, Inc. is a corporation formed to build, develop and lease a "mall" type shopping center. It completed its Urban Mall four years ago, at which time it had already agreed on leases for 100% of its space. The leases all provided a guarantee of no less than 3,000 parking spaces for the customers or invitees of the tenants. It also promised the ratio of parking space to building space would not be diminished, i.e., that if store space increased, parking spaces would increase in at least the same ratio as existed when the mall opened.

Within two years, it was clear that the mall was not a success, perhaps because it was a town-center mall rather than a suburban one. Urbino Mall, Inc. had lost two tenants to bankruptcy, and its own income was seriously in jeopardy because some of its rental was a percentage of the gross of some tenants, but only after those tenants had gross sales of $500,000 or more. Most tenants were not grossing that much; traffic was light, and both landlord and tenants were finding the situation difficult. So was the Pure Life Ins. Co., which had financed the building of the mall.

After some discussions with Pure, Urbino decided to try to get a large discount store in the mall hoping to vitalize the business of all its tenants. For this purpose, Urbino entered into negotiations with Winborne Stores, Inc., the corporate operator of a large chain of discount houses. Winborne and Urbino entered into an agreement. Urbino, with financing guaranteed by Pure Ins. Co., would build an additional wing on the store and provide no less than 100,000 square feet of store space for Winborne, who in turn agreed to pay a substantial rental. The agreement also provided that Urbino would build an additional parking facility adjacent to the new wing and provide spaces for an additional 800 cars.

With finances provided by Pure, Urbino began work on the new wing and on the parking lot. The wing was finished in due time, as was the lot. Winborne, as provided in the lease, deposited $10,000 with Urbino upon completion and began to prepare for moving in. At this point, and before Winborne moved in, a large portion of the parking lot adjacent to the Mall, including a large portion of that just completed to comply with the Winborne agreement, was condemned by the City. Its purpose was to implement a program of that would clear "urban blight" areas, build a small park, and widen a highway. Winborne, on discovering this, immediately notified Urbino that it regarded Urbino in breach, since Urbino could not furnish the lot as prescribed. Winborne also took the position that the lease was terminated for breach and that it was entitled to recover its deposit.

193

Urbino at first attempted to negotiate, but has now consulted our firm, because Winborne has remained adamant. An initial conversation with Urbino's manager, Joan Finian, indicates that the parking lot construction probably cost, apart from the new wing on the mall itself, at least $8,000. Urbino wants to get someone in the new wing, hopefully Winborne, and any delay is deadly. Finian concedes, however, that many retailers regard the parking space commitment as a very serious part of the agreement. She says it would adversely and seriously affect the gross sales of Winborne since these spaces cannot be provided, but that she and her company are willing to reduce the Winborne rent substantially if need be. Have we got anything to bargain with? Can we keep Winborne in there? What other lines of development are possible?

Problem 44

First Bank & Trust Co. of Charlesville v. Mott

Matthew Gottlieb Mott worked for many years in a responsible position, first as a teller, and later as an officer, at the First Bank. Two years ago, a bank audit revealed, for the first time, that there were serious shortages dating back twenty years. For 18 months, auditors and investigators worked on the case and eventually discovered that the source of the shortages was the embezzlement by Mott, which had taken place over a long period of time. The total shortages were determined to be $133,000. However, those actually traceable to Mott amounted to only about $100,000. The other shortages may have been due to Mott's extremely adroit techniques in embezzlement — it was shown that he used several different devices — or they may have been due to embezzlement by others. No other embezzlement has been identified, however. Mott died, probably by suicide, about six months ago. He cannot, therefore, be questioned by the usual authorities.

What was apparently Mott's first embezzlement, some twenty years ago, involved the amount of.$1,000. A few days after that embezzlement occurred, Mott opened a bank account for $1,000 in the Valley Bank of Charlesville. Other than the coincidence of those two events, there is nothing to indicate that the embezzlement and the bank account are related. Three months later, a similar pair of events occurred, this time with $2,500. The $3,500 bank account thus established, Mott purchased a single premium term life policy for $2,500, a policy that will now pay the sum of $50,000. The named beneficiary is Mott's wife, Irene.

During the twenty years between the first embezzlement and the suicide, Mott maintained the bank account in Valley Bank, but no other pair of coincidences occurred with respect to that account. That is, no deposit occurred in the Valley Bank that bears any temporal or quantitative relationship to the embezzle-ments that have been identified as occurring during those years. The bank account dropped at one point to a low of about $10. At Mott's death it contained $5,000. A counterpart savings account in the same bank, which was created by transfers from the bank account and bears the same account number except for a prefix indicating a savings account rather than a checking account, held some $15,000 at his death.

We represent the bank. What remedies has the bank? What immediate action should be taken, if any?

Problem 45

Ferrell v. Slocum

Ferrell wished to erect two small commercial buildings for an investment. For this purpose, he sought two vacant lots, not necessarily together. He heard that Slocum owned two lots, which in fact adjoined one another, and he approached Slocum about buying these. Ferrell hoped to buy two lots from a single owner for a better price than if he purchased two lots from two different owners. As it turned out, he was able to get Slocum's price down somewhat on this basis.

Ferrell had looked at the zoning maps of the town before he began searching for lots. One of the Slocum lots was on the corner of Wettach and Aycock Streets. The other was adjacent to this, but faced only on Aycock Street. Ferrell remembered that all of the lots facing Wettach Street were zoned for commercial buildings. He was not sure, however, about Aycock, and he asked Slocum about this. Slocum told him, yes, the Aycock street lot was also zoned commercial. This was not true, but it accorded with Ferrell's memory, and he did not check it. What Ferrell did not know was that the City of Chapelapolis was in the process of re-zoning Wettach Street to residential. In fact the re-zoning was completed before Ferrell purchased.

Ferrell and Slocum eventually reached agreement on the sale of the two lots for $50,000. The price was allocated $30,000 to the corner lot and $20,000 to the Aycock Street lot. The two lots were to be conveyed at different times because Slocum had a tenant in a small building on the Aycock Street lot whose lease did not expire until May. In accord with the contract, Slocum conveyed the Wettach Street lot on March 1, accepting the payment of $30,000 at that time. He conveyed the Aycock Street lot on April 15, accepting the balance of the contract price at that time.

In July, Ferrell discovered that the Aycock Street lot had never been zoned commercial, but had always been residential. He discovered that the lots with

195

residential zoning were valued at only around $15,000 each. Had they been zoned commercial, they would have been worth close to the price he paid for them.

Ferrell called on Slocum in mid-August. He told Slocum he wanted to call the deal off, and would give Slocum a deed if Slocum would return the money. Slocum said he wanted to do the right thing, and would think it over. A couple of days later, Slocum told Ferrell he had decided the only right thing to do was to stand by his deals. Consequently, he refused to return the money.

Ferrell considered this matter further. In December he wrote Slocum a formal letter, again offering to return the land and demanding return of the money. Ferrell also stated that if Slocum would not agree, Ferrell would have no choice but to sue for damages. Slocum did not answer the letter and Ferrell has retained our firm to represent him against Slocum.

Preliminary evaluation of the case suggests that we are apt to have conflicting evidence on the issue of Slocum's scienter. Please consider the remedies we may claim and recommend an approach to the remedies side of the case. Prepare to back your strategy or recommendation.

Problem 46

Montoya v. Vukovik

Twenty years ago, Tom and June Vukovik opened the Town Club, a restaurant and bar on the 16th floor of a building in downtown Chapelapolis. The business was organized so that only members of the club and their guests could enjoy the facilities. There was a membership fee (paid annually), a smaller monthly charge, and then regular menu and drink prices. During this time, the club operated smoothly and very profitably for the Vukoviks, who in form were employees, but who in fact had conceived and operated the whole thing.

Members during this period were always businessmen and no one else ever applied. One room was reserved for men only, but in other rooms, men could bring women guests. Three years ago, a lawyer, Helen Montoya, applied for membership. She was denied membership on the ground that she was a woman and that the club was intended for male membership only. After some bitter exchanges, the Vukoviks agreed to put it to a vote of the members. The members after reasonable notice and a full discussion, voted approximately 75% to 20% (with 5% absent) against admission of women.

Ms. Montoya then filed suit for damages under a state statute which provided that "all places of public accommodation shall be open without discrimination and shall serve all customers equally. . . . " There were a number of procedural points involved, and eventually the trial judge, after hearings, ruled in favor of the Vukoviks, holding that the statute had no application because the club was a bona fide private club. The case was appealed, and there were briefs and arguments in the intermediate court of appeal and later in the Supreme Court of the State. The state Supreme Court held that the club was not a bona fide club and that it was subject to the statute.

On remand, the trial judge entered a judgment for damages in the sum of $10, and Ms. Montoya again appealed. The intermediate appellate court held that Ms. Montoya, though not suffering pecuniary loss, was nevertheless entitled to substantial and not merely nominal damages. The Supreme Court of the state denied certiorari and the case was remanded to the trial court for entry of a judgment for substantial damages.

The trial judge entered a judgment of $1,000, but denied Ms. Montoya's motion for reasonable attorneys' fees, which she claimed in the amount of $10,-000. The trial judge also refused to impose punitive damages. Ms. Montoya again appealed, and after an argument in the intermediate court of appeals, the Supreme Court of the state granted certiorari to determine whether attorneys' fees and punitive damages should be awarded against the Vukoviks. On what basis should attorneys' fees be granted or denied in this case? Punitive damages?

Problem 47

Le Clef v. Windsor

Eloise Buffet grew up in the state of Lincoln. Twenty years ago, she was a famous movie star. She married Senator Stone of Lincoln in a dramatic and well-publicized courtship and wedding, and the couple were more or less constantly in the news. They had two unusually attractive children and Stone was considered a presidential candidate very likely to win an election, but he died of cancer eight or nine years ago.

Five or six years ago, Buffet, still in the news, but retired from public life, married Jean Paul Le Clef, a French painter of considerable renown and took his name. Unfortunately for her, Eloise Buffet Le Clef had fired the public imagination. Although she sought privacy, it was quite difficult for her to attain it. Photographers and writers constantly sought interviews, which were always refused. Some, however, followed her constantly with long-range lenses and sophisticated audio equipment.

197

One Windsor, a professional news and feature photographer, has been constantly following Le Clef for months, taking pictures of her in public places and attempting to get close for shots of her or her children at close range. He has at times touched her, talked to her, and shouted at her. Occasionally he has made threats. He has published one or two photographs so obtained. Once, disguised as a waiter, he penetrated a party which Le Clef attended and was able to photograph her in a swim suit.

Mrs. Le Clef has hired body guards, but to little avail. She consults a lawyer for whom you work. Assume that there are no criminal law solutions or that the criminal law solutions are unacceptable. You sit in on the client conference. What matters should you consider?

Problem 48

Malley v. Amontilato Hotel Corp.

Amontilato Hotel Corporation is your client. Amontilato owns and operates a large number of hotels in 58 different cities of the United States and seven other countries. In addition, it operates some related enterprises, including motels and other special places of accommodation.

Amontilato owns and operates the Park Lake Hotel in the City of Park Lake. The entire area, comprising two counties with Park Lake at the center, is a major tourist area, featuring luxury hotels and luxury recreation. Amontilato overbooks rooms at all its hotels in a deliberate policy of keeping rooms occupied at the maximum level. Very often cancellations or no-shows balance the overbooking. When this does not happen, Amontilato managers have standing arrangements with other nearby hotels or motels to take the overbooked Amontilato guests. Where Amontilato hotels have been paid in advance for a night's charge as a guarantee of arrival, and the guest is forced to accept another hotel because of over-booking, the Amontilato managers usually arrange with the substitute hotel to make no charge to the guest and to accept a coupon from Amontilato as the guest's payment. The substitute hotel or motel then bills Amontilato its regular room rate, or sometimes, its room rate with a discount. Thus Amontilato hotels sometimes make an additional profit when they overbook because the guest pays one rate while the hotel is able to get a substitute room at a cheaper rate.

The Park Lake area hotels and motels belong to an association for the pursuit of common interests. This association performs various acts of neutral publicity, answering queries and so on. The Amontilato hotel in Park Lake has an arrangement with the Lakeside Hotel for receiving any oversells that the Amontilato hotel, Park Lake, may have. This is a profitable arrangement for Amontilato. However, oversells by Amontilato, which commands national prestige, have

198

adverse effects on all other operators (except Lakeside, since Amontilato's over-sells are always channelled to Lakeside).

James Malley booked a room with Park Lake, the Amontilato hotel, and prepaid the first night's charge to guarantee the room. Nevertheless, when he and his wife arrived, they were told the hotel had no room for them and they could accept a room, without additional charge for the first night, at Lakeside. Malley refused to do this, drove fifty miles and found a small "cabin" with maid service in the same general luxury area. Malley paid $160 a day for this accommodation which was $40 a day higher than the Park Lake charge. They stayed two weeks. Malley sued. The Park Lake Association (the trade association) filed an amicus brief in support of Malley's claim, and the trial judge awarded a total of $4,000. Amontilato's local lawyers have been instructed to lodge an appeal. You are in the general counsel's office and are asked to summarize, in preparation for a brief, the elements of damages that might be recovered and prepare any argumentation that occurs to you.

Problem 49

Palmer v. Vickers Industries, Inc.

Vickers Industries operates a plant on Foundry Avenue. One of its plant managers, Allen, became aware that a machine used in the plant would occasionally blow out excessive steam through a vent. The vent released the steam to the outside at sidewalk level by means of a horizontal pipe which penetrated the brick wall of the factory about three feet above ground level. Had the machine been working safely, the amount of steam would have been so small that it would have vaporized by the time it reached the outside; but as Allen knew, the eruption of steam was increasing and was a serious threat to pedestrians outside. Allen and financial officers of the company decided not to repair the machine or to redirect the vent. Instead they constructed a small shield or hood over the vent, with the intention of directing the steam downward and thus minimizing its potential for harming a pedestrian.

Another officer of the company, Branson, knew of the steam danger. He was on the walk near the steam vent one day as a pedestrian, Palmer, walked close to the vent. At that moment, Branson heard a gurgling noise which was associated with a steam eruption. He reacted quickly, pushing Palmer away from the vent. Unfortunately, Palmer, surprised by the push, lost his balance and fell into the street. A delivery truck operated by Cimino, a driver for the Vickers company, ran over him. Cimino said he was only a few feet from Palmer when

199

he fell into the street and was unable to stop or even hit the brakes. Palmer was seriously and permanently injured and suffers partial paralysis.

After suit was filed in this case, Vickers did two things which a jury could find amounted to a cover-up attempt. First, it transferred Allen to another city, and second it "lost" all documents relating to the machinery and to Allen's modification. The trial judge admitted evidence of these acts over Vickers' objections.

Palmer's claims for medical expense, lost wages, and pain and suffering were submitted to the jury, which found in Palmer's favor, assessing damages at $1,200,000. The jury also assessed punitive damages in the sum of $1,000,000 against Vickers, and $10,000 against Allen. No punitive award was made against Branson. Vickers appeals the punitive award only. Is the evidence sufficient to warrant a punitive award or should the punitive portion of the judgment be reversed?

Problem 50[5]

United Citrus Workers vs. Citrus Growers
Cooperative

A new problem has surfaced in connection with the agreement between the United Citrus Workers and the Citrus Growers Cooperative (recently formalized by the area citrus growers) about health insurance for the workers and their dependents. Lydia Muniz has again provided us with the information, but has indicated that part of the problem is access to information. We must verify the details as best we can.

The agreement between the workers and the growers provided that the contributions of the growers will be tied to annual profits of the growers. In negotiating the initial agreement, the growers' contributions were based on past financial statements from which the parties estimated future profits and anticipated contributions by the growers to the health insurance fund.

Unfortunately, the growers have reported to the United Citrus Workers that profits have fallen off over the past year and in accordance with the agreement, the growers' contributions to the fund will be cut. To the extent the growers' contributions are decreased, payroll deductions from the workers are increased.

---

[5] See Problem 6-10 above.

Muniz has reason to believe that the growers have had a more profitable year, evidenced by major purchases of new equipment and rumored increases in salaries for supervisors (who are not associated with the United Citrus Workers).

The United Citrus Workers are becoming extremely frustrated. This latest development follows an earlier problem that the workers were able to resolve with the growers. That problem involved poor internal management by the growers. One of the growers had failed to make its full contributions, resulting once again in higher payroll deductions from the workers themselves. That problem has now been resolved, and the workers have been made whole, but the workers are extremely suspicious now. They do not believe that the recent reports of lower profits are accurate and want to know what they can do to protect themselves from either poor management or false reporting by the growers.

It appears that the current agreement does not provide a means for the workers to review the basis for the growers' calculations of profit. Ms. Muniz and I have an appointment early next week to discuss possible remedies. Please review the possibilities and report back to me in time for our appointment.

Problem 51

Frank v. Chanson

Frank the Furrier is an exclusive fur salon in Megalopolis. The salon sells furs on a retail basis to a wealthy, cosmopolitan, clientele of men and women. The owners of Frank the Furrier, Harry and Felice Frank, live on the upper floor of the spacious brownstone that houses both their business and their home. Frank the Furrier sells coats and stoles of both trapped and cage-bred animals.

Human Friends of Furry Animals ("HUFFA") is a loosely organized group that is dedicated to the protection of animals; more specifically, the group directs its attention to preventing the commercial exploitation of animals. For the past several days, HUFFA sympathizers have gathered outside Frank the Furrier and engaged in the following activities: (1) chanted slogans and carried placards that read, "Fur is Dead," "Fur is found on beautiful animals and ugly people," "Buy a Fur and Slip into Something Dead," "You can never wear a brand new fur," and "Fur Hurts"; (2) attempted to prevent the salon's customers from entering the building; and (3) obstructed the parking places immediately in front of the salon by standing three and four abreast in the street immediately in front of the building.

Pierre Chanson has, for a number of years, been active in animal rights activities and is the leading spokesperson for HUFFA. He has been seen daily at the recent demonstrations.

201

Part II

Yesterday, when the Franks came down from their apartment and attempted to open the front doors of the salon, they discovered that the door locks had been jammed shut with epoxy glue.

The Davis Firm
From: Charles Davis

Harry and Felice Frank, the owners of Frank the Furrier, have provided us with the above information, which is true to the best of their knowledge. They claim that the demonstrators have trespassed on their property and that the chanting and placards have embarrassed their clients and substantially cut their sales.

Once we have explored the possible solutions to these problems, the Franks also want us to look into the possibility of bringing criminal charges against Pierre Chanson for damage to the doors of the salon. They believe Chanson has been involved in other animal rights activities and might even be connected to groups that have engaged in criminal activities in other states.

In addition to the disruption to their business, both of the Franks are extremely upset and feel that they cannot escape the turmoil that the demonstrators have introduced into their lives.

They want us to stop the demonstrators from blocking the entrance to the salon. They also want us to ensure that the few parking places in front of the salon, which are at a premium in Megalopolis, are not obstructed. Finally, they want to know what kind of damages they might recover from the demonstrators for the economic harm and emotional turmoil they have been subjected to.

The Center for the Protection of Animal Rights
From: Roberta Shields

Pierre Chanson has consulted us in connection with the recent activities of HUFFA related to the Frank the Furrier salon. We have agreed to represent Chanson and HUFFA in connection with any action the Franks might bring.

Last night, Chanson was served with a temporary restraining order forbidding Chanson and any member of HUFFA, as well as any of Chanson's associates in any other animal rights organizations, from harassing the Furrier customers, from blocking parking spaces, from blocking entrance into the salon, and "from otherwise interfering with the salon's business."

The Davis firm represents the Franks. Chanson is concerned about a number of things. First, though he is the "spokesperson" for HUFFA, he does not have a membership list, and has little way of contacting the various people who have been demonstrating. Secondly, he read in the paper that someone had jammed the front doors of the salon shut with epoxy glue, and he knows nothing about who might have done that. He is concerned, though, that he might be a suspect, since he has been connected with animal rights groups that have openly engaged in similar tactics. He himself has never used such tactics. We can deal with that later, but for now, we need to know the following things:

1. Can we get the TRO dissolved?

2. Can we prevent a preliminary or permanent injunction?

APPENDIX OF CASES

LINCOLN NATIONAL LIFE INSURANCE CO.
v.
THE BROWN SCHOOLS, INC.
Texas Court of Appeals, 1988
757 S.W.2d 411

DRAUGHN, Justice . . . .

The essential facts are undisputed. Lincoln provided insurance for medical, hospital coverage and other benefits to Texas A & M University employees and their dependents. The policy covered Mason Rittman, an employee of Texas A & M, and his daughter, Rebecca. Rebecca became eligible to receive benefits under this policy when she was hospitalized in a facility owned and operated by appellee Brown. The policy obligated Lincoln to pay Mr. Rittman benefits for a twenty-four month period during which Rebecca received treatment from Brown. Rittman assigned these benefits due him under the policy to Brown on an assignment form issued by Brown. Lincoln, in compliance with this assignment, paid the money due under the policy directly to Brown. Although the policy expired in July 1983, Lincoln erroneously continued to pay Brown benefits for treatment rendered on behalf of Rittman until February 1984. The overpayments were due solely to Lincoln's mistake. Brown was unaware of the policy terms, and made no representations to induce Lincoln to continue the payments beyond the policy terms.

The trial court granted Brown's motion for summary judgment and denied restitution to Lincoln National for the overpayments. The court also granted Lincoln's motion for partial summary judgment against it's insured, Rittman, and ordered the cause against Rittman set for trial on certain disputed facts.

The issue to be decided in this case is simple: Is an insurer entitled to restitution for overpayment made to a hospital on behalf of its insured, where the overpayment was due solely to insurer's mistake as to the amount payable under the policy? The resolution of this issue, however, is not so simple. It involves competing equitable principles, and because of its unique fact situations is a case of first impression in Texas.

204

Generally, any party who has paid funds due to a mistake of fact is entitled to restitution, if the receiving party has not materially changed its position in reliance on the payment. [ ]. Restitution in such cases is grounded on the equitable principle that one who, under influence of mistake of fact, has paid money to another not entitled to it, ought not to suffer unconscionable loss nor unjustly enrich the other. See RESTATEMENT OF RESTITUTION § 1 (1937).

Notwithstanding the general rule, there is no universal principle that one who makes a mistake in paying another is always entitled to restitution. If there is some other reason which makes it unequitable or inexpedient, restitution will be denied the paying party. See RESTATEMENT OF RESTITUTION ch. 2 Introductory Notes (1937). Two interrelated exceptions to restitution under such circumstances have developed. One is indicated in the general rule as stated in the Bryan case: If the receiving party has materially changed its position in reliance on the payment, restitution is precluded.

In the case before us, a strong argument could be made that the appellee, Brown, materially changed its position by rendering medical and hospitalization services to the insured, in reliance on continued payments by the insurer under the assignment of insurance benefits. However, the trial court in its summary judgment favoring Brown specifically found there was no evidence that Brown changed its position to its detriment in reliance upon the mistaken payments by Lincoln . . . . However, . . . we find without regard to this issue, another equitable basis for affirmance of the summary judgment denying restitution in this case.

The Nebraska Supreme Court addressed a situation essentially similar to this case in Federated Mutual Insurance Company v. Good Samaritan Hospital, 191 Neb. 212, 214 N.W.2d 493 (1974). That court concluded the hospital was under no duty to make restitution to the insurance company where the overpayments were due solely to the insurance company's mistake. Just as in this case, the benefits were paid directly to the hospital because of a right-to-payment agreement executed by the insured. The court held in favor of the hospital, finding the insurance carrier was not entitled to restitution because (1) the overpayment was made due solely to the insurer's mistake and lack of care; (2) the hospital made no misrepresentations to induce the payment; and (3) the hospital acted in good faith without prior knowledge of the mistake. The court also found there was no evidence that the hospital changed its position to its detriment in reliance upon the mistaken payment. The parties there, as here, stipulated to these facts. The court grounded its decision on the rationale of the RESTATEMENT OF RESTITUTION § 14(1) (1937):

> A creditor of another or one having a lien on another's property who has received from a third person any benefit in discharge of the debt or lien, is under no duty to make restitution therefor, although the discharge was given by mistake of the transferor as to his interests or duties, if the transferee made no misrepresentations and did not have notice of the transferor's mistake.

We agree with this approach and find it applicable to the facts of this case. Here, Lincoln knew its own policy payment provisions, but failed to notify Brown as to these provisions; and Lincoln alone made the mistake of paying beyond its responsibility. Brown made no misrepresentations, had no knowledge or notice of appellant's mistake, extended valuable services based on the assignment of payment by the insured, was not unjustly enriched, and simply had no reason to suspect that any of the payments for services rendered were in error. In the normal course of such business, the hospital has no responsibility to determine if an insurance carrier is properly tending to its business.

Lincoln makes a spirited argument for recovery based on the law of contractual assignments, and the general rule that one who has paid money to another contracting party is entitled to restitution. Lincoln asserts that a special relationship exists between it and Brown because of the assignment of the policy benefits by its insured to Brown; that by entering into such a contractual relationship with Lincoln, Brown had every right to inquire of Lincoln regarding the terms of the policy. As stated, we have no real quarrel with the general principle of restitution and strict contractual assignment law as stated by appellant, but we do not view this as an issue to be determined strictly by the law relevant to assignment of contracts. The assignment in this case was not a formal assignment of the insurance contract to Brown. Rather, it was the usual insurance benefits assignment in hospital cases which merely facilitated the payment of the insured's debt to his creditor Brown. Regardless of the contractual vehicle which created it, the problem is one covered by equitable principles of restitution.

These principles make a distinction between mistaken insurance payments made to the insured and those made to an innocent third party creditor of the insured. A critical element mandating restitution in mistake-of-fact payment cases is unjust enrichment. Some authorities regard it as prerequisite for restitution. See Annotation, Right of Insurer Under Health Or Hospitalization Policy To Restitution of Payments Made Under Mistake, 79 A.L.R.3d 1113, 1116 (1977). Here the appellee extended medical services and was paid. There was no unjust enrichment. We regard Brown's position as analogous to that of a bona fide purchaser. It innocently paid value (medical services) for title to the money it received and is, thereby, under no duty to restore it to the insurer. This approach represents the theoretical basis for the Restatement's position on innocent third-party creditors in such situations. RESTATEMENT OF RESTITUTION § 13(a) comment a; § 14(1) comment a (1937); See also Federated Mutual v. Good Samaritan Hospital, 214 N.W.2d at 494-95.

Being in the position of a bona fide purchaser for value, appellee was not required to show a change of position in reliance on the overpayment. This is so because the doctrine of bona fide purchaser is grounded on an assumption of a change of position. It has been suggested that the defense of bona fide purchaser "may be nothing more than an instance of change of position grown doctrinaire." 45 Harv.L.Rev. 1342 (1931-32). It follows that had appellee known of the policy's monetary limitations, or had it received money in excess of services rendered, the result would be different.

There is no moral issue involved here. This exception to the general rule allowing restitution for money paid under mistake of fact is simply an equitable limitation that places the loss, as between two innocent parties, on the one who has created the situation and was in the best position to have avoided it. Appellant, possessing the policy and the knowledge of its terms, made the mistake and, as between it and the appellee hospital, it must bear the loss.

We affirm the summary judgment.

Notes

Would the insurer in *Lincoln National* be permitted to recover against either the purchaser of the policy which was mistakenly overpaid or against the beneficiary who received the additional medical benefits?

LAKE RIVER CORP. v. CARBORUNDUM CO.
769 F.2d 1284 (7th Cir. 1985)

POSNER, Circuit Judge.

. . . . Carborundum manufactures "Ferro Carbo," an abrasive powder used in making steel. To serve its midwestern customers better, Carborundum made a contract with Lake River by which the latter agreed to provide distribution services in its warehouse in Illinois. Lake River would receive Ferro

207

Carbo in bulk from Carborundum, "bag" it, and ship the bagged product to Carborundum's customers. The Ferro Carbo would remain Carborundum's property until delivered to the customers.

Carborundum insisted that Lake River install a new bagging system to handle the contract. In order to be sure of being able to recover the cost of the new system ($89,000) and make a profit of 20 percent of the contract price, Lake River insisted on the following minimum-quantity guarantee: In consideration of the special equipment [i.e., the new bagging system] to be acquired and furnished by LAKE-RIVER for handling the product, CARBO-RUNDUM shall, during the initial three-year term of this Agreement, ship to LAKE-RIVER for bagging a minimum quantity of [22,500 tons]. If, at the end of the three- year term, this minimum quantity shall not have been shipped, LAKE-RIVER shall invoice CARBORUNDUM at the then prevailing rates for the difference between the quantity bagged and the minimum guaranteed. If Carborundum had shipped the full minimum quantity that it guaranteed, it would have owed Lake River roughly $533,000 under the contract.

After the contract was signed in 1979, the demand for domestic steel, and with it the demand for Ferro Carbo, plummeted, and Carborundum failed to ship the guaranteed amount. When the contract expired late in 1982, Carborundum had shipped only 12,000 of the 22,500 tons it had guaranteed. Lake River had bagged the 12,000 tons and had billed Carborundum for this bagging, and Carborundum had paid, but by virtue of the formula in the minimum-guarantee clause Carborundum still owed Lake River $241,000--the contract price of $533,000 if the full amount of Ferro Carbo had been shipped, minus what Carborundum had paid for the bagging of the quantity it had shipped.

When Lake River demanded payment of this amount, Carborundum refused, on the ground that the formula imposed a penalty. At the time, Lake River had in its warehouse 500 tons of bagged Ferro Carbo, having a market value of $269,000, which it refused to release unless Carborundum paid the $241,000 due under the formula. Lake River did offer to sell the bagged product and place the proceeds in escrow until its dispute with Carborundum over the enforceability of the formula was resolved, but Carborundum rejected the offer and trucked in bagged Ferro Carbo from the East to serve its customers in Illinois, at an additional cost of $31,000.

Lake River brought this suit for $241,000, which it claims as liquidated damages. Carborundum counterclaimed for the value of the bagged Ferro Carbo when Lake River impounded it and the additional cost of serving the customers affected by the impounding. The theory of the counterclaim is that the impounding was a conversion, and not as Lake River contends the assertion of a lien. The district judge, after a bench trial, gave judgment for both parties. Carborundum ended up roughly $42,000 to the good: $269,000 + $31,000 - $241,000 - $17,000, the last figure representing prejudgment interest on Lake River's damages. (We have rounded off all dollar figures to the nearest thousand.) Both parties have appealed.

The only issue that is not one of damages is whether Lake River had a valid lien on the bagged Ferro Carbo that it refused to ship to Carborundum's customers — that, indeed, it holds in its warehouse to this day. Although Ferro Carbo does not deteriorate with age, the domestic steel industry remains in the doldrums and the product is worth less than it was in 1982 when Lake River first withheld it. If Lake River did not have a valid lien on the product, then it converted it, and must pay Carborundum the $269,000 that the Ferro Carbo was worth back then. . . . .

Lake River has not been very specific about the type of lien it asserts. We think it best described as a form of artisan's lien, the "lien of the bailee, who does work upon or adds materials to chattels...." Restatement of Security § 61, comment on clause (a), at p. 165 (1941). Lake River was the bailee of the Ferro Carbo that Carborundum delivered to it, and it did work on the Ferro Carbo — bagging it, and also storing it (storage is a service, too). If Carborundum had refused to pay for the services that Lake River performed on the Ferro Carbo delivered to it, then Lake River would have had a lien on the Ferro Carbo in its possession, to coerce payment. [ ] But in fact, when Lake River impounded the bagged Ferro Carbo, Carborundum had paid in full for all bagging and storage services that Lake River had performed on Ferro Carbo shipped to it by Carborundum. The purpose of impounding was to put pressure on Carborundum to pay for services not performed, Carborundum having failed to ship the Ferro Carbo on which those services would have been performed.

Unlike a contractor who, having done the work contracted for without having been paid, may find himself in a box, owing his employees or suppliers money he does not have — money he was counting on from his customer — Lake River was the victim of a breach of a portion of the contract that remained entirely unexecuted on either side. Carborundum had not shipped the other 10,500 tons, as promised; but on the other hand Lake River had not had to bag those 10,500 tons, as it had promised. It is not as if Lake River had bagged those tons, incurring heavy costs that it expected to recoup from Carborundum, and then Carborundum had said, "Sorry, we won't pay you; go ahead and sue us."

A lien is strong medicine; it clogs up markets, as the facts of this case show. Its purpose is to provide an effective self-help remedy for one who has done work in expectation of payment and then is not paid. The vulnerable position of such a person gives rise to "the artisan's privilege of holding the balance for work done in the past." A lien is thus a device for preventing unjust enrichment — not for forcing the other party to accede to your view of a contract dispute. "The right to retain possession of the property to enforce a possessory lien continues until such time as the charges for such materials, labor and services are paid." [ ]. Since here the charges were paid before the lien was asserted, the lien was no good. . . . .

The hardest issue in the case is whether the formula in the minimum-guarantee clause imposes a penalty for breach of contract or is merely an effort to liquidate damages. Deep as the hostility to penalty clauses runs in the common law, [ ], we still might be inclined to question, if we thought ourselves free to do so, whether a modern court should refuse to enforce a penalty clause where the signator is a substantial corporation, well able to avoid improvident commitments. Penalty clauses provide an earnest of performance. The clause here enhanced Carborundum's credibility in promising to ship the minimum amount guaranteed by showing that it was willing to pay the full contract price even if it failed to ship anything. On the other side it can be pointed out that by raising the cost of a breach of contract to the contract breaker, a penalty clause increases the risk to his other creditors; increases (what is the same thing and more, because bankruptcy imposes "deadweight" social costs) the risk of bankruptcy; and could amplify the business cycle by increasing the number of bankruptcies in bad times, which is when contracts are most likely to be broken. But since little effort is made to prevent businessmen from assuming risks, these reasons are no better than makeweights.

A better argument is that a penalty clause may discourage efficient as well as inefficient breaches of contract. Suppose a breach would cost the promisee $12,000 in actual damages but would yield the promisor $20,000 in additional profits. Then there would be a net social gain from breach. After being fully compensated for his loss the promisee would be no worse off than if the contract had been performed, while the promisor would be better off by $8,000. But now suppose the contract contains a penalty clause under which the promisor if he breaks his promise must pay the promisee $25,000. The promisor will be discouraged from breaking the contract, since $25,000, the penalty, is greater than $20,000, the profits of the breach; and a transaction that would have increased value will be forgone.

On this view, since compensatory damages should be sufficient to deter inefficient breaches (that is, breaches that cost the victim more than the gain to the contract breaker), penal damages could have no effect other than to deter some efficient breaches. But this overlooks the earlier point that the willingness to agree to a penalty clause is a way of making the promisor and his promise credible and may therefore be essential to inducing some value-maximizing contracts to be made. It also overlooks the more important point that the parties (always assuming they are fully competent) will, in deciding whether to include a penalty clause in their contract, weigh the gains against the costs — costs that include the possibility of discouraging an efficient breach somewhere down the road — and will include the clause only if the benefits exceed those costs as well as all other costs.

On this view the refusal to enforce penalty clauses is (at best) paternalistic — and it seems odd that courts should display parental solicitude for large corporations. But however this may be, we must be on guard to avoid importing our own ideas of sound public policy into an area where our proper judicial role is more than usually deferential. The responsibility for making innovations in the common law of Illinois rests with the courts of Illinois, and not with the federal courts in Illinois. And like every other state, Illinois, untroubled by academic skepticism of the wisdom of refusing to enforce penalty clauses against sophisticated promisors, [ ], continues steadfastly to insist on the distinction between penalties and liquidated damages. [ ]. To be valid under Illinois law a liquidation of damages must be a reasonable estimate at the time of contracting of the likely damages from breach, and the need for estimation at that time must be shown by reference to the likely difficulty of measuring the actual damages from a breach of contract after the breach occurs. If damages would be easy to determine then, or if the estimate greatly exceeds a reasonable upper estimate of what the damages are likely to be, it is a penalty.

The distinction between a penalty and liquidated damages is not an easy one to draw in practice but we are required to draw it and can give only limited weight to the district court's determination. Whether a provision for damages is a penalty clause or a liquidated-damages clause is a question of law rather than fact . . . .

Mindful that Illinois courts resolve doubtful cases in favor of classification as a penalty, [ ], we conclude that the damage formula in this case is a penalty and not a liquidation of damages, because it is designed always to assure Lake River more than its actual damages. The formula — full contract price minus the amount already invoiced to Carborundum — is invariant to the gravity of the breach. When a contract specifies a single sum in damages for any and all breaches even though it is apparent that all are not of the same gravity, the specification is not a reasonable effort to estimate damages; and when in addition the fixed sum greatly exceeds the actual damages likely to be inflicted by a minor breach, its character as a penalty becomes unmistakable. This case is within the gravitational field of these principles even though the minimum-guarantee clause does not fix a single sum as damages.

Suppose to begin with that the breach occurs the day after Lake River buys its new bagging system for $89,000 and before Carborundum ships any Ferro Carbo. Carborundum would owe Lake River $533,000. Since Lake River would have incurred at that point a total cost of only $89,000, its net gain from the breach would be $444,000. This is more than four times the profit of $107,000 (20 percent of the contract price of $533,000) that Lake River expected to make from the contract if it had been performed: a huge windfall.

Next suppose (as actually happened here) that breach occurs when 55 percent of the Ferro Carbo has been shipped. Lake River would already have received $293,000 from Carborundum. To see what its costs then would have been (as estimated at the time of contracting), first subtract Lake River's anticipated profit on the contract of $107,000 from the total contract price of $533,000. The difference — Lake River's total cost of performance — is $426,000. Of this, $89,000 is the cost of the new bagging system, a fixed cost. The rest ($426,000-$89,000 = $337,000) presumably consists of variable costs that are roughly proportional to the amount of Ferro Carbo bagged; there is no indication of any other fixed costs. Assume, therefore, that if Lake River bagged 55 percent of the contractually agreed quantity, it incurred in doing so 55 percent of its variable costs, or $185,000. When this is added to the cost of the new bagging system, assumed for the moment to be worthless except in connection with the contract, the total cost of performance to Lake River is $274,000. Hence a breach that occurred after 55 percent of contractual performance was complete would be expected to yield Lake River a modest profit of $19,000 ($293,000 - $274,000). But now add the "liquidated damages" of $241,000 that Lake River claims, and the result is a total gain from the breach of $260,000, which is almost two and a half times the profit that Lake River expected to gain if there was no breach. And this ignores any use value or salvage value of the new bagging system, which is the property of Lake River — though admittedly it also ignores the time value of money; Lake River paid $89,000 for that system before receiving any revenue from the contract.

To complete the picture, assume that the breach had not occurred till performance was 90 percent complete. Then the "liquidated damages" clause would not be so one-sided, but it would be one-sided. Carborundum would have paid $480,000 for bagging. Against this, Lake River would have incurred its fixed cost of $89,000 plus 90 percent of its variable costs of $337,-000, or $303,000. Its total costs would thus be $392,000, and its net profit $88,000. But on top of this it would be entitled to "liquidated damages" of $53,000, for a total profit of $141,000 — more than 30 percent more than its expected profit of $107,000 if there was no breach.

The reason for these results is that most of the costs to Lake River of performing the contract are saved if the contract is broken, and this saving is not reflected in the damage formula. As a result, at whatever point in the life of the contract a breach occurs, the damage formula gives Lake River more than its lost profits from the breach — dramatically more if the breach occurs at the beginning of the contract; tapering off at the end, it is true. Still, over the interval between the beginning of Lake River's performance and nearly the end, the clause could be expected to generate profits ranging from 400 percent of the expected contract profits to 130 percent of those profits. And this is on the assumption that the bagging system has no value apart from the contract. If it were worth only $20,000 to Lake River, the range would be 434 percent to 150 percent.

Lake River argues that it would never get as much as the formula suggests, because it would be required to mitigate its damages. This is a dubious argument on several grounds. First, mitigation of damages is a doctrine of the law of court-assessed damages, while the point of a liquidated-damages clause is to substitute party assessment; and that point is blunted, and the certainty that liquidated-damages clauses are designed to give the process of assessing damages impaired, if a defendant can force the plaintiff to take less than the damages specified in the clause, on the ground that the plaintiff could have avoided some of them. It would seem therefore that the clause in this case should be read to eliminate any duty of mitigation, that what Lake River is doing is attempting to rewrite the clause to make it more reasonable, and that since actually the clause is designed to give Lake River the full damages it would incur from breach (and more) even if it made no effort to find a substitute use for the equipment that it bought to perform the contract, this is just one more piece of evidence that it is a penalty clause rather than a liquidated-damages clause. See Northwest Collectors, Inc. v. Enders, 74 Wash.2d 585, 594, 446 P.2d 200, 206 (1968).

But in any event mitigation would not mitigate the penal character of this clause. If Carborundum did not ship the guaranteed minimum quantity, the reason was likely to be — the reason was — that the steel industry had fallen on hard times and the demand for Ferro Carbo was therefore down. In these circumstances Lake River would have little prospect of finding a substitute contract that would yield it significant profits to set off against the full contract price, which is the method by which it proposes to take account of mitigation. At argument Lake River suggested that it might at least have been able to sell the new bagging equipment to someone for something, and the figure $40,000 was proposed. If the breach occurred on the first day when performance under the contract was due and Lake River promptly sold the bagging equipment for $40,000, its liquidated damages would fall to $493,000. But by the same token its costs would fall to $49,000. Its profit would still be $444,000, which as we said was more than 400 percent of its expected profit on the contract. The penal component would be unaffected. . . . .

We do not mean by this discussion to cast a cloud of doubt over the "take or pay" clauses that are a common feature of contracts between natural gas pipeline companies and their customers. Such clauses require the customer, in consideration of the pipeline's extending its line to his premises, to take a certain amount of gas at a specified price — and if he fails to take it to pay the full price anyway. The resemblance to the minimum - guarantee clause in the present case is obvious, but perhaps quite superficial. Neither party has mentioned take-or-pay clauses, and we can find no case where such a clause was even challenged as a penalty clause — though in one case it was argued that such a clause made the damages unreasonably low. [ ]. If, as appears not to be the case here but would often be the case in supplying natural gas, a supplier's fixed costs were a very large fraction of his total costs, a take-or-pay clause might well be a reasonable liquidation of damages. In the limit, if all the supplier's costs were incurred before he began supplying the customer, the contract revenues would be an excellent measure of the damages from breach. But in this case, the supplier (Lake River, viewed as a supplier of bagging services to Carborundum) incurred only a fraction of its costs before performance began, and the interruption of performance generated a considerable cost saving that is not reflected in the damage formula.

The fact that the damage formula is invalid does not deprive Lake River of a remedy. The parties did not contract explicitly with reference to the measure of damages if the agreed-on damage formula was invalidated, but all this means is that the victim of the breach is entitled to his common law damages. See, e.g., Restatement, Second, Contracts § 356, comment a (1981). In this case that would be the unpaid contract price of $241,000 minus the costs that Lake River saved by not having to complete the contract (the variable costs on the other 45 percent of the Ferro Carbo that it never had to bag). The case must be remanded to the district judge to fix these damages.

[Discussion of other damages issues is omitted.]

CAMPBELL SOUP CO. v. WENTZ
172 F.2d 80 (3d Cir. 1948)

Separate actions by the Campbell Soup Company against George B. Wentz and another and Walter M. Lojeski to enjoin further sale to others of carrots under contract to plaintiff and to compel specific performance of contract. From a judgment for the defendants, 75 F.Supp. 952, the plaintiff appeals.

GOODRICH, Circuit Judge.

These are appeals from judgments of the District Court denying equitable relief to the buyer under a contract for the sale of carrots. The defendants in No. 9648 are the contract sellers. The defendant in No. 9649 is the second purchaser of part of the carrots which are the subject matter of the contract.

The transactions which raise the issues may be briefly summarized. On June 21, 1947, Campbell Soup Company (Campbell), a New Jersey corporation, entered into a written contract with George B. Wentz and Harry T. Wentz, who are Pennsylvania farmers, for delivery by the Wentzes to Campbell of all the Chantenay red cored carrots to be grown on fifteen acres of the Wentz farm during the 1947 season. Where the contract was entered into does not appear. The contract provides, however, for delivery of the carrots at the Campbell plant in Camden, New Jersey. The prices specified in the contract ranged from $23 to $30 per ton according to the time of delivery. The contract price for January, 1948 was $30 a ton.

The Wentzes harvested approximately 100 tons of carrots from the fifteen acres covered by the contract. Early in January, 1948, they told a Campbell representative that they would not deliver their carrots at the contract price. The market price at that time was at least $90 per ton, and Chantenay red cored carrots were virtually unobtainable. The Wentzes then sold approximately 62 tons of their carrots to the defendant Lojeski, a neighboring farmer. Lojeski resold about 58 tons on the open market, approximately half to Campbell and the balance to other purchasers.

On January 9, 1948, Campbell, suspecting that Lojeski was selling it 'contract carrots,' refused to purchase any more, and instituted these suits against the Wentz brothers and Lojeski to enjoin further sale of the contract carrots to others, and to compel specific performance of the contract. The trial court denied equitable relief. We agree with the result reached, but on a different ground from that relied upon by the District Court.

. . . . A party may have specific performance of a contract for the sale of chattels if the legal remedy is inadequate. Inadequacy of the legal remedy

215

is necessarily a matter to be determined by an examination of the facts in each particular instance.

We think that on the question of adequacy of the legal remedy the case is one appropriate for specific performance. It was expressly found that at the time of the trial it was 'virtually impossible to obtain Chantenay carrots in the open market.' This Chantenay carrot is one which the plaintiff uses in large quantities, furnishing the seed to the growers with whom it makes contracts. It was not claimed that in nutritive value it is any better than other types of carrots. Its blunt shape makes it easier to handle in processing. And its color and texture differ from other varieties. The color is brighter than other carrots. The trial court found that the plaintiff failed to establish what proportion of its carrots is used for the production of soup stock and what proportion is used as identifiable physical ingredients in its soups. We do not think lack of proof on that point is material. It did appear that the plaintiff uses carrots in fifteen of its twenty-one soups. It also appeared that it uses these Chantenay carrots diced in some of them and that the appearance is uniform. The preservation of uniformity in appearance in a food article marketed throughout the country and sold under the manufacturer's name is a matter of considerable commercial significance and one which is properly considered in determining whether a substitute ingredient is just as good as the original.

The trial court concluded that the plaintiff had failed to establish that the carrots, 'judged by objective standards,' are unique goods. This we think is not a pure fact conclusion like a finding that Chantenay carrots are of uniform color. It is either a conclusion of law or of mixed fact and law and we are bound to exercise our independent judgment upon it. That the test for specific performance is not necessarily 'objective' is shown by the many cases in which equity has given it to enforce contracts for articles — family heirlooms and the like — the value of which was personal to the plaintiff.

Judged by the general standards applicable to determining the adequacy of the legal remedy we think that on this point the case is a proper one for equitable relief. There is considerable authority, old and new, showing liberality in the granting of an equitable remedy. We see no reason why a court should be reluctant to grant specific relief when it can be given without supervision of the court or other time-consuming processes against one who has deliberately broken his agreement. Here the goods of the special type contracted for were unavailable on the open market, the plaintiff had contracted for them long ahead in anticipation of its needs, and had built up a general reputation for its products as part of which reputation uniform appearance was important. We think if this were all that was involved in the case specific performance should have been granted.

The reason that we shall affirm instead of reversing with an order for specific performance is found in the contract itself. We think it is too hard a bargain and too one-sided an agreement to entitle the plaintiff to relief in a court of conscience. For each individual grower the agreement is made by filling in names and quantity and price on a printed form furnished by the buyer. This form has quite obviously been drawn by skilful draftsmen with the buyer's interests in mind.

Paragraph 2 provides for the manner of delivery. Carrots are to have their stalks cut off and be in clean sanitary bags or other containers approved by Campbell. This paragraph concludes with a statement that Campbell's determination of conformance with specifications shall be conclusive.

The defendants attack this provision as unconscionable. We do not think that it is, standing by itself. We think that the provision is comparable to the promise to perform to the satisfaction of another and that Campbell would be held liable if it refused carrots which did in fact conform to the specifications.

The next paragraph allows Campbell to refuse carrots in excess of twelve tons to the acre. The next contains a covenant by the grower that he will not sell carrots to anyone else except the carrots rejected by Campbell nor will he permit anyone else to grow carrots on his land. Paragraph 10 provides liquidated damages to the extent of $50 per acre for any breach by the grower. There is no provision for liquidated or any other damages for breach of contract by Campbell.

The provision of the contract which we think is the hardest is paragraph 9, set out in the margin.[6] It will be noted that Campbell is excused from accepting carrots under certain circumstances. But even under such circumstances the grower, while he cannot say Campbell is liable for failure to take the carrots, is not permitted to sell them elsewhere unless Campbell agrees. This is the kind of provision which the late Francis H. Bohlen would call 'carrying

---

[6] 'Grower shall not be obligated to deliver any Carrots which he is unable to harvest or deliver, nor shall Campbell be obligated to receive or pay for any Carrots which it is unable to inspect, grade, receive, handle, use or pack at or ship in processed form from its plants in Camden (1) because of any circumstance beyond the control of Grower or Campbell, as the case may be, or (2) because of any labor disturbance, work stoppage, slow-down, or strike involving any of Campbell's employees. Campbell shall not be liable for any delay in receiving Carrots due to any of the above contingencies. During periods when Campbell is unable to receive Grower's Carrots, Grower may with Campbell's written consent, dispose of his Carrots elsewhere. Grower may not, however, sell or otherwise dispose of any Carrots which he is unable to deliver to Campbell.'

217

a good joke too far.' What the grower may do with his product under the circumstances set out is not clear. He has covenanted not to store it anywhere except on his own farm and also not to sell to anybody else.

We are not suggesting that the contract is illegal. Nor are we suggesting any excuse for the grower in this case who has deliberately broken an agreement entered into with Campbell. We do think, however, that a party who has offered and succeeded in getting an agreement as tough as this one is, should not come to a chancellor and ask court help in the enforcement of its terms. That equity does not enforce unconscionable bargains is too well established to require elaborate citation.

The plaintiff argues that the provisions of the contract are separable. We agree that they are, but do not think that decisions separating out certain provisions from illegal contracts are in point here. As already said, we do not suggest that this contract is illegal. All we say is that the sum total of its provisions drives too hard a bargain for a court of conscience to assist.

This disposition of the problem makes unnecessary further discussion of the separate liability of Lojeski, who was not a party to the contract, but who purchased some of the carrots from the Wentzes.

The judgments will be affirmed.

Notes

Notes

Notes

Notes

Notes

Notes